Comparing Black Deaths in Custody, Police Brutality, and Social Justice Solutions

Janelle Christine Simmons
Independent Researcher, USA

A volume in the Advances in Criminology, Criminal Justice, and Penology (ACCJP) Book Series

IGI Global
PUBLISHER of TIMELY KNOWLEDGE

Published in the United States of America by
IGI Global
Information Science Reference (an imprint of IGI Global)
701 E. Chocolate Avenue
Hershey PA, USA 17033
Tel: 717-533-8845
Fax: 717-533-8661
E-mail: cust@igi-global.com
Web site: http://www.igi-global.com

Library of Congress Cataloging-in-Publication Data

Names: Simmons, Janelle Cristine, 1978- author.
Title: Comparing Black deaths in custody, police brutality, and social justice solutions / by Janelle Cristine Simmons.
Description: Hershey, PA : Information Science Reference, [2023] | Includes bibliographical references. | Summary: "This book addresses the topic of Black Deaths in Custody which describes actions that lead to the death of Black people while they are in the process of being detained by a law enforcement agent or were already detained, focusing on three core countries where Black Deaths in Custody appear to occur at higher rates"-- Provided by publisher.
Identifiers: LCCN 2022024505 (print) | LCCN 2022024506 (ebook) | ISBN 9781799893042 (hardcover) | ISBN 9781799893066 (ebook)
Subjects: LCSH: Police brutality. | Black people--Violence against. | Discrimination in law enforcement. | Racism. | Social justice.
Classification: LCC HV7936.P725 S56 2023 (print) | LCC HV7936.P725 (ebook) | DDC 363.2/32--dc23/eng/20220714
LC record available at https://lccn.loc.gov/2022024505
LC ebook record available at https://lccn.loc.gov/2022024506

This book is published in the IGI Global book series Advances in Criminology, Criminal Justice, and Penology (ACCJP) (ISSN: pending; eISSN: pending)

British Cataloguing in Publication Data
A Cataloguing in Publication record for this book is available from the British Library.

Advances in Criminology, Criminal Justice, and Penology (ACCJP) Book Series

ISSN:pending
EISSN:pending

Editor-in-Chief: Liam J. Leonard, Winchester University, UK

MISSION

Criminology has never been more relevant. Violence, serial murder, crime and victimization continue to remain an unfortunate staple of society. Crime is a key issue globally, nationally, and regionally. Law enforcement personnel within the criminal justice system must keep pace with ever changing modes of crime. As officials work to predict and prevent crimes, as well as apprehend offenders, they will need to devise new tools and strategies to preserve the safety of society and ensure proper justice is served.

The **Advances in Criminology, Criminal Justice, and Penology (ACCJP)** Book Series explores emerging research behind crime control strategies, crime motivation, new methods and the utilization of technology for committing illegal acts, criminal justice and reform strategies, and the effects of crime on society and its victims. The publications contained within this series are valuable resources for government officials, law enforcement officers, corrections officers, prison management, criminologists, sociologists, psychologists, forensic scientists, security specialists, academicians, researchers, and students seeking current research on international crime.

COVERAGE

- Prisons
- Serial Killers
- Hacking
- Serial Murder
- Victimology
- Criminal Psychology
- Restorative Justice
- Policing
- Criminal Justice Systems
- Gaming

The Advances in Criminology, Criminal Justice, and Penology (ACCJP) Book Series (ISSN pending) is published by IGI Global, 701 E. Chocolate Avenue, Hershey, PA 17033-1240, USA, www.igi-global.com. This series is composed of titles available for purchase individually; each title is edited to be contextually exclusive from any other title within the series. For pricing and ordering information please visit http://www.igi-global.com/book-series/advances-criminology-criminal-justice-penology/212650. Postmaster: Send all address changes to above address.

Titles in this Series

For a list of additional titles in this series, please visit:
http://www.igi-global.com/book-series/advances-criminology-criminal-justice-penology/212650

Restorative Justice and Practices in the 21st Century
Holli Vah Seliskar (Purdue University Gloal, USA)
Information Science Reference • © 2023 • 324pp • H/C (ISBN: 9781668461457) • US $215.00

Realizing the Purpose and Benefits of Juvenile Transfer to Criminal Court
Joseph B. Sanborn, Jr. (University of Central Florida (Retird), USA)
Information Science Reference • © 2023 • 516pp • H/C (ISBN: 9781799879237) • US $245.00

Cases on Crimes, Investigations, and Media Coverage
Liam James Leonard (University of Winchester, UK)
Information Science Reference • © 2023 • 254pp • H/C (ISBN: 9781799896685) • US $215.00

Paths to the Prevention and Detection of Human Trafficking
Sharon K. Andrews (University of Houston-Clear Lake, USA) and Caroline M. Crawford (University of Houston-Clear Lake, USA)
Information Science Reference • © 2022 • 422pp • H/C (ISBN: 9781668439265) • US $215.00

Comparative Criminology Across Western and African Perspectives
Simeon P. Sungi (United States International University-Africa, Kenya) and Nabil Ouassini (Prairie View A&M University, USA)
Information Science Reference • © 2022 • 322pp • H/C (ISBN: 9781799828563) • US $250.00

Handbook of Research on Present and Future Paradigms in Human Trafficking
Essien D. Essien (University of Uyo, Nigeria)
Information Science Reference • © 2022 • 488pp • H/C (ISBN: 9781799892823) • US $295.00

For an entire list of titles in this series, please visit:
http://www.igi-global.com/book-series/advances-criminology-criminal-justice-penology/212650

IGI Global
PUBLISHER of TIMELY KNOWLEDGE

701 East Chocolate Avenue, Hershey, PA 17033, USA
Tel: 717-533-8845 x100 • Fax: 717 533-8661
E-Mail: cust@igi-global.com • www.igi-global.com

Table of Contents

Foreword

Dr. Janelle Christine Simmons synthesizes the legal historiography of a significant portion of Euro-America to offer this worthy detailing of the reinforced symmetrical construction of systemic racial profiling and mass incarceration throughout Western nation-states. Beginning in Great Britain, Western legal precedence creates a historical blueprint and accounting of the overlapping legal systems that targeted African and African descended communities from before the trans-Atlantic slave trade until after The Cold War. Dr. Simmons' consolidation of the legal historiography of the aforementioned Great Britain, along with The United States, Australia and South Africa offers a baseline comprehension into the style of laws required to criminalize the movement, group economics, political solidarity and cultural unity of Africans and African Americans throughout the known world.

Dr. Simmons adds to the growing voice of historians and economists asserting that the legalized apartheid and cultural exploitation of African, Black and Aboriginal communities the world over was to the direct socio-economic benefit of Euro-American communities and their descendants. Noting that inherited wealth continues to be the largest form of private wealth distribution throughout Western nations, Dr. Simmons' retracing of the legal historiography of racial apartheid yields the well-defined conclusions of systemic racism echoed in previous anthropological and economic investigations into the construction of whiteness composed by 20th-century scholars Melville Herskovits and Charles E. Silberman.

Beginning with Great Britain, Simmons encapsulates Euro-American colonialism as the socio-political and economic time machine through which subsequent English national offshoots, namely the United States, Australia and South Africa, transported centuries old notions of White supremacy and Eurocentricity to Native American, African and Aboriginal societies. Simmons' cross-cultural comparison and contrasting of race-based legislation throughout these Western nations is a true service to average citizens in need of source material itemizing the commonality of institutional racism worldwide.

Simmons dissects Australia's 1869 Aboriginal Protection Act in tandem to America's plethora of Jim and Jane Crow laws and Black codes to illuminate the near exact impacts of family separations, economic malfeasance and population controls white-dominated governments exacted upon Black and Aboriginal communities to maintain socio-economic racial caste systems. Moreover, cultural indoctrinations of "one-drop" rules in the United States & "Half-castes" in Australia reinforced fallacious notions of Euro-American racial purity. Reactionary laws were often passed by the racist government practitioners of these bigoted pseudo-sciences to restrict the expansion of Black/Aboriginal home ownership and often forcibly displace existing Black and Aboriginal subdivisions.

The socio-economic investment in systems of whiteness through legalized surveillance, displacement and incarceration throughout Jim and Jane Crow racial apartheid eras often go overlooked or explained away as incidental to minimize the practical and economic implications of race-based apartheid throughout the West. Dr. Simmons locates her historiography at the center of this omission by detailing the creation of racialized communities in Victoria & New South Wales, Australia. The Neglected Children and Juvenile Offenders Act (1904) & The Aborigines (Training of Children) Act (1923) are two of the downunder's most notorious legal vehicles for monitoring and interfering in family planning and community development of Aboriginal families. The institutionalizing of generations of Aboriginal communities - places large cross-sections of Aboriginal youth development squarely within the jurisdiction of the state. The mirroring of similar legislation by other Western nations extending all the way to The United States' 2004 adoption of No Child Left Behind statutes illustrates the West's consistent investment in the destruction of communities of color through the enactment of legislation purported to cure racial ills.

Not to be outdone by the United States and Australia, Dr. Simmons' adds the South Africa Act of 1910 for the further compounding of the predictable outcomes from well-crafted legislation built on the social and cultural practices of Euro-American colonialism. Built on the precedence of the 1866 Pass Laws, after the first decade of the 20th-century, it was now legal and cultural practice for Black South Africans to carry written "passes" permitting them to work and travel in their ancestral homelands. Similar to Great Britain, the United States and Australia, South Africa also banned interracial marriage and instituted stringent social taboos against whites cohabitating with indigenous South Africans.

By 1945, the Urban Areas Act mandated that Blacks and whites in South Africa could only live in the same residence if the Black residences were hired as the domestic servants of white homeowners. The racial and social implications of such economic caste hierarchies were severe and permanent brands in the minds and psyches of citizens locally and globally. To be white is to be innocent, prosperous, credible, and worthy. To be Black is to be hapless, suspicious, impoverished, and culpable. Such social definitions help to explain that even today, when the legal record between Blacks and whites are near equal, throughout the Western worlds, Africans and Aboriginal laborers are undercompensated by 33%, over-incarcerated by 67% and overrepresented within lower socio-economic measurements by over 80%.

Dr. Simmons' historiography of the Euro-American race system is a reliable explanation of the required ordinances legal systems employ to manufacture over-inflated and devastating racial disparities in vital life metrics of home ownership, bodily safety, and generational wealth. Connecting legal principles with cultural practice becomes a useful standard for seeing the interplay between societal pillars of government, religion, and economics. Dr. Janelle Christine Simmons' approach to expanding her gaze to view multiple Western societies adds further distinction to this work that is a crucial addition to anyone looking to accurately contextualize racial disparities throughout the Western world.

Ronald A. Allen
Independent Researcher
February 20th, 2023

Ronald A. Allen *is a Historian, Theologian, and Educator as well as the Founder, POP Debate/The Exodus Conference and an Instructor: 8th Grade Nonfiction Writer.*

Preface

This book continues in describing a history of relationships. The majority of the relationships illuminated here have to do with the oppressor and the oppressed. In *Analyzing Black History Through Racial Profiling by Police,* I began with introducing the reader to the history that predates police brutality such as Islam and Slavery, Transatlantic Slavery, the 13th Amendment and then Slave Patrols. In *Comparing Black Deaths in Custody, Police Brutality, and Social Justice Solutions*, we will journey on a deeper exploration of the issues in order to come up with plausible solutions.

As previously stated, I am one who is self-read and self-traveled in much of my understanding of the history of Africa and Africans and Blacks in America. Outside of taking a class regarding North Africa and Islam, I hardly ever learned more than topics regarding slavery, etc. As I began to teach psychology in and across inner-city colleges such as the College of New Rochelle in the Bronx and Harlem, I was introduced to theorists such as Frantz Fanon, whose work I have come to respect and love. It is through these works and experiences and other relationships that I had established (i.e., both personal and work-related) that my eyes were opened to a deeper issue of injustice and inequalities that still exist. In fact, as I have worked on these two books, I have been continuously harassed by the police and even disrespected by the Black community as they want to be "right" with the White man. It is a new form of oppression.

While this book focuses on issues that mostly deal with the oppression of the body, many of my Black sisters and brothers continued to be oppressed in their minds. This phenomenon is not limited to the Black experience but continues to be an issue worldwide. While I am multiracial, I see this as being more dangerous than blatant racism. It stinks of what Fanon and Hilton in analyzing Fanon refers to as being what happens when the Black man insists on being accepted by the White man in order to do better financially. It is a slippery slope that often leads to compromises that causes one to lose themselves. This type of self-enforced acculturation leads to a deadening in many ways of one's culture and one's true liberty. This is what causes someone to be a person who has Black or Brown skin and then wears a White mask. It is what Frantz Fanon decried and Hilton critiqued. It is what I stand against!

To address this and many other issues, the author introduces transitioning governments and laws, which are necessary to understanding the shifting scene of events when it came to the Indigenous or Black man anywhere. Second, an introduction to various case studies such as America, Australia, and South Africa (i.e., Chapters 1, 2, and 3) are noted. As one who was born in America with a British upbringing/Background, and am also part Australian and South African (i.e., White); the author found these cases of blatant enslavement and racism to be the starkest. A discussion of Great Britain did not take place as the history is too vast. Nonetheless, one may want to look at case studies such as Canada and/or Great Britain. Third, then many of the names of the victims of police brutality are discussed (Chapter 4), further social justice issues are examined (Chapter 5) and solutions are proffered (Chapter 6). This is all done in order to establish the historical contexts for further acts of police brutality and the reality of living to address them; and calling for a reform of the police rather than allow police forces worldwide to manipulate the public, abuse the public, and punish the public for reporting crimes – that they were hired to address.

As previously stated, due to what I experienced previously with the police from working with them at the Bronx District Attorney's Office (i.e., having the most respect for them), studying with police officers and other government agents at John Jay College of Criminal Justice during my first Master's program and surviving 9/11, and then being assaulted (2013), and harassed by the police who I thought would fight for a trial and protect me – I am personally not devoid of strong emotions. This history, these testimonies, these deaths are felt by me, as the author, personally. Nonetheless, the author has striven to be as accurate as possible by relying on the text while also sharing personal vignettes so that the reader can have both sides of the story. In fact, if such acts continue, many of us will be living in a police state and looking towards *1984* written by George Orwell. It is imperative for scholars worldwide to partner with activists to address all forms of injustice including the attempted brainwashing, and oppression of free thought seated in each of our minds!

ORGANIZATION OF THE BOOK

This book contains a Preface, a Foreword, Acknowledgment, an Introduction, and eight solid chapters with a final conclusion.

Introduction. The Introduction brings continuance from Stop-And-Frisks to the basis of this book, which is a further exploration of issues that led up to grave forms of police brutality. It begins by focusing on some of the general history that led to the chosen cases and personal experiences of the other. The reader will soon learn of lynchings in the South, Aboriginal suicide (i.e., murdered by the police or correctional officers) in Australia; and South Africans suiciding (i.e., who were political leaders, anti-apartheid and killed by the police or prison guards).

Chapter 1. In Chapter 1, a discussion of transitioning governments and laws takes place regarding America. For example, what happened when America was no longer a colony but a free country that fought a civil war to set Blacks free from 1863 to 1865? Even after the Civil War and the assassination of former President Lincoln, unofficial slavery took place through Black Codes and Jim Crow Laws down South. This history and its surrounding issues are explored.

Chapter 2. In Chapter 2, a comparison of Western laws takes place. British, American, Australian and South Africans laws are compared as the backdrop for the historical events that led to the establishment of said laws. The impact of some of these laws on various comparative countries are briefly touched upon. Also, the laws of each country/region can and will be compared for a final analysis

Chapter 3. In Chapter 3, one will be introduced to America. Before America was established, it was known as the New World. The New World was then found and colonized. Eventually, the country known as the United States of America was established. The history of the establishment of the country as well as the injustices levied on people of color are established and discussed.

Chapter 4. In Chapter 4, one will be introduced to Australia. What happened when the British came to establish a prison colony for the Irish? How did this impact the Aborigine? What was it like for Aborigines to be raped and have their land stolen and called savages? How did the British law supplant original Aboriginal law and traditions? What happened when Australia became a Commonwealth Democracy? Did Aborigines have rights? Issues like these and more are discussed as the history is laid down and there is some comparison between the Aboriginal people of the Americas.

Chapter 5. In Chapter 5, the country of South Africa is introduced and its tribes alike. The complexity of the case of South Africa is explored. While the Dutch and the British first settled South Africa and then warred for and over it, this country's history is longer and more complex than America, for example. After slavery, which came to its shores in the 1600 and 1700s – came Apartheid. Apartheid is an Afrikaner word meaning separateness. Thus, tribes and races were separated.

This form of separateness created a gravesite of injustices. While the author once sat with her "friend's" mother, Mrs. Hogi, and discussed the Jim Crow South and learned that many Black people desired to be alone rather than integrate – and for some it was a better situation; those who grew up under Apartheid never had a chance to make such a choice. This government-imposed circus of separateness was established by the invader and oppressor to benefit himself and his family and his people group to the detriment of the original inhabitants of the land. This and more is discussed in Chapter 3 – extensively!

Chapter 6. In Chapter 6 titled "Say Their Names," the names of many of the documented fallen are listed and discussed via newspaper articles, artworks/pieces, etc. Say His Name! Michael Brown! Say His Name! Eric Garner! Say Her Name! Sandra Bland! Just as the case of George Floyd was used as a pivotal case along with Amadou Diallo to introduce the preceding book, these three cases were focused on to continue an in-depth discussion about the social justice issue and crime of being Black in America.

Chapter 7. In Chapter 7, titled "Social Justice Issues Examined," myriad of social justice issues are examined. This chapter deals with the hate that has been perpetuated merely based on color and perceived class status. KB in Dark Skin (2021) states the following: "Where can we take all the hate that we're hauling? Laws only help but they never could dissolve it!" These sentiments are the basis for the discussion that takes place in this chapter. What are the social justice issues? Why do they matter? What can we do about them?

Chapter 8. In Chapter 8, "An Examination of Solutions," one is brought to an in depth discussion of various solutions based on the works garnered for this book. While the list is not extensive, it is a list of the most probable and possible solutions. These solutions can be utilized by grassroot organizers, educators, ministers, politicians, and the like.

Conclusion. In this closing chapter, an overview of what has taken place in the previous chapters takes place. A final statement is made on the content of the book. In addition, a final conglomerate list of solutions and recommendations are given as well as future research suggestions.

In a world where presidents can be interrogated for maintaining laws that keep traditional values between a man and a woman such as Sections 14.74 and 14.79 of the criminal code of Liberia; but police can run rampant in various Westernized countries and stop people of color at exponential rates shows an inequality of justice. Countries have the right to maintain what they believe to be God-ordained sanctions. However, governments do not have the right to harass and harangue and increase costs for people of color or anyone else simply for existing. While this analysis seems simplistic, it is more complex than one thinks. Why is it okay for a State to fight for sex consent of a child and pornographic activity to be approved such as in the 8th Circuit in Omaha, Nebraska in 2019, but a man can be beaten to death or choked to death by a police officer because he is Black and has allegedly committed some obtuse crime such as selling loosies as in the case of Eric Garner? It appears that many citizens worldwide are focusing on the wrong thing and fighting for the wrong causes.

In the Book of James, there is a reference and an argument made about faith versus works. In the preface of the preceding work on this topic, I noted that I had hopes that I was effectuating through prayer. However, without writing the book, without standing against tyranny and injustice and without protesting minor and major attacks on my person, my color (i.e., brown-skinned girl), my race (i.e., African American/Multi-Racial), my gender (i.e., Female), my religion (i.e., Pentecostal Born-Again Christian who is Jewish by lineage), and my nationality (i.e., American); I would have faith in God and that things could change without the actual perpetuating work. And if I did the work without faith, it would be meaningless, led by nothing but possibly mere pride.

James, the "brother" of Jesus states the following in Chapter 2:26:

For as the body without the spirit is dead, so faith without works is dead also.

Now, I give this promise to you! I will never lose my faith in Jesus Christ of Nazareth, my Jewish Messiah, and I will never stop fighting for that which is good until I give up the ghost. For the New Testament via the Apostle Paul in Galatians 6:9 states the following:

For as the body without the spirit is dead, so faith without works is dead also.

May we never tire of fighting for that which will make this world a better place and allow us to focus on our families, friends, and communities in ways that matter (i.e., *tikkun olam* or Repairing the World)!

Sincerely,

Janelle Christine Simmons
Independent Researcher, USA

Acknowledgments

"You can cage the singer but not the song." – Harry Belafonte

"But a caged bird stands on the grave of dreams

His shadow shouts on a nightmare scream

His wings are clipped, and his feet are tied

So he opens his throat to sing"

– Maya Angelou from Poem "I Know Why the Caged Bird Sings"(1969)

First, as always, I would like to acknowledge my family worldwide. With all my heart, I wish to address those who I spent the most time with as I grew up such as the Simmons', the Donovans, the Adams, the Richards, and the Famous' (i.e., Thanks for the Bermudian Genealogy!) I'd also like to thank extended surprise family members that I have found and interacted with along the way. May we continue to rise up!

Second, I would like to continue to extend an extended acknowledgement to all those I have learned from such as family members and friends – especially my elders. I would also like to thank institutions that I attended such as Jack and Jill (Pre-school), 1st grade at the Lutheran School of Flushing, P.S. 229 – Emmanuel Kaplan/COMPASS (i.e., 2nd to 5th grade), P.S. 24 – Andrew Jackson (i.e., 6th grade), I.S. 237 – Rachel L. Carson, Francis Lewis High School (Majored in Social Sciences), Michigan State University (B.A. – Psychology, Minor – Pre-Law, Honors College Member, Psi Chi Member, Golden Key National Honors Society), John Jay College of Criminal Justice

(M.A. – Forensic Psychology, Psi Chi Member), Torch Trinity Graduate University (i.e., formerly known as Torch Trinity Graduate School of Theology) (M.Div.), Liberty University (Ed.S. – Curriculum and Instruction and Ed.D. in Educational Leadership, Kappa Delta Pi Member) and Walden University (Partially completed Ph.D. in Psychology with a Specialization in I/O; Invited to Join Honors Society).

To shorten this acknowledgement, I ask you to refer to the preceding book titled Analyzing Issues from Slavery to Racial Profiling by the Police. In addition to those I acknowledged before from universities I attended to religious leaders; I would like to take the time to thank additional people here.

Third, I would like to acknowledge a man of God who passed away too soon, Rabbi Fenchel of Sha'ar Adonai of New York, NY who was always very welcoming as I transitioned from a megachurch to a Messianic Congregation. After two years of attending this multicultural congregation on and off, I chose to attend Beth El, a Two-Testament Synagogue also located in Manhattan led by Rabbi Bruce Cohen. Rabbi Cohen's teaching was simple and yet profound. His exposition of the Scripture and his welcoming congregation helped me to marinate in the Word. It also helped me to understand my Jewish holidays and the meaning of maintaining certain Old Testament laws as well as how to live them. Finally, I would like to acknowledge a third Messianic congregation and religious leader – that of Rabbi Ben of Kehilath HaDerekh Messianic Congregation located in Manhattan. While I only visited this congregation for a number of months in person, I am able to view sermons online. As an ex-paratrooper and a Messianic Jew – I find solace that he will continue to share the Gospel with Jew and Gentile alike.

Fourth, I would like to extend my thanks to Ron A. Allen who shared my vision for the purpose of both authored books. He has written the Foreword for Analyzing Issues from Slavery to Racial Profiling by Police, and now this book. I first met Ron in 2014 as we both worked side-by-side in a Baptist Church known as Downtown Baptist Church (i.e., now known as Old Town Community Baptist) in Alexandria, Virginia. I served as a Church Intern working across several departments and Ron was working as the Youth Pastor. We spent many days in the Basement arguing about my position towards the Black Community and my multicultural stance. Nine years later, I can say that Ron and I are not only brother and sisters in Christ, but friends and colleagues still working for the cause of freedom and social justice! I thank him for his integrity in standing against all odds.

Fifth, I would also like to extend my thanks and gratitude to libraries that I have visited online or in person. I would like to thank Liberty University in

Lynchburg, VA, my Alma Mater for their online library, which I have access to as an alumnus. I would like to continue to extend my heartfelt thanks to Saint Joseph University in Philadelphia, PA for being gracious enough to host me as a visitor. In addition, I would like to thank John Jay College of Criminal Justice in New York City, and the National Law Enforcement Museum in Washington, D.C. for their assistance and tutelage in regard to various topics of the development of the police force, slave patrols, et al.

Additionally, I would like to thank Brampton Public Library in Toronto and their lovely librarian Agnes who assisted me with finding books on Islam, Slavery, and Black Deaths in Custody or Police Brutality. She was very helpful in showing me the computer and search engines and telling me general areas to search for said information. I even thank Queens University in Belfast and Michael – albeit a failed attempt where library access is limited to students and faculty who allowed me to peruse the exhibit titled "Friel Reimagined: A Playwright's Works in Progress," and still work on this manuscript in the attached café!

I would also like to thank the Schomburg Center of Harlem. This library has been a staple in the Harlem community for decades. I have fond memories of completing genealogical research at this locale approximately 25 years ago. I also was able to hear a talk from Joe Morton on May 2, 2016 at the Schomburg Center for Black Culture.

Figure 1. Joe Morton being interviewed on a Panel at the Schomburg Center on May 2, 2016
Source: Janelle Christine Simmons, Ed.D.

Additionally, due to their research catalog, I was able to access their online portal and have been able to substantiate further claims made in this book as well as others. Additionally, several of their photo exhibits have been referenced in this work.

Without the support and tutelage of the institutions and people mentioned, I would never have been able to come this far or complete these works. It would have been impossible to complete "Comparing Black Deaths in Custody, Police Brutality, and Social Justice Solutions." I am forever thankful! May God Bless You All and May We Continue to Rise Up!

"

Introduction

Perhaps it is easy for those who have never felt the stinging darts of segregation to say, "Wait."

But when you have seen vicious mobs lynch your mothers and fathers at will and drown your sisters and brothers at whim; when you have seen hate filled policemen curse, kick and even kill your black brothers and sisters; when you see the vast majority of your twenty million Negro brothers smothering in an airtight cage of poverty in the midst of an affluent society. . . .

We know through painful experience that freedom is never voluntarily given by the oppressor; it must be demanded by the oppressed. - Martin Luther King, Jr. – "Letter from a Birmingham Jail"[1]

This chapter focuses on introducing the continuation of information and the analysis of issues regarding Black Deaths in Custody in regard to police brutality from its preceding and associated book titled "Analyzing History from Slavery through Racial Profiling by [the] Police." It begins with a discussion about new calls for police reforms and the latest well-known case of police brutality regarding Tyre Nichols. Thereafter, one is introduced with the remainder of the contents of this book titled "Comparing Black Deaths in Custody, Police Brutality and Social Justice Solutions." Topics such as Transitioning Governments and Law, various Case Studies on America, Australia and South Africa as well as the names of some of the deceased will be reviewed briefly.

INTRODUCTION

After I completed the initial manuscript, which was only to bear this title (i.e., the title of this book), I was met with a dilemma. The contract I signed called for approximately 300 pages but I had written over 600. I put in a request to the Book Producer/Editor if I may split this book in two and sign two new book contracts. I was informed that I may. It was during this process that the case of Tyre Nichols materialized to my chagrin. I began the last book with the case of George Floyd and to see another "brother" beaten and terrorized by the police for a routine traffic stop that went wrong was all wrong in my mind.

Figure 1. Picture of Tyre Nichols
Source: Sainz (2023)

The Case of Tyre Nichols

Tyre Nichols is an African American male who at 29-years-old was beaten by the police and this beating occurred during a routine traffic stop that turned into a police chase (Burke, 2023; Diaz, 2023; Finkel, 2023; Sainz, 2023; Sanchez & Morales, 2023). It was alleged that he had been pulled over for reckless driving, but it was never substantiated (Burke, 2023). Like George Floyd who also died while in "police custody" (Burke, 2023; Harrelson &

Levin, 2022; Sanchez & Morales, 2023; Sharpton, 2022; The White House, n.d.), he was being arrested when the incident occurred. While some police departments tried to explain an influx of Black Deaths in Custody, which can be defined by some as a murder that can/does happen in a prison, in a jail, or even in a psychiatric ward (Athwal, 2002) – as being related to new recruits and an influx of retirees (Sanchez & Morales, 2023); there is no excuse for murder without cause, especially by a police officer who has sworn to protect and serve.

The officers who had beaten Tyre Nichols are suffering the consequences of their actions (Burke, 2023; Diaz, 2023; Finkel, 2023; Sainz, 2023; Sanchez & Morales, 2023). All five officers (i.e., Tadarrius Bean, Demetrius Haley, Emmitt Martin III, Desmond Mills, Jr., and Justin Smith were all fired on January 20, 2023 (Burke, 2023). Additionally, they have also been charged with second-degree murder (Burke, 2023; Diaz, 2023; Finkel, 2023; Sainz, 2023; Sanchez & Morales, 2023). Currently, Tyre's artwork is on billboards throughout the desert, but where is he (Finkel, 2023)? With that being said, this case continues the discussion that begs the question; "What is wrong with the criminal justice system/legal system in America?" Also, "What is wrong with the Police Force in America?" These questions extend to the other case study countries such as Australia and South Africa.

MAIN FOCUS OF CHAPTER

Issues, Controversies, Problems

The main focus of this chapter titled "Introduction" is/was to serve as an introduction to the topic of this book. This Introduction leads into Chapter 1 of this book (Previously Chapter 9) titled "Transitioning Governments and Laws." In "Transitioning Governments and Laws," the author introduces the reader to the initial types of governments in each of the chosen countries noted as case studies. She delineates how the country was established briefly and/or what government looked like in each country. This sets the foundation for how the Transatlantic Slave Trade began (D. Glover, personal communication, September 9, 2014; Hughes & Meltzer, 1956; National Park Service, n.d.), and how slavery was established in each country as well as how human rights issues arose, which led to police brutality and oppressive regimes (e.g., Apartheid).

Within these three chosen case studies, i.e., America, Australia, and South Africa; a pattern arises (D. Glover, personal communication, September 9, 2014; Harrelson & Levin, 2022; Hughes & Meltzer, 1956; United Nations, 2022). This pattern itself, like a formula for the destruction of any people group of color in and of itself is an issue and a controversy. Let's say that is Point 1! Second, in each case study, there appears to be the issue of an "invader" (D. Glover, personal communication, September 9, 2014; Fanon, 2008; Hilton, 2011; Hughes & Meltzer, 1956). Caucasians or those with White skin from European regions and countries saw the resources, the spices, and the women and land associated with people that they had categorized as being barbaric or lesser (D. Glover, personal communication, September 9, 2014; Fanon, 2008; Harrelson & Levin, 2022; Hilton, 2011; Hughes & Meltzer, 1956). Ironically, as in the case of South Africa or even the United States of America, trade had begun before war and subjugation became a rule of thumb. Thus, it would appear that if Caucasians as a group of people were sincerely honest—they would have to say that to trade at that level—the people they were interacting with could hardly be called barbarians.

Third, instead of paying for items and resources and a workforce, Europeans decided to invade the land, begin wars and then to separate tribes and enslave individuals to do their work (Blight, 2018; Davidson, 1964; D. Glover, personal communication, September 9, 2014; Harrelson & Levin, 2022; Hughes & Meltzer, 1956; United Nations, 2022). Fourth, once enslaved, Europeans continued to perpetuate conflicts between differing tribes (i.e., a reality which still happens today – e.g., the Yoruba and Ebo tribes of Nigeria), separate families, destroyed languages and cultures; and did their best to break the spirit of the African and of the Indigenous tribes (Blight, 2018; Davidson, 1964; D. Glover, personal communication, September 9, 2014; Hughes & Meltzer, 1956; United Nations, 2022) to the lands of countries like Australia through acts like beatings, humiliation, rape, etc. (Davidson, 1964; Fanon, 2008; Hilton, 2011). Slave Codes were enacted to control the slave population (United Nations, 2022; Vandiver, Giacopassi, & Curley, 2003). Fifth, even after seemingly showing a modicum of humanity and establishing laws within each form of government that ended slavery; they found new ways to enslave those of darker skin such as the use of Black Codes throughout the Caribbean and the Americas and Jim Crow Laws in America (Blight, 2018; Harrelson & Levin, 2022; Hughes & Meltzer, 1956; Irons, 2002; Olson, 1944; United Nations, 2022; Woodward, 1966). Sixth, thereafter, once laws such as the aforementioned -- were eradicated, the process of assimilating never came. African Americans, for example, still do not out earn as a collective group Caucasians, etc. Moreover, there are still realities like glass ceilings, etc. This and other issues and controversies such as eugenics and forced sterilizations of Indigenous Populations will be discussed within this book.

As noted in the Preface, this book will also address topics like comparative laws (Chapter 2), America as a Case Study (Chapter 3), Australia as a Case Study (Chapter 4), South Africa as a Case Study (Chapter 5), the names of many African Americans who were killed during arrests, while in custody and even some in their homes without cause (Chapter 6). Afterwards, social justice issues will be examined (Chapter 7), and there will be an examination of solutions (Chapter 8). Finally, a conclusion will be proffered. From these explorations, the author hopes that the reader will come on a journey of learning about slavery and the history that led to an unusual pattern of Black Deaths in Custody worldwide. While these three countries are…and serve only as a few examples; there are a myriad of countries and governments that have continued to perpetuate this cycle of racism, mental and physical rape, self-hate and eventually the out and out murder of citizens who happen to bare a complexion that some detest or who represent a race that some choose to detest.

As noted in the Preface, this book will also address topics like transitioning governments (Chapter 1), comparative laws (Chapter 2), America as a Case Study (Chapter 3), Australia as a Case Study (Chapter 4), South Africa as a Case Study (Chapter 5), the names of many African Americans who were killed during arrests, while in custody and even some in their homes without cause (Chapter 6). Afterwards, social justice issues will be examined (Chapter 7), and there will be an examination of solutions (Chapter 8). Finally, a conclusion will be proffered. From these explorations, the author hopes that the reader will come on a journey of learning about slavery and the history that led to an unusual pattern of Black Deaths in Custody worldwide. While these three countries are…and serve only as a few examples; there are a myriad of countries and governments that have continued to perpetuate this cycle of racism, mental and physical rape, self-hate and eventually the out and out murder of citizens who happen to bare a complexion that some detest or who represent a race that some choose to detest.

CONCLUSION

In conclusion, this chapter focused on introducing the main issue of this book, which was police brutality. Unlike the first book, this chapter looks at it through the story of Tyre Nichols. Moreover, this book continues the history from where the last book ends (i.e., slave patrols and the like) and transitions to the changing laws, history of the countries of the chosen case studies, the countries themselves, and even the names of many of those whose crime was being Black in America (BBIA)[2], and therefore were murdered by the police. In the case of Tyre Nichols, he lost his life fleeing from the police for a basic traffic stop that went terribly wrong.

REFERENCES

Athwal, H. (2002, November 11). *Black deaths in custody.* IRR UK. https://irr.org.uk/article/black-deaths-in-custody/

Blight, D. W. (2018). *Frederick Douglass: Prophet of freedom.* Simon & Schuster.

Burke, M. (2023, March 4). Fired Memphis EMT said police impeded Tyre Nichols' care by refusing to remove handcuffs. *MSN.* https://www.msn.com/en-us/news/other/fired-memphis-emt-said-police-impeded-tyre-nichols-care-by-refusing-to-remove-handcuffs/ar-AA18dJM2

Davidson, B. (1964). *The African past: Chronicles from antiquity to modern times.* Grosset & Dunlap.

Diaz, J. (2023, February 24). Deaths in custody are a crisis, but data on them is a black hole, a new report says. *MPR News.* https://www.mprnews.org/story/2023/02/23/npr-police-custody-deaths

Fanon, F. (2008). *Black skin, white mask.* Grove Press.

Finkel, J. (2023, March 4). *Tyre Nichols' photography will soar on desert x billboards.* Yahoo. https://www.yahoo.com/news/tyre-nichols-photography-soar-desert-152359697.html

Harrelson, A., & Levin, M. (2022). *Lift your voice: How my nephew George Floyd's murder changed the world.* Post Hill Press Book.

Hilton, B. T. (2011). Frantz Fanon and Colonialism: A Psychology of Oppression. *Journal of Scientific Psychology*, 45–59.

Irons, P. (2002). *Jim Crow's children: The broken promise of the Brown decision*. Penguin Books.

National Park Service. (n.d.). *The middle passage*. NPS. https://www.nps.gov/afbg/learn/historyculture/upload/FINALMiddlePassage.pdf

Olson, E. (1944). The slave code in colonial New York. *The Journal of Negro History*, *29*(2), 147–165. doi:10.2307/2715308

Sainz, A. (2023, February 17). 5 Memphis police officers plead not guilty in death Tyre Nichols. *ABC7*. https://abc7chicago.com/tyre-nichols-case-memphis-police-officers-plead-not-guilty-cops/12831166/

Sanchez, R., & Morales, M. (2023, February 11). 'A recipe for disaster.' Deadly encounter in Memphis comes at a critical time in American policing. *CNN*. https://www.cnn.com/2023/02/11/us/tyre-nichols-memphis-police-law-enforcement/index.html

Sharpton, A. (2022). *Righteous trouble makers: Untold stories of the social justice movement in America*. Hanover Square Press.

The White House. (n.d.). *Fact sheet: President Biden to sign historic executive order to advance effective, accountable policing and strengthen public safety*. The White House. https://www.whitehouse.gov/briefing-room/statements-releases/2022/05/25/fact-sheet-president-biden-to-sign-historic-executive-order-to-advance-effective-accountable-policing-and-strengthen-public-safety/

United Nations. (2022, March 25). *Resistance to slavery and unity against racism: Rhythms of resistance*. UN. https://www.youtube.com/watch?v=VUhHhW1__sg

Vandiver, M., Giacopassi, D.J. & Curley, M.S. (2003). The Tennessee slave code: A legal antecedent to the inequalities in modern capital cases. *Journal of Ethnicity in Criminal Justice, 1*(3-4_, 67-89. doi:. doi:10.1300/j222voln03_04

Woodward, C. V. (1966). *The strange career of Jim Crow*. Oxford University Press.

ENDNOTES

1 Source: https://www.africa.upenn.edu/Articles_Gen/Letter_Birmingham.html.

2 BBIA is a term that was created by the author in 2023. It denotes the dual reality of Blacks in America as opposed to Caucasians or even Africans. The experience and perception of Blacks in America differs from almost any other people group significantly due to realities such as slavery, institutionalized racism and the continued "passing over" for lighter skinned minorities or "model minorities" who come to America – after the fact.

Chapter 1
Transitioning Governments and Laws

ABSTRACT

This chapter focuses on governments, what type of government each country has, and how these governments transitioned as laws changed regarding within each country. Some references will be made to Australian and South African laws in comparison to the United States. For example, South Africa was a tribal land that became an Apartheid state that then became a democracy. The chapter will mainly focus on introducing the reader to each system of government and discuss any transitions in types of government. These instances will be reviewed, analyzed, and discussed. For more specific country-case-specific laws, see the three chapters on case studies.

My hip hop will rock and shock the nation like the Emancipation Proclamation...
-Wu Tang Clan, Da' Mystery of Chessboxin', 1993

DOI: 10.4018/978-1-7998-9304-2.ch001

INTRODUCTION

MAIN FOCUS OF THE CHAPTER

The main focus of this chapter is to introduce different types of government specific to this book and the countries that have been introduced previously. Therefore, the reader will briefly learn about the Apartheid government of South Africa, Colonization (i.e., of America, Australia, and South Africa), and the UK/British Commonwealth and then Commonwealth Democracy as well as Democracies in general – and specifically to the United States. The author will also introduce how each government was/is dictates its governmental structure and how grievances are addressed. With that being said, let's begin delving into this topic.

Government

"Much of American law itself, whether we're aware of it or not, is codified to protect the very system of white supremacy pioneers like Thurgood Marshall and Pauli Murray aimed to dismantle" (Sharpton, 2022, p. 180).

Government is a term that describes "an organization with the authority and power to make and enforce laws and enact policy to control an area of land or a group of people" (Johnson, 2006; Open Education Sociology Dictionary, 2022), which is "a nation, state, or other political entity founded on law and united by a compact of the people for the common good" (Central Intelligence Agency, n.d., p. 1). According to Philpott (2010) regarding American governance, the government is "any entity of the legislative or judicial branch, any executive agency, military department, government corporation, or independent establishment, the United States Postal Service, or any nonappropriated - fund instrumentality of the Armed Forces (FAR 8.701)" (p. 104). It is a form of authority that leads one to hold an office and make the final decisions for the people (Fasenfast, 2010) who live in a certain region. Throughout the world, there are various governments (Central Intelligence Agency, n.d.; Fasenfast, 2010). These governments had/have a myriad of laws (Central Intelligence Agency, n.d.; Fasenfast, 2010; Johnson,

2006). In fact, governments must learn to communicate with their constituents in order to convey messages, etc. (Carter, Kemper, Brown & Phillips, 2009).

In the case of the three countries that this book focuses on, the governments range from being an Apartheid state to a Democracy. However, each of them began by initially being tribal.

Figure 1. Picture of a Native American Tribe
Source: NonDoc Media, LLC. (2019).

Tribes and Their Governments

A tribe is defined as "a group of people, often of related families, who live together, sharing the same language, culture, and history, especially those who do not live in towns or cities (Cambridge University Press, 2022). Thus, each tribe lives/lived in different regions (Cambridge University Press, 2022; Lynch, 1976; Peterson, 2022). They also had different responsibilities (The Arizona Board of Regents, 2022; M. Wilcox, personal communication, September 21, 2022). In regions like South Africa, the White man believed Indigenous people to be lazy or too weak to complete manual labor (M. Wilcox, personal communication, September 21, 2022).

In America, there were hundreds of tribes (Legends of America, 2022; Petersen, 2022). Before Christopher Columbus arrived in America, the tribes lived freely and lived regionally but no person could own the land (Petersen, 2022). The concept was foreign to the Indigenous people of America. They were however assigned to take care of different sections of the land by assignment such as North, South, East and West (The Arizona Board of Regents, 2022). For some tribes, there were war chiefs, peace chiefs, etc. (Petersen, 2022; The Arizona Board of Regents, 2022) with a navigation of dualism (The Arizona Board of Regents, 2022).

Therefore, without the White man's help, indigenous people had been practicing self-governance, natural healing, assignment of roles and responsibilities (The Arizona Board of Regents, 2022; Petersen, 2022; M. Wilcox, personal communications, September 21, 2022). The fact is that "… most Native nations had governing systems that supported their core cultural values, strengthened social relationship, resolved disputes, advanced their priorities, and responded to the circumstances they faced" (The Arizona Board of Regents, 2022, p. 1). Regardless, the tribes across regions and countries knew how to work the earth, heal holistically, and survive (The Arizona Board of Regents, 2022; Petersen, 2022; M. Wilcox, personal communication, September 21, 2022). Also, when Caucasians came and when they enforced armed militaries to take the land of the Indigenous people, the Native Americans resisted some charges, avoided, or retreated from others, and eventually a remnant survived (Petersen, 2022).

America was tribal (Legends of America, 2022; Petersen, 2022). Australia was tribal and had been inhabited by its native people called Aborigines (Chang, 2019). South Africa was also tribal (Golden, 2004; Holland, 1989; Lynch, 1976; Noah, 2019; M. Wilcox, personal communication, September 21, 2022), and currently consists of approximately 10 recognized tribes and has 11 official languages (Golden, 2004; Lynch, 1976; M. Jacobs, personal communication, August 27, 2021; M. Wilcox, personal communication, September 21, 2022). While no one owned the land, there were often conflicts between tribes (Holland, 1989; Noah, 2019; M. Wilcox, personal communication, September 21, 2022). Nonetheless, the tribes tried to coexist. Then the White man came with a position of "divide and conquer" (Lynch, 1976; Noah, 2019; Petersen, 2022; M. Wilcox, personal communication, September 21, 2022; M. Wilcox, personal communication, September 23, 2022).

The New World/America

The New World had been unsettled. In 1607, the first successful establishment of a colony occurred in Jamestown, Virginia (Srividhya, Hutchings & Wright, 2009) and in some records it was by 1609 (National Park Service, 2020). To have a colony, the process of colonization must take place. A colony is a land that has been "taken" by another country and has that country's laws and regulations imposed upon it. At that time, colonies in America were mostly established by Great Britain (National Park Service, 2020; Srividhya, Hutchings & Wright, 2009). Great Britain was and still is a Commonwealth as it is part of the United Kingdom (Commonwealth Secretariat, 2019; Nexus Partnerships Limited, 2020). This system of government will be further discussed below.

Australia

In 1770, Possession Island was possessed by James Cook under the British Empire (Bringing Them Home, n.d.). By 1788 (Bringing Them Home, n.d.; Maxwell-Stewart & Oxley, 2020), Port Jackson became a settlement, and it was at that point that Australia was officially colonized (Chang, 2019; Healing Foundation, 2022) and founded as a full Commonwealth (Australian Law Reform Commission, 2022; International Work Group in Indigenous Affairs, n.d.; Maxwell-Stewart & Oxley, 2020) on January 26 (Chang, 2019). and the Aborigines and the British began to have armed conflicts (Bringing Them Home, n.d.) as several laws began to be implemented. Most of the laws that were implemented in force regarding Aborigines began at the middle of the 19th century (Find and Connect, 2021; Gipps, 1840). This made Australia a Commonwealth (Commonwealth Secretariat, 2019; Nexus Partnerships Limited, 2020). A commonwealth is a "nation, state, or other political entity founded on law and united by a compact of the people for the common good: (Central Intelligence Agency, n.d., p. 1).

In 1900, a constitution was established, and Australia began the road to being a Commonwealth with democratic principles (Commonwealth Secretariat, 2019; Gardbaum, 2013; Morales, 2022; Museum of Australian Democracy, n.d.; Nexus Partnerships Limited, 2020). In 1901, Australia becomes a Commonwealth denoted by the British Parliament (Commonwealth Secretariat, 2019; Nexus Partnerships Limited, 2020). The constitution began with the following words: "An Act to constitute the Commonwealth of Australia" (Museum of Australian Democracy, n.d.).

Figure 2. Picture of the Front page of the Australian Constitution
Source: Australian Broadcasting Corporation (2016). https://www.abc.net.au/news/2016-08-01/front-cover-of-australian-constitution/7680186?nw=0.

After 121 years, the Commonwealth of Australia has worked towards transforming its nation, addressing grievances, and making amends to the Aborigines (Chang, 2009; Bringing Them Home, n.d.; Healing Foundation, 2022). South Africa took a different journey.

South Africa

By the 1600s and 1700s, Dutch and British settlers had met the shores and lands of South Africa (Holland, 1988; South African History Online, n.d.; M. Wilcox, personal communication, September 21, 2022; M. Wilcox, personal communication, September 23, 2022). Their main interactions had been with the Dutch East Indian Company (Holland, 1988) as well as merchants (Boshoff, 2018; South African History Online, n.d.). For all intents and purposes despite the division between the Dutch and the British, South Africa was a Commonwealth with Dutch colonies (South African History Online, n.d.). Its capital was Cape Town (South African History Online, n.d.; M. Wilcox, personal communications, September 21, 2022). On May 31, 1910, the four colonies became known as the Union of South Africa and were a self-governing colony under British control (South African History Online, n.d.; M. Wilcox, personal communication, September 21, 2022; M. Wilcox, personal communication, September 23, 2022). The country had officially been colonized (South African History Online, n.d.; M. Wilcox, personal communication, September 21, 2022). And eventually, South Africa was deemed by the British to become self-governing (Holland, 1988; M. Wilcox, personal communication, September 21, 2022).

By 1912, the White Union of South Africa allowed Blacks to make laws, but they were not allowed to administer laws (Holland, 1988). The African National Conference was formed in 1912 on January 8th (Dubow, 2000; Holland, 1989; South African History Online, n.d.; M. Wilcox, personal communication, September 21, 2023). A conference was held, and the African Native National Congress (ANNC) was formed in the 1960s, as Black South Africa's response to being colonized and introduced to further measures of Apartheid (Dubow, 2000; Holland, 1989; South African History Online, n.d.; M. Wilcox, personal communication, September 21, 2022).

Soon, the British created a prison colony on Robben Island (South African History Online, n.d.; M. Wilcox, personal communication, September 21, 2022). That prison colony as depicted by the Robben Island Museum had political prisoners who fought for their rights against the State of Apartheid.

One of the most notable prisoners was Nelson Mandela who became the first Democratic President of South Africa after Apartheid ceased to exist (South African History, n.d.; M. Wilcox, personal communication, September 21, 2022; M. Wilcox, personal communication, September 23, 2022).

Figure 3. Picture of a Native American tribe
Source: Michael Wilcox of Tusk Adventures & Tours, Taken on September 21, 2023 at Robben Island Museum.

Figure 4. Janelle Christine Simmons, Ed.D. laying in a prison bed mock-up of a typical holding cell before reaching Robben Island as a prison transport
Source: Source: Michael Wilcox of Tusk Adventures & Tours, Taken on September 21, 2023 at Robben Island Museum.

Robben Island also was conducive in creating alliances as prisoners struggled to survive (M. Wilcox, personal communication, September 21, 2022; M. Wilcox, personal communication, September 23, 2022). Eventually, South African became a Commonwealth Democracy which contains a Commonwealth Charter.

What is a Commonwealth/Commonwealth Charter?

The Commonwealth Charter is a union of nations called member states that have committed to "the development of free and democratic societies and the promotion of peace and prosperity to improve the lives of all the people of the Commonwealth" (Commonwealth Secretariat, 2022, p. 1). There are 54 independent countries[1] in total that span across Africa, Asia, Europe, and the Pacific, which includes the United Kingdom (Community Secretariat, 2019; Nexus Partnerships Limited, 2020).[1] Sixty percent (60%) of all member countries have constituents under the age of 29 years old (Nexus Partnerships Limited, 2020). The Commonwealth represents 2.5 billion (Nexus Partnerships Limited, 2020) of approximately 8 billion people on the face of this earth. Out of the Commonwealth grew nations that chose to be pure democracies or Commonwealth democracies (Gardbaum, 2013). They also agree to certain principles such as the Lusaka Declaration of the Commonwealth on Racism and Racial Prejudice Zambia, 1979 (Commonwealth Secretariat, 2019). There is no overriding constitution for all member nations (Commonwealth Secretariat, 2019; Gardbaum, 2013). This differs from a democracy.

What is a Democracy?

According to the Central Intelligence Agency (n.d.), a democracy is a "form of government in which the supreme power is retained by the people, but which is usually exercised indirectly through a system of representation and delegated authority periodically renewed" (p. 1). Gardbaum (2013) goes further and defines democracy as a "[…] 'new commonwealth of constitutionalism' – 'the new model' for short – refers to a common general structure or approach underlying the bill of rights introduced in recent years in Canada (1982), New Zealand (1990), the UK (1998), the Australian Capital Territory (2004) and […] the state of Victoria (2006) (p. 1). Additionally, European democracy speaks to Europe and not to Australia or even South Africa or the United States

(Dahrendorf, 2003). The process involves a codified bill of rights (Gardbaum, 2013). Its roots come from the Greek (Encyclopedia Britannica, 2022).

The word democracy comes from the Greek. It contains two Greek words, which are as follows: *demos* and *kratos* (Encyclopedia Britannica, 2022). *Demos* means "people," and *kratos* means "rule" (Encyclopedia Britannica, 2022). The principle of the people being the rulers of the government began in the middle of the 5th century BCE in places like Athens (Encyclopedia Britannica, 2022). The *demos* were citizens by birth or were naturalized (Encyclopedia Britannica, 2022). In Italy, the part of the *demos* that could vote were that or the noble class, until there was protest (Encyclopedia Britannica, 2022). According to the Central Intelligence Agency (n.d.), a democracy is a "form of government in which the supreme power is retained by the people, but which is usually exercised indirectly through a system of representation and delegated authority periodically renewed" (p. 1).

While England was a monarchy, the King's councils began in order to handle grievances and became a basic function that led to a parliament, which by the 15th century became representative of a modern form of representation of passing bills and enacting laws (Encyclopedia Britannica, 2022). The difference in this democratic process is that the final decision is always made and approved or disapproved of by the monarchy (Encyclopedia Britannica, 2022). By the 16th century, during the Reformation period – the idea of a government having a means by which there were checks and balances – was finally established (Schaeffer, 2005). By 1782, England had had a constitutional crisis and by 1830, the principle of electing a Prime Minster, etc. changed the face of government in England (Encyclopedia Britannica, 2022). Eventually, the voting process was extended from 5% of the population to 7% of those twenty years and older in 1832, and then to male suffrage (1867, 1884, and 1918); and then suffrage for women (1928) (Encyclopedia Britannica, 2022).

America

While Britain had originally colonized the New World, there were 13 colonies (Connecticut, Delaware, Georgia, Maryland, Massachusetts, New Hampshire, New Jersey, New York, North Carolina, Pennsylvania, Rhode Island, South Carolina, Virginia), which each had their own localize government (US Citizenship and Immigration Services, n.d.). Eventually, a new nation was born called the United States of America (Encyclopedia Britannica, 2022; Smith, 2021). The argument was over taxation from the King and freedom of religion (US Citizenship and Immigration Services, n.d.). Additionally, they were angered over the fact that they were forced to give free board to British soldiers (US Citizenship and Immigration Services, n.d.). After a war with Britain that began in Massachusetts, the thirteen colonies won their independence and became the first thirteen states of the United States of America (US Citizenship and Immigration Services, n.d.; Smith, 2021). In 1776, key leaders met in Philadelphia and Thomas Jefferson penned the Declaration of Independence and it was accepted on July 4, 1776 (US Citizenship and Immigration Services, n.d.).

Eleven years later, the Constitution was penned on September 17, 1787 (Library of Congress, n.d; Smith, 2021; University of Minnesota Human Rights Library, n.d; US Citizenship and Immigration Services, n.d.). The Constitution of the United States of America was/is a document that establishes the principles that Americans and other residents will live by and sets forth the inalienable rights that they are due such as freedom of speech and freedom of religion (Library of Congress, n.d; Smith, 2021; US Citizenship and Immigration Services, n.d.; University of Minnesota Human Rights Library, n.d). Most likely, the idea of checks and balances that was introduced during the Reformation period (Schaeffer, 2005), was introduced into the idea of having a tripartite government.

Figure 5. Picture of the Declaration of Independence
Source: Bing Images. (2022). https://www.walmart.com/ip/Declaration-Of-Independence-Nthe-First-Printing-The-Also-Known-As-Dunlop-Broadside-Printed-By -John-In-Philadelphia-4-July-1776-Poster-Print-Granger-C/780 871696.

IN CONGRESS, JULY 4, 1776.

A DECLARATION

BY THE REPRESENTATIVES OF THE

UNITED STATES OF AMERICA,

IN GENERAL CONGRESS ASSEMBLED.

Signed by ORDER and in BEHALF of the CONGRESS,

JOHN HANCOCK, PRESIDENT.

ATTEST.
CHARLES THOMSON, SECRETARY.

Figure 6. Picture of part of the Constitution of the United States of America
Source: Marshall (2019)

After the United States had been established as a democracy, Australia followed over 100 years later. South Africa was to become a democracy over 200 years after America had been established as one. However, South Africa is a Commonwealth Democracy.

South Africa

Each democracy and commonwealth democracy has a constitution (Gardbaum, 2013; M. Wilcox, personal communication, September 23, 2022). After Apartheid ended and the first presidential election of South Africa took place in 1994, a constitution was crafted in 1996 (Golden, 2004; Karimi, 2013; Marshall, 2019; Nelson Mandela Foundation, 2022; Noah, 2019; South African History Online, n.d.; van Vuuren, 2015; M. Wilcox, personal communication, September 21, 2022; M. Wilcox, personal communication, September 23, 2022; Willoughby-Herald, 2015). However, there was a time when it was not a democracy. South Africa had been known as an Apartheid State (M. Wilcox, personal communication, September 21, 2023; M. Wilcox, personal communication, September 23, 2022).

What is an Apartheid State?

The term apartheid is defined as "apartness" or "separateness" (Golden, 2004; Holland, 1988; Karimi, 2013; Lynch, 1976; Marshall, 2019; Nelson Mandela Foundation, 2022; Noah, 2019; South African History Online, n.d.; van Vuuren, 2015; M. Wilcox, personal communication, September 21, 2022; M. Wilcox, personal communication, September 23, 2022; Willoughby-Herald, 2015). In South Africa, the principle of apartheid had been applied for hundreds of years to some extent. However, in 1948, it became a government known as Apartheid (Golden, 2004; Holland, 1988; Karimi, 2013; Lynch, 1976; Marshall, 2019; Nelson Mandela Foundation, 2022; Noah, 2019; South African History Online, n.d.; van Vuuren, 2015; Willoughby-Herald, 2015). As a system of government, Blacks and other non-Whites were other and were to be "controlled" (Golden, 2004; Holland, 1988; Karimi, 2013; Lynch, 1976; Marshall, 2019; Nelson Mandela Foundation, 2022; Noah, 2019; South African History Online, n.d.; van Vuuren, 2015; M. Wilcox, personal communication, September 21, 2022; M. Wilcox, personal communication, September 23, 2022; Willoughby-Herald, 2015). Tribes such as the Xhosa and Zulu were turned against each other (Noah, 2019). Tribes were also separated by regions on homelands (Lynch, 1976; M. Wilcox, personal communication, September 21, 2022; M. Wilcox, personal communication, September 23, 2022).

By continuing to make race distinctions, a caste system was created (Golden, 2004; Holland, 1988; Noah, 2019; van Vuuren, 2015; M. Wilcox, personal communication, September 21, 2022; M. Wilcox, personal communication, September 23, 2022; Willoughby-Herald, 2015). At the top of the caste were Whites and at the bottom of the caste were Blacks (Golden, 2004; Holland, 1988; Noah, 2019; South African History Online, n.d.; van Vuuren, 2015; M. Wilcox, personal communication, September 21, 2022; M. Wilcox, personal communication, September 23, 2022; Willoughby-Herald, 2015). In 1949, the South African Citizen Act was enacted (i.e., Act No. 44 of 1949), which made provision for any South African Citizen (South African History Online, n.d.) or whatever that was supposed to mean. After that, a myriad of acts, etc. were instituted that brought about more and more division and oppression to non-White citizens, especially non-Whites and more specifically Black South Africans (South African History Online, n.d.; M. Wilcox, personal communication, September 21, 2022; M. Wilcox, personal communication, September 23, 2022).

And though there had been restrictions on the media regarding Apartheid South Africa (Holland, 1988; Lynch, 1976; South African History Online, n.d.), the revolution was still being written about, photographed and televised (Simmons, 2014) to the outer regions of the world (Golden, 2004; Holland, 1988; Lynch, 1976; Karimi, 2013; Nelson Mandela Foundation, 2022; South African History Online, n.d.; van Vuuren, 2015; M. Wilcox, personal communication, September 21, 2022; M. Wilcox, personal communication, September 23, 2022; Willoughby-Herald, 2015). After numerous human rights atrocities, a domestic and international war was lodged against the Apartheid government of South Africa[2] (Golden, 2004; Holland, 1988; Lynch, 1976; Karimi, 2013; Nelson Mandela Foundation, 2022; South African History Online, n.d.; van Vuuren, 2015; M. Wilcox, personal communication, September 21, 2022; M. Wilcox, personal communication, September 23, 2022; Willoughby-Herald, 2015). Eventually, South Africa became a democratic nation and held its first democratic elections in 1994 (Marshall, 2019; Nelson Mandela Foundation, 2022; South African History Online, n.d.; M. Wilcox, personal communication, September 21, 2022; M. Wilcox, personal communication, September 23, 2022). By 1996, a constitution was formed (Marshall, 2019).

Figure 7. Picture of the Constitution of South Africa
Source: Wikimedia (2020) https://commons.wikimedia.org/wiki/File:Constitution_of_the_Republic_of_South_Africa_Amendment_Act_1996_from_Government_Gazette.djvu.

REPUBLIC OF SOUTH AFRICA

GOVERNMENT GAZETTE

STAATSKOERANT

VAN DIE REPUBLIEK VAN SUID-AFRIKA

CAPE TOWN, 29 MARCH 1996
KAAPSTAD, 29 MAART 1996

No. 17068

PRESIDENT'S OFFICE	KANTOOR VAN DIE PRESIDENT

A Change Was Still to Come: Transitioning Governments

Just as England, part of Great Britain, which is part of the United Kingdom changed from a pure monarchy to a Commonwealth democracy (Dahrendorf, 2003; Encyclopedia Britannica, 2022); other countries had transitioning governments as well. The New World went from being a colony of Great Britain to being an independent nation with a democratic form of government (Encyclopedia Britannica, 2022). Australia went from being colonized to being a Commonwealth to being a Commonwealth democracy (Australian Law Reform Commission, 2022; International Work Group in Indigenous Affairs, n.d.; Maxwell-Stewart & Oxley, 2020).

South Africa went from being colonized to being an Apartheid State to becoming a Commonwealth democracy (Golden, 2004; Holland, 1988; Lynch, 1976; Karimi, 2013; Nelson Mandela Foundation, 2022; South African History Online, n.d.; van Vuuren, 2015; Willoughby-Herald, 2015).

Just because governments shifted, did not mean that they were perfect. It also did not mean that democracy extended to all inhabitants, residents, or citizens. In America, slavery existed until the early 19th century (Smith, 2021). In Australia, Aborigines did not have voting rights until 1967. In South Africa, Black Africans were being massacred at almost every protest (Golden, 2004; Holland, 1988; Lynch, 1976; Karimi, 2013; Nelson Mandela Foundation, 2022; South African History Online, n.d.; van Vuuren, 2015; Willoughby-Herald, 2015). And yet changes came.

For Australia, change came gradually (Chang, 2019). But for South Africa, change came after painful clashes, losses, and years of belittlement that the original people were the least of all races because of the color of their skin (Golden, 2004; Holland, 1988; Karimi, 2013; Lynch, 1976; Nelson Mandela Foundation, 2022; Noah, 2019; South African History Online, n.d.; van Vuuren, 2015; Willoughby-Herald, 2015). However, for America, change came through a Civil War and the writing of Amendments to the Constitution. That is, at least in theory.

By 1865, the 13th Amendment was passed which ended slavery (Smith, 2021; U.S. Citizenship & Immigration Services, n.d.). Yet, Black Codes were instituted to maintain cheap labor after the South had lost the Civil War (A&E Television Networks, LLC., 2022; Smith, 2021) while also maintaining segregation (Alchin, 2017) throughout certain states such as Alabama, Florida, Georgia, Louisiana, Mississippi, North Carolina, Tennessee, and Virginia

(Alchin, 2017). These laws began around 1865 (A&E Television Network, LLC, 2022; Anti-Defamation League, 2018; National Park Service, 2018a).

Jim Crow laws were established from the 1880s to the 1960s to keep Blacks in a subservient role (A&E Television Networks, LLC, 2022a; Anti-Defamation League, 2018; Haygood, 2013; National Park Service, 2018a; Smith, 2021). Jim Crow laws were a specific set of laws that were local and state statutes to legalize racial segregation not unlike apartheid laws (Smith, 2021). These laws separated the way of life for millions of people from where they could congregate, what bathroom, waiting room or water fountain they would use (A&E Television Networks, LLC, 2022a; Anti-Defamation League, 2018; Smith, 2021). It would take the Civil Rights Movement to put an end to many of these unjust laws (Belafonte & Shnayerson, 2011; Haygood, 2013; Smith, 2021). However, segregation (Philpott, 2010) would continue, which could be considered a milder form of Apartheid. This reality would exist for decades within the United States.

Figure 8. Picture of Jim Crow
Source: Library of Congress (2022)

Solutions and Recommendations

In this chapter, the solutions are self-explanatory. First, the fact is that in each region, there were tribes. For example, America was tribal (Legends of America, 2022; Petersen, 2022). Australia was tribal and had been inhabited by its native people called Aborigines (Chang, 2019). South Africa was also tribal (Golden, 2004; Holland, 1989; Lynch, 1976; Noah, 2019; M. Wilcox, personal communication, September 21, 2022), and currently consists of approximately 10 recognized tribes and has 11 official languages (Golden, 2004; Lynch, 1976; M. Jacobs, personal communication, August 27, 2021; M. Wilcox, personal communication, September 21, 2022). Therefore, tribes had their own practices, responsibilities, and their own laws to regulate their actions, and the use of the land (Chang, 2019; Legends of America, 2022; Petersen, 2022; The Arizona Board of Regents, 2022).

Second, once these tribes and tribal lands were colonized by Europeans, the tribesmen fought, and many died to re-establish their position. Then new governments were established that promised freedom (Australian Law reform Commission, 2022; M. Jacobs, personal communication, August 27, 2021; M. Wilcox, personal communication, September 21, 2022; M. Wilcox, personal communication, September 23, 2022; Smith, 2021). Through those governments, protest came and continued (Belafonte & Shnayerson, 2022; M. Jacobs, personal communication, August 27, 2021; Noah, 2019; M. Wilcox, personal communication, September 21, 2022). Protest brought about changes to the law that were more just (Belafonte & Shnayerson, 2022; M. Jacobs, personal communication, August 27, 2021; Noah, 2019; M. Wilcox, personal communication, September 21, 2022).

CONCLUSION

In conclusion, land demarcations with human inhabitants have some form of a government. Even before European powers came, the Indigenous people had a form of government within their tribes and had agreements with neighboring tribes. There were people trained as peace and war chiefs. There were medicine men. There were directives.

After European powers came and colonized many of these lands, new forms of government were imposed. America began with 13 colonies that became 13 independent states. Australia was established as a Commonwealth and then in 1900, a Commonwealth democracy. South Africa was a Commonwealth after the Dutch lose power to Britain, and then became an Apartheid State and then was re-admitted into the Commonwealth. Regardless, today, each is or resembles a democracy and has democratic processes operating.

In other words, governments transition. Even if a country does not change its form of government, things change. Much of this change has had to do with the establishing of constitutions and new laws. Many of these new laws eventually brought new freedoms such as suffrage laws and the right to vote. Citizens began to be able to participate in the government in a new way. The world was able to see what the establishment of a democracy looks like when in 1994, Nelson Mandela voted in the 1994 election and found himself to be the first democratic president of South Africa.

However, each of these countries, like so many other colonized nations, had a dark past. There were many grievances to address. Many of these grievances were addressed through laws. In the next chapter, Chapter 10, the reader will learn how some laws became more oppressive and how other laws were written, adopted, and established in practice to address heinous human rights violations, etc. These laws are compared across the three cases (i.e., in an extensive fashion) chosen for this book, which are America, Australia and South Africa.

REFERENCES

A&E Television Networks. (2022). Civil rights movement. *History.com.* https://www.history.com/topics/black-history/civil-rights-movement

A&E Television Networks. (2022a). Jim Crow laws. *History.com.* https://www.history.com/topics/early-20th-century-us/jim-crow-laws

Alchin, L. (2017). *Black codes.* American Historama. https://www.american-historama.org/1866-1881-reconstruction-era/blackcodes.htm#:~:text=Definition%20and%20Summary%3A%20The%20Black%20Codes%20were%20a,War%20at%20the%20beginning%20of%20the%20Reconstruction%20Era

Anti-Defamation League. (2022). *Civil rights movement.* ADL. https://www.adl.org/education/resources/backgrounders/civil-rights-movement

Australian Law Reform Commission. (2022). *Australian law as applied to Aborigines: August 28, 2010.* ALRC. https://www.alrc.gov.au/publication/recognition-of-aboriginal-customary-laws-alrc-report-31/4-aboriginal-customary-laws-and-anglo-australian-law-after-1788/australian-law-as-applied-to-aborigines/

Belafonte, H., & Shnayerson, M. (2011). *My song: A memoir.* Knopf Publishers.

Boshoff, J. J. (2018, January). *The search for the slave ship Meermin. Developing a methodology from finding intertidal shipwrecks.* University of South Africa. https://uir.unisa.ac.za/bitstream/handle/10500/24734/dissertation_boshoff_j.pdf;sequence=1

Bringing Them Home. (n.d.). *Historical context: The stolen generations.* BTH. https://bth.humanrights.gov.au/significance/historical-context-the-stolen-generations?msclkid=e1774539cf4711ec8c533f37dc49e321

Cambridge University Press. (2022). *Tribe.* Cambridge University Press. https://dictionary.cambridge.org/dictionary/english/tribe?msclkid=0c83111dd03d11ec9f800a425784bb04

Carter, E.L., Kemper, K.R., Brown, A. & Phillips, J.C. (2009). *"Executing the powers with which it is in trusted": Justifications, definitions and limitations of government speech. 14 Communications, Law and Policy, 14*(4), 453-478. doi:10.1080/10811680903238019

Central Intelligence Agency. (n.d.). *Field listing: Government type.* CIA. https://www.cia.gov/the-world-factbook/field/government-type/

Chang, C. (2019, January 21). How early Australians treated Aboriginal people. *News.com.* https://www.news.com.au/national/politics/how-early-australians-treated-aboriginal-people/news-story/e984d3a453382c59a1d5d81f99a9ad8c

Commonwealth Secretariat. (2019). *Commonwealth declarations*. Commonwealth Secretariat. https://production-new-commonwealth-files.s3.eu-west-2.amazonaws.com/s3fs-public/202201/Commonwealth%20Declarations%20Booklet.pdf?VersionId=V5eWs7gRYjOcPeco80v0nJ0UrOcS3iNb

Commonwealth Secretariat. (2022). *Commonwealth charter*. Commonwealth Secretariat. https://thecommonwealth.org/charter?msclkid=64c91d17d08311ec9ec693da6e83bf9a

Dahrendorf, R. (2003, October). A definition of democracy. *Journal of Democracy, 14*(4), 101–114. doi:10.1353/jod.2003.0067

Dubow, S. (2000). *The African National Congress.* Johannesburg, South Africa: Jonathan Ball Publishers.

Encyclopedia Britannica. (2022). *Democracy.* Britannica. https://www.britannica.com/topic/democracy

Fasenfest, D. (2010, October). Government, governing, and governance. *Critical Sociology, 36*(6), 771-774. file:///C:/Users/janel/Downloads/36_6.pdf. DOI: . doi:10.1177/0896920510378192

Find and Connect. (2021). *The Aborigines protection act 1886 (1887-1890).* Find and Connect. https://www.findandconnect.gov.au/guide/vic/E000432?msclkid=ec9ee398cf4511ec9b478069421f9580

Gardbaum, S. (2013, February). *The new commonwealth model of constitutionalism.* Cambridge University Press.

Gipps, G. (1840). *1840: 4 Victoria, No. 8. An act to prohibit the Aboriginal natives of New South Wales from having fire arms or ammunition in their possession, without the permission of a magistrate.* Kathy Stavrou. https://www.kathystavrou.net/caught-in-the-act/act5-1840.html?msclkid=86b2337bcf4711ecb557cec86ca930f3

Golden, M. (2014, Winter). *Carnegie corporation in South Africa: A difficult past leads to a commitment to change.* Carnegie. https://media.carnegie.org/filer_public/f3/54/f354cbf9-f86c-4681-8573-c697418ee786/ccny_cresults_2004_southafrica.pdf

Haygood, W. (2013). *The butler: A witness of history.* Atria Books.

Healing Foundation. (2022). *Who are the stolen generations?* Healing Foundation. https://healingfoundation.org.au/who-are-the-stolen-generations/#:~:text=The%20Stolen%20Generations%20refers%20to%20a%20period%20in,Aboriginal%20children%20to%20be%20removed%20from%20their%20parents

Holland, H. (1989). *The struggle: A history of the African National Congress.* Grafton Paperback.

International Work Group for Indigenous Affairs. (n.d.). *Indigenous peoples of Australia.* IWGIA. https://iwgia.org/en/australia#:~:text=The%20Indigenous%20World%202022%3A%20Australia%20Written%20on%2001,Australians%20in%202021%20was%20estimated%20to%20be%20881%2C600

Johnson, A. G. (2006). *Privilege, power, and difference.* McGraw Hill Companies.

Karimi, F. (2013, December 5). Nelson Mandela, anti-apartheid icon and father of modern South Africa, dies. *CNN.* https://www.cnn.com/2013/12/05/world/africa/nelsonmandela/index.html?msclkid=15894e81ced611ecbfb54ac0c0c85ad5

Legends of America. (2022). *Native American tribes list.* Legends of America. https://www.legendsofamerica.com/na-tribelist/?msclkid=e81c0039d03c11ecaf9b4525ddec4ae0

Library of Congress. (n.d.). *The fourteenth amendment.* Library of Congress. https://constitution.congress.gov/constitution/amendment-14/

Library of Congress. (n.d.). *The fifteenth amendment.* Library of Congress. https://constitution.congress.gov/constitution/amendment-15/

Lynch, H. (Ed.). (1976). *The great contemporary issues series – Set 1, Vol. 5: Black Africa.* New York, NY: The New York Times Arno Press.

Marshall, B. (2019, September 17). *U.S. Constitution signed September 17, 1787.* MLWGS. https://mlwgs.com/u-s-constitution-signed-september-17-1787/

Maxwell-Stewart, H., & Oxley, D. (2020). Convicts and the colonization of Australia, 1788-1868. *Digital Panopticon.* https://www.digitalpanopticon.org/Convicts_and_the_Colonisation_of_Australia,_1788 1868

Morales, E.P. (2022, January). *Unraveling abolition: Legal culture and slave emancipation in Columbia.* New York, NY: Cambridge University Press.

Museum of Australian Democracy. (n.d.). *Commonwealth of Australia Constitution Act 1900 (UK).* FoundingDocs. https://www.foundingdocs.gov.au/scan-sid-91.html

National Park Service. (2018a). *Jim Crow laws.* Retrieved on February 3, 2022 from https://www.nps.gov/malu/learn/education/jim_crow_laws.htm

Nelson Mandela Foundation. (2022). *The archive at the center of memory: Timeline.* Nelson Mandela Foundation. https://www.nelsonmandela.org/content/page/timeline?msclkid=320c32c9ced611ecb984658f100a6b7f

Nexus Partnerships Limited. (2020). *The commonwealth.* Commonwealth of Nations. https://www.commonwealthofnations.org/commonwealth/

Noah, T. (2019). *Born a crime: Stories from a South African childhood.* Spiegel and Grau.

Open Education Sociology Dictionary. (2022). Government. *Sociology Dictionary.* https://sociologydictionary.org/government/?msclkid=69710078d03911ec896ef2ae3a565911

Petersen, T.T. (2022, August 12). *Military conquest of the prairie: Native American resistance, evasion & survival, 1865-1890.* Liverpool University Press.

Philpott, D. (2010). *A guide to federal terms and acronyms* (2nd ed.). The Scarecrow Press, Inc.

Schaeffer, F. A. (2005). *How should we then live?* Crossway Books.

Sharpton, A. (2022). *Righteous trouble makers: Untold stories of the social justice movement in America.* Hanover Square Press.

Smith, W. (2021, February 17). *Amend: The fight for America.* [Net Series]. Netflix.

South African History Online. (n.d.). English settlement in South Africa. *South African History Online.* https://www.sahistory.org.za/article/english-settlement-south-africa?msclkid=913ee8bfcdba11eca89fcce63fef6f72

Srividhya, S., Hutchings, K., & Wright, J. M. (2009). *Debating the slave trade: Rhetoric of British national identity, 1759-1815*. Taylor & Francis Group.

The Arizona Board of Regents. (2022). *Tribe*. Azregents. https://azregents.edu/

United States Citizenship and Immigration Services. (n.d.). *Intermediate level: Establishing independence*. USCIS. https://www.uscis.gov/sites/default/files/document/lesson-plans/Intermediate_establishing_independence_handouts.pdf?msclkid=5152e848d10611ec849a49e419e34f13

University of Minnesota Human Rights Library. (n.d.). *All Amendments to the United States Constitution*. HR Library. http://hrlibrary.umn.edu/education/all_amendments_usconst.htm?msclkid=2ff06db1cff911eca379a664ac2ef6af

Van Vuuren, H. (2015). Apartheid, guns and money: A tale of profit. Auckland Park, South Africa: Jacana Media (Pty) Ltd.

Vrieland, D. (2022). *Dr. King comes to Grosse Pointe*. Academia Letters. *Article, 4541*. doi:10.20935/AL4541

Willoughby-Herald, T. (2015). *Waste of a White skin*. University of California Press. doi:10.1525/california/9780520280861.001.0001

KEY TERMS AND DEFINITIONS

Apartheid: A policy of keeping the races "separate" or "apart" from one another.

Civil Rights: A specific class of rights that protect citizens (e.g., United States citizens) and their freedoms.

Civil Rights Movement: A movement launched from approximately 1954 to 1968, which aimed at ending discrimination, institutional racism, segregation, and the like within the United States. Some of its leaders were people like Medgar Evers, Louis Farrakhan, Martin Luther King, Jr., Malcolm X, et al.'

Commonwealth: A union of nations, specifically 54 that work towards the common good, consisting of 2.5 billion members.

Democracy: Coming from *demos* and *kratos*. Meaning a government that is ruled by the people.

Government: a body of governance or entity that contains various branches to administer services throughout various jurisdictions.

Human Rights: Rights that are deemed inherent to any human being on the face of the earth regardless of their country of origin.

Jim Crow Laws: Laws that were instituted by the White man during the reconstruction period after the Civil War had ended. These laws sought to maintain segregation of the races; mainly Whites and Blacks.

Tribe: A group of people who are kin and bound by said kinship as well as demarking a certain/particular territory of land.

Tribal Law: A form of governance that is specific to a tribe.

ENDNOTES

1 See List of 54 Commonwealth Nations.

2 Michael Wilcox is a licensed tour guide who owns Tusk Adventures and Tours. He was my guide for two tours in Cape Town on September 21, 2022 and September 23, 2022 respectively. He noted that Robben Island had many political prisoners. Many of these prisoners were housed in atrocious living conditions because they were protesting the Apartheid government, which included his uncle R.C. Wilcox who acted as the Minister of Sports for Nelson Mandela while at Robben Island.

APPENDIX 1

List of 54 Commonwealth Nations

Antigua and Barbuda (Caribbean and Americas)
Australia (Pacific)
Bahamas (Caribbean and Americas)
Bangladesh (Asia)
Barbados (Caribbean and Americas)
Belize (Caribbean and Americas)
Botswana (Africa)
Brunei Darussalam (Asia)
Cameroon (Africa)
Canada (Caribbean and Americas)
Cyprus (Europe)
Dominica (Caribbean and Americas)
Fiji (Pacific)
Gambia (Africa)
Ghana (Africa)
Guyana (Caribbean and Americas)
Grenada (Caribbean and Americas)
India (Asia)
Jamaica (Caribbean and Americas)
Kenya (Africa)
Kingdom of Eswatini (Africa)
Kiribati (Pacific)
Lesotho (Africa)
Malawi (Africa)
Malaysia (Asia)
Maldives (Asia)
Malta (Europe)
Mauritius (Africa)
Mozambique (Africa)
Namibia (Africa)
Nauru (Pacific)
New Zealand (Pacific)
Nigeria (Africa)

Papa New Guinea (Pacific)
Pakistan (Asia)
Rwanda (Africa)
Saint Lucia (Caribbean and Americas)
Samoa (Pacific)
Seychelles (Africa)
Sierra Leone (Africa)
Singapore (Asia)
Solomon Islands (Pacific)
South Africa (Africa)
Sri Lanka (Asia)
St. Kitts and Nevis (Caribbean and Americas)
St. Vincent and Grenadines (Caribbean and Americas)
Tonga (Pacific)
Trinidad and Tobago (Caribbean and Americas)
Tuvalu (Pacific)
Uganda (Africa)
United Kingdom (Europe)
United Republic of Tanzania (Africa)
Vanuatu (Pacific)
Zambia (Africa)

Chapter 2
A Comparative Analysis of Laws Amongst Western Powers Through the 20th Century

ABSTRACT

This chapter focuses on the laws of America, Australia, Britain (i.e., as a foundation for America, Australia, and South Africa), and South Africa. By exploring the laws of these countries, the author hopes to establish a timeline of events. While Britain is not a main focus of this book, the British Empire has influenced multiple countries worldwide. Moreover, due to colonization, Britain played a major role in America, Australia, and South Africa. By analyzing precipitating events, one can examine when new laws were implemented and the effects of said laws. Then these laws, i.e., the laws of each country/region can and will be compared for a final analysis.

"I don't give a damn about your legislation, middle finger until we are talking about reparations..."-Neelam, Ride on My Enemies (2020)

"We are the ones, 'Cause Pac did a lot more for me than Barack, so look – ladadadadada... The pen is greater than the sword!" -Andy Mineo, Vendetta (2015)

DOI: 10.4018/978-1-7998-9304-2.ch002

INTRODUCTION

The first study abroad program that I completed was offered by Michigan State University (Simmons, 2011). I went to Sydney and Canberra in 1997-1998 to study Comparative Legal Systems, Criminal Justice and the like. I was able to study at NSW and at Canberra University and was taught by professors such as Dr. John Hudzik as well as attend lectures from native Australians (Simmons, 2011). Even while in Australia, my interactions with some police were questionable. And yet, I was also trained by a number of the police detectives or got a drink with them from the bar and sat and chatted about everything from criminal apprehension to the treatment of Aborigines and the issue of Aborigines "suiciding." It was in this country that I became twenty (20) years old and was challenged almost every day to see situations "rightly."

To be frank, it does not matter whether one lives in the United States or Australia or anywhere in between if their civil liberties (i.e., as citizens) are threatened for no reason. Lockwood (1970) addresses this point in stating the following in regard to the United States of America: "The sad truth is that civil liberties and constitutional guarantees are largely a myth in this country in A.D. 1970. Anyone who has ever stood in a police station in a large city watching prisoners being booked will know what I mean" (p. 30). Lockwood (1970) continues and notes that the individual rights that were initially written or listed in documents such as the Bill of Rights "[…] are often applied by our so-called law enforcement agencies in such a way as to deny many people their rights […]" (p. 30). The referenced bill of rights are codified (Gardbaum, 2013), and yet, can still be violated by law enforcement officials, etc. This is not only the truth when it comes to the United States but also to countries like Australia and South Africa.

MAIN FOCUS OF CHAPTER

This chapter will focus on comparing significant laws across the three cases listed in Chapters 3-5. Thus, the main focus of this chapter will be examining the acts, amendments, bills and laws that were passed that affected Black Africans and Aborigines and Black Americans for at least the last 100 years or so. In each country, separateness was valued. This separateness meant advancing the lives and livelihoods of White people at the expense of African or Black people or Indigenous people. Thus, many of the laws appear to be similar in nature such as Black Codes, Jim Crow Laws, Apartheid Laws, etc. Laws such as these usually came after the taking of the land.

Issues, Controversies, Problems

The issues and controversies and problems are so beyond the scope of this chapter that the author has decided to limit the discussion to some of the most poignant highlights. The human rights abuses that have occurred worldwide, especially due to colonization can hardly be addressed nor remedied. Biko (n.d.) stated the following: "White society collectively owes the blacks so huge a debt that no one member should automatically expect to escape from the blanket of condemnation that needs must come from the black world" (p. 8). Nonetheless, the author will do her best to give a general outline and highlight various laws that occurred around similar topics throughout America, Australia and South Africa.

America

America has had a colored history as has been referenced to thus far. America was once known as the New World. Settlers came and took the land. While this section of this chapter will not focus on land use issues, it should be noted that the land could not be owned. America had been established as a land with tribes on it. When the British came, this concept was eroded. It should be noted that each act was a form of genocide and the genocide would have continued if the act(s) had not ceased. According to the United Nations, Section 5 of Resolution 96 genocide did not only include massacres but forced cultural assimilation, sterilization[1] and dehumanization, which were all forms of the theft of freedom and rights (Hilton, 2011). Regardless, acts, amendments, bills, codes, laws, etc. were established on a repetitive basis to control the resources, which included Non-White individuals.

Eventually, colonies were established in the New World, i.e., 13 of them (Dahrendorf, 2003). Native American Indians were diseased, raped and continued to be exterminated and later even sterilized so that their kind could not procreate (Hilton, 2011; Petersen, 2022). The Dawes Act came in 1887, 111 years after America was founded (Hilton, 2011). The land of Native American Indians could be broken up and this led to suffering and poverty (Hilton, 2011; Petersen, 2022). Other Acts were passed that greatly impacted the Native American and address disenfranchising him such as the Indian Reorganization Act of 1934 or the Wheeler-Howard Act of 1934 led the Federal government to purchase land and create more reservations thus redistributing land back to the Native Americans (Hilton, 2011). Eventually, the Native Americans or Indigenous peoples of America formed a resistance against military conquests and various other antagonistic acts by the White man, and continued to fight (Petersen, 2022), and even negotiated trades. Concurrently, Africans were brought to the Americas.

Then the first Africans were enslaved in America (Srividhya, Hutchings & Wright, 2009). Soon, slave codes had been instituted which did everything from restricting movement to banning weapons (Swift, 2022). By the time, America was fully America, the conversation turned to slaves. Was a slave a whole person? The answer was a declarative – "No!"

Three/Fifths Law

The Three-Fifths law (Blight, 2018) was established in America in 1787 in Philadelphia (African American Registry, 2022; Legal Dictionary, n.d.). During the Constitutional Convention, Whites were concerned that Blacks would outnumber them and also there were other issues like taxes and counting the population of each state (Legal Dictionary, n.d.). Thus, during censuses, slaves would only be counted as 60% of a person (African-American Registry, 2022; Legal Dictionary, n.d.). Northern states were concerned that since slaves could not vote, the South should not count slaves to "increase" their populations (Legal Dictionary, n.d.). Due to the vote, Southern states were able to bolster their electoral votes by 30% (Legal Dictionary, n.d.). Eventually seats were reapportioned – known as "slave seats" to address that injustice (Blight, 2018). By the time a slave was no longer considered 3/5 of a person, freed Black men had other issues to contend with at the time (Blight, 2018). As soon as slavery ended, Black Codes were enacted (Blight, 2018; Khan Academy, 2022; Spruill, 2016).

Black Codes

Black codes were also instituted after the Civil War via the Confederate states (Blight, 2018) just as Slave codes had been in place during slavery. These codes were highly restrictive (Blight, 2018; Smith, 2021; Spruill, 2016). They maintained the social strata (Blight, 2018; Smith, 2021; Spruill, 2016), and worked to return the Black man and woman to a place of servility (Blight, 2018). In other words, they were meant to maintain White supremacy (Khan Academy, 2022).

They were created with the intent that Black people would never succeed in America (Blight, 2018; Khan Academy, 2022; Smith, 2021; Spruill, 2016). Blacks were restricted from voting (Khan Academy, 2022; Smith, 2022). In addition, many Blacks were economically restricted and then forced to go back and work for the plantations they had left as slaves (Blight, 2018; Khan Academy, 2022; Smith, 2021). If they chose not to comply, they were often beaten, fined and/or arrested (Khan Academy, 2021; Smith, 2021). According to Blight (2018), the "Freedman's Bureau agents reported over and again about violence against ex-slaves, including whippings. Ritualistic torture, and murders" (p. 473). Black Codes eventually made way for Jim Crow Laws (Blight, 2018; Khan Academy, 2022; Smith, 2021; University of Minnesota Human Rights Library, n.d.).

Jim Crow Laws

When the Civil War was won, an Amendment was added called the 13th Amendment (Blight, 2018; Hughes & Meltzer, 1956; Smith, 2021; University of Minnesota Human Rights Library, n.d). Once passed, Blacks who had been slaves were now considered "free" (Blight, 2018; Hughes & Meltzer, 1956; Smith, 2021; University of Minnesota Human Rights Library, n.d.). The White populace was not happy, and they came up with laws to restrict the movements of Blacks in America before and after slavery (Belafonte & Shnayerson, 2011; Blight, 2018; Haygood, 2013; Hughes & Meltzer, 1956; Johnson, 2006; Khan Academy, 2022; National Park Service, 2018a; Smith, 2011) such as housing restrictions (Vrieland, 2022). The laws that helped to permanently establish segregation and to promote segregation were known as Jim Crow Laws (Belafonte & Shnayerson, 2011; Blight, 2018; Haygood, 2013; Johnson, 2006; Khan Academy, 2022; National Park Service, 2018a; Smith, 2011).

Jim Crow Laws were a set of laws that were both local and state statutes that were established to legalize racial segregation (Belafonte & Shnayerson, 2011; Blight, 2018; Haygood, 2013; Johnson, 2006; National Park Service, 2018a; Smith, 2021). These laws were put into place almost as soon as the Civil War ended by the White populace (Belafonte & Shnayerson, 2011;

Blight, 2018; Haygood, 2013; Johnson, 2006; National Park Service, 2018a; Smith, 2021). Basically, these laws separated Blacks and Whites in almost all public spaces save work (Belafonte & Shnayerson, 2011; Blight, 2018; Haygood, 2013; Johnson, 2006; National Park Service, 2018a; Smith, 2021). They enabled "legal segregation" to take place (Hughes & Meltzer, 1956).

Blacks had to attend different schools, utilize different bathrooms, and water fountains, etc. (Belafonte & Shnayerson, 2011; Haygood, 2013; Johnson, 2006; National Park Service, 2018a; Smith, 2021). This separation was known as segregation. The applicable term to describe this phenomenon is "segregated facilities." Segregated facilities were defined by Philpott (2010) as follows:

any waiting room, work areas, rest rooms and wash rooms, restaurants and other eating areas, time clocks, locker rooms, and other storage or dressing areas, parking lots, drinking fountains, recreation entertainment areas, transportation, and housing – utilities provided for employees, that are segregated by explicit directive or are in fact segregated in the basis of race, color, religion, or national origin because of habit, local custom, or otherwise (FAR 52.222-21(a)) (p. 88).

Figure 1. Picture of water fountains showing the effects of Jim Crow laws
Source: https://www.researchgate.net/figure/Jim-Crow-era-segregated-water-fountains-The-spatial-segregation-of-the-races-was-overtly_fig5_332580025.

These laws not only brought division and reinforced the self-righteousness of Caucasians, but it also caused emotional, physical and spiritual damage to African-Americans and other minority groups within the United States.

While Jim Crow laws were instituted to keep Blacks and Whites separate, the One-Drop rule was the basis for making sure that Blacks and Whites would not intermingle on a more personal level. In other words, Whites were penalized for having even one drop of African/Black blood (Snipp & Liebler, 2012). Therefore, it was not in their best interests to miscegenate with non-Whites.

One-Drop Rule/Law

Another law, which was put into place was that of the one-drop law or one-drop rule (African American Registry, 2022; Bradt, 2010; Johnson, 2006; Library of Virginia, 1924; Pose, 2009; Smith, 2021; Snipp & Liebler, 2012). According to Johnson (2006), the rule basically stated that being "White" was equivalent to being pure. Thus, being Black was less pure (Johnson, 2006; Smith, 2021), and therefore Blacks were a blemish on society (Smith,

Figure 2. Registration of birth and color – Virginia
Source: Library of Virginia – 1924 (Pose, 2009).

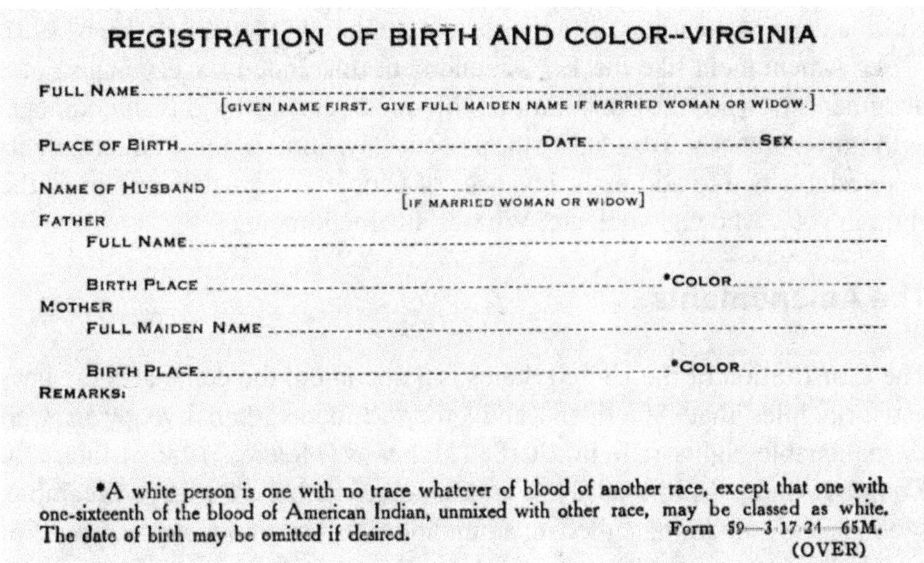

REGISTRATION OF BIRTH AND COLOR--VIRGINIA

FULL NAME....................
[GIVEN NAME FIRST. GIVE FULL MAIDEN NAME IF MARRIED WOMAN OR WIDOW.]

PLACE OF BIRTH.................... DATE.................... SEX....................

NAME OF HUSBAND ....
[IF MARRIED WOMAN OR WIDOW]

FATHER
FULL NAME....................

BIRTH PLACE .... *COLOR....................

MOTHER
FULL MAIDEN NAME ....

BIRTH PLACE.................... *COLOR....................

REMARKS:

*A white person is one with no trace whatever of blood of another race, except that one with one-sixteenth of the blood of American Indian, unmixed with other race, may be classed as white. The date of birth may be omitted if desired. Form 59—3 17 21—65M.

(OVER)

2021). Moreover, even having one drop of blood that was African meant that one could not be considered White (African American Registry, 2022;

Bradt, 2010; Johnson, 2006; Library of Virginia, 1924; Pose, 2009; Smith, 2021; Snipp & Liebler, 2012).

The 'One-Drop' rule was based on the foundational truth that White people were superior due to biology and culture (Snipp & Liebler, 2012). It was rooted in racism and racist doctrines (Snipp & Liebler, 2012). It wound up being influential for over 100 years (Snipp & Liebler, 2012). Technically, the one-drop rule had been established since 1565. However, it was not legislated until later. In the colony of Virginia, in 1682, it was considered an abomination for a Black person to have sex with a White person (Snipp & Liebler, 2012). Sadly, there were penalties for breaking miscegenation principles or laws. For example, in VA, the penalty for having a mixed-race baby was severe (Snipp & Liebler, 2012). A mixed-race baby born to a slave would be a slave for the rest of their life and if born to a White woman; the child would be an indentured servant until the age of 30 (thirty) (Snipp & Liebler, 2012). Many of these laws had been instituted by the Ku Klux Klan who had established that it was a privilege to be White and to have a White birthright (Blight, 2018; Snipp & Liebler, 2012). In fact, to secure this belief, the Ku Klux Klan decided to maintain order through Black Codes, Miscegenation laws and by sending "[…] hooded night riders […] to terrorize colored people by tarring-and-featherings, beatings, and murders" (Hughes & Meltzer, 1956, p. 198).

An Amendment like the 13th Amendment that ended slavery is part of a document known as the Constitution. This document has various amendments as the government had to adapt to the present-day. Some of these Amendments were established to address grievances of people groups such as slaves, the right to vote, who can vote, etc. What is an amendment?

The Amendments

The Constitution of the United States is a document the delineates the laws and principles that Americans and other residents shall live by as well as inalienable rights (Blight, 2018; Hughes & Meltzer, 1956; Library of Congress, n.d.; Smith, 2021). The Constitution began with a preamble, sections and something called an amendment (Library of Congress, n.d.) of which there were ten (10) original Amendments (University of Minnesota Human Rights Library, n.d.). Amendments are additions or changes to the original Constitution (Library of Congress, n.d.). The original Constitution was deemed an authoritative text from March 4, 1789 (University of Minnesota Human Rights Library, n.d.; Smith, 2021). Of the 33 Amendments proposed, there are 27 ratified Amendments (Library of Congress, n.d.; University of Minnesota Human Rights Library, n.d.). Several of these Amendments directly align to this discussion.

First, the First Amendment stated Americans can freely exercise their religion, speak freely, have the right to publish in the press, and to assemble peaceably (University of Minnesota Human Rights Library, n.d.). Second, the Second Amendment which a "well regulated" militia was necessary and that citizens had the right to possess and carry their own weapons for protection (University of Minnesota Human Rights Library, n.d.). Third, the Thirteenth Amendment of 1865 outlawed/abolished slavery (Smith, 2021; University of Minnesota Human Rights Library, n.d.). The literal wording is as follows:

"Section 1.

Neither slavery nor involuntary servitude, except as a punishment for crime whereof the party shall have been duly convicted, shall exist within the United States, or any place subject to their jurisdiction."

"Section 2.

Congress shall have power to enforce this article by appropriate legislation"

Fourth, the Fourteenth Amendment of 1868 noted that no State can deprive an individual of certain inalienable rights such as liberty, life, and property unless due process has been followed and all are to be equally protected under the laws (Blight, 2018; Smith, 2021; University of Minnesota Human Rights Library, n.d.). Fifth, the Fifteenth Amendment of 1870 states that no citizen can be denied the right to vote in a free election (University of Minnesota Human Rights Library, n.d.). Sixth, the 19th Amendment of 1920 states the right to vote cannot be "revoked" due to one's sex (University of Minnesota Human Rights Library, n.d.). Seventh, the 24th Amendment of 1964 stated that the right to vote could not be revoked just because someone failed to pay their poll tax (University of Minnesota Human Rights Library, n.d.). Thereafter, there are more Amendments that address different issues. Nonetheless, America was to be established on its own terms in 1776 and thereon.

To "make America great," many people who were not White or were not male were often overlooked, used, and taken advantage of at almost all points of its history (Hughes & Meltzer, 1956). Like America, Australia had a colored past. However, with some of the same goals that colonization brings, some of the laws were the same or at least comparatively so. While Australia did not have segregation in the form it existed in in America, there was still a form of separateness and there were eventually reservations.

Australia

In 1770, James Cook claimed possession of Possession Island and raised the British flag (Bringing Them Home, n.d.). By 1788 (Bringing Them Home, n.d.; Maxwell-Stewart & Oxley, 2020), Port Jackson becomes a settlement and the Aborigines, and the British begin to have armed conflicts (Bringing Them Home, n.d.) as several laws were began to be implemented. Most of the laws that were implemented in force regarding Aborigines began at the middle of the 19th century (Find and Connect, 2021; Gipps, 1840). This law prohibited Aborigines or Half-Castes from having weapons or ammunition in their possession without permission in New South Wales (24/2/1838-11/7/1846) (Gipps, 1840). The Aboriginal Protection Act of 1869 was formed and then was extended to other regions of Australia and basically stated that the government could act in the best interests of Aborigines (Victoria) (Bringing Them Home, n.d.). This "acting in the best interests" also included forcibly removing their children from their homes (Bringing Them Home, n.d.). This Act was extended over the years and across the provinces of Australia (Bringing Them Home, n.d.; Find and Connect, 2021).

In provinces like Victoria, the Aborigines Protection Act 1886 (1887 – 1890) was established (Find and Connect, 2021). Basically, the term Aborigine was re-defined and therefore Half-Caste were not considered Aborigine and were therefore forced off of their reserves/reservations (Find and Connect, 2021). By 1897, in Queensland, the Aboriginal Protection and Restriction of the Sale of Opium Act was established and made legal the right for locals to be removed from reserves by the Chief Protector and for their children to be institutionalized in dormitories (Bringing Them Home, n.d.).

In 1900, the Constitution for the country is formulated (Museum of Australian Democracy, n.d.). Even though there was a constitution in 1900, in 1901, Australia becomes a federation and Aborigines are not counted in the census (Bringing Them Home, n.d.). However, certain laws do not apply to them (Bringing Them Home, n.d.). In 1905, the Aborigines Act (WA) made the Chief Protector the official guardian of Aborigines under the age of 16 (Bringing Them Home, n.d.). In 1909, the Aborigines Protection Act (NSW) ensured that the Aborigines Protection Board could have custody over children were found to be neglected in some fashion via the Neglected Children and Juvenile Offenders Act of 1905 for New South Wales (Bringing Them Home, n.d.). By 1911, the Aborigines Act (SA) allowed the Chief Protector to be able to move Aborigines and half-castes at will and to still serve as the legal guardian (Bringing Them Home, n.d.). In 1915, the Aborigines Protection Amending Act of New South Wales ensured that the Aboriginal Protection Board could separate Aboriginal children from their families and did not have to prove neglect (Bringing Them Home, n.d.).

In 1923, the Aborigines (Training of Children) Act of 1923 was instituted (Find and Connect, 2018). Basically, the definitions of Aborigine and half-caste were extended so that the State could take possession of any Aboriginal child and hold them in a facility until they turned age 18 (i.e., somewhat equivalent to Foster Care in the United States if a child is deemed a ward of the State) (Find and Connect, 2018). By 1934, the Aborigines Act combined the laws of 1911 and 1923 (Find and Connect, 2018). A year later, the Infants Welfare Act of Tasmania was passed, and Indigenous children could be removed from their parents/families (Bringing Them Home, n.d.). This law extended from 1928 to 1980 where the head teacher had powers equivalent to a constable (Bringing Them Home, n.d.). By 1937, assimilation is adopted as the formal policy for dealing with natives (Bringing Them Home, n.d.).

Due to these grievous acts, Aborigines mark January 26th as their day of mourning in 1938 (Bringing Them Home, n.d.). By 1940, in New South Wales, the Aborigines Protection Board no longer had power to remove Indigenous children from their parents and is renamed the Aborigines Welfare Board and then is abolished in 1969 (Bringing Them Home, n.d.). In 1948, Australia adopts the Universal Declaration of Human Rights via the "newly-formed" organization known as the United Nations (Bringing Them Home, n.d.). The next year, Australia ratifies the Convention on the Prevention and Punishment of the Crime of Genocide, and it comes full sway in 1951 (Bringing Them Home, n.d.).

Until 1965, the Director of Native Welfare was literally the legal guardian for all "Aboriginal" children (Bringing Them Home, n.d.). In 1996, the Aboriginal Lands Trust Act is passed, and Aborigines are recognized as possibly having land rights (Find and Connect, 2018). Moreover, a promise from 1836 is kept as far as having lands reserved (Chang, 2019). In 1967, the Constitution is amended (Bringing Them Home, n.d.). Aborigines are finally able to vote (Bringing Them Home, n.d.) as of May 27, 1967 (Chang, 2019). Thus, Aborigines were considered to be full Australian citizens and had finally been included in the census (Chang, 2019). Another country that had been colonized like Australia was that of South Africa. By 1969, all provinces/states repealed any and all laws regarding forceful removal of Aboriginal children (Bringing Them Home, n.d.). By 1972, Aborigines begin to protest at the capital in Canberra and fight for land rights (Bringing Them Home, n.d.).

In 1975, the Racial Discrimination Act of 1975 is passed (Bringing Them Home, n.d.; Commonwealth Consolidated Acts, n.d.). This act bars all forms of racial discrimination (Commonwealth Consolidated Acts, n.d.). Finally in 1976, Aborigines are granted Aboriginal Land Rights in the Northern Territory by the Aboriginal Land Rights [Northern Territory] Act, which provided for Aboriginal land ownership, recognized said ownership and granted land rights to approximately 11,000 Aboriginal people while other Aborigines could lodge a claim (Bringing Them Home, n.d.; Find and Connect, 2018). By 1980, a program called Link-Up (NSW) Aboriginal Corporation was founded to assist Aborigines to trace and reunite with missing family members (Australians Together, 2022; Bringing Them Home, n.d.). This program was then extended to all provinces (Bringing Them Home, n.d.). Further strives were made toward rectifying some of the heinous outcomes of previous legislation that was put forth to advance the White race. Legislation was passed in 1983 that stated if foster services are needed, Aboriginal children are to be placed with Aboriginal families (Bringing Them Home, n.d.). After being implemented in NT legislation, the following provinces followed: NSW (1987), Victoria (1989), South Australia (1993), Queensland and the ACT (1999), Tasmania (2000) and Western Australia (2006) (Bringing Them Home, n.d.).

In 1987, the Northern territory held elections and for the first time ever Aboriginal people experienced compulsory voting (Bringing Them Home, n.d.). In 1988, a massive protest took place, which came to be known as the Bicentennial of British Settlement in Australia (Bringing Them Home,

Figure 3. Badge: White Australia has a Black history
Photographer: Heath Warwick.
Source: Museums Victoria (Pose, 2009).

n.d.; Pose, 2009). Aborigines wanted the hegemonic society of Australia to acknowledge that their history was founded in Blackness (Bringing Them Home, n.d.; Pose, 2009). And so, they did.

In 1991, the Council for Aboriginal Reconciliation was established (Bringing Them Home, n.d.). It was hoped that in ten years, there would be a full reconciliation (Bringing Them Home, n.d.). In addition, in the same year, a report was presented by the Royal Commission into Aboriginal Deaths in Custody Bringing Them Home, n.d.). It was found that 43% of the cases of those who had died in custody were originally children who had been removed from their families (Bringing Them Home, n.d.). With this hope, comes another in 1992. In a High Court of Australia case named Mabo v. Queensland, it is finally determined and declared that certain lands do have native titles. In other words, the Aborigines existed in the land before White Europeans came (Bringing Them Home, n.d.), which means they did not find anything. Rather, they were ignorant of Australia's existence. Due to that fact, in 1993, the Native Title Act is passed (Bringing Them Home, n.d.; Find and Connect, 2018). The Natives of the land can make land claims on land that is not freehold or privately-owned lands (Bringing Them Home, n.d.; Find and Connect, 2018).

In 1998, the Native Title Amendment Act of 1998 is enacted and amends how Aborigines can claim land (Bringing Them Home, n.d.; Find and Connect, 2018). At the same time, National Sorry Day is instituted on May 26 (Bringing Them Home, n.d.). A year later, the Federal Parliament passes a "motion" and expresses its deep regret over removing "stolen children" from their families and homelands (Bringing Them Home, n.d.). A 'Walk for Reconciliation" also begins on May 28, of 1998 (Bringing Them Home, n.d.).

More laws follow. In 1999, the Federal Parliament issues a formal apology regarding stolen children and their forced removal from their families of origin and their homelands (Bringing Them Home, n.d.). In 2001, the Northern Territory Government repealed mandatory sentencing laws and apologizes to stolen children (Bringing Them Home, n.d.). In 2002, a Reconciliation Progress Report is published in the Social Justice Report of 2001 Bringing Them Home, n.d.). Concurrently, the first stolen child receives money from the New South Wales Victims Compensation tribunal due to injuries and sexual assault she had endured as a stolen child (Bringing Them Home, n.d.). Others were not so lucky and in 2003 the Aboriginal and Torres Strait Islander Social Justice Commissioner publicly criticizes the government for not providing further settlements and forms of reparation (Bringing Them Home, n.d.). Still, more "I'm sorry" statements are issued in 2004 by the Commonwealth Government (Bringing Them Home, n.d.). And by 2005, 'National Sorry Day' is seen as a National Day of Healing (Bringing Them Home, n.d.).

A Stolen Generations compensation board is set up in Tasmania via the Stolen Generations of Aboriginal Children Act of 2006 (Bringing Them Home, n.d.; Find and Connect, 2018). By 2007, the first Stolen Generation case is completed successfully (Bringing Them Home, n.d.). Thereafter, there are more apologies and acknowledgements that the Aboriginal and Torres Strait Islander people were in the country first (Bringing Them Home, n.d.).

Also, key people garner awards (Bringing Them Home, n.d.). Still, there is the question about the land. Like the concept of Liam Neeson in the movie "Taken," the lands of South Africa like that of the Aborigines and the Native American Indians had been taken too. Moreover, restrictive laws had been formed for centuries.

South Africa

By the time that modern South Africa was officially colonized, it was 1910 (South African History Online, n.d.). He had advocated racial segregation and based on this Act; he had removed coloreds from an active voter registration (Lynch, 1976). It was at that time that the South Africa Act of 1910 was implemented (Lynch, 1976). Certain acts, amendments, bills, etc. began to take place. Ironically, Gandhi established the first peace colony or settlement in 1912 (November 17, 1970) (Lynch, 1976). In 1913, the Native Land Act was established, which basically stated that there was or would be limited land acquisition, and it forced Blacks to purchased land on Black reserves (Holland, 1988; South African History Online, n.d.; Willoughby-Heard, 2015).

A law that had been on the books since 1866, was the Pass Laws (South African History Online, n.d.), which then had several amendments. In fact, prior to that, slaves who were at the Cape had to carry passes (M. Wilcox, personal communication, September 21, 2022) since 1709 (South African History Online, n.d.). The pass laws were then converted to the Passbooks (Holland, 1988; Lynch, 1976; South African History Online; United Nations, 2021). The premise was the same. Black South Africans needed passes to work, to travel, etc. The pass laws also worked to make Blacks settle in certain areas (South African History Online, n.d.), which was akin to reserves and forced settlements (Lynch, 1796). They had major restrictions on their movements and the purpose was to control them and know who they were communicating and relating with (Holland, 1988; Lynch, 1976; Nelson Mandela Foundation, 2022; South African History Online; United Nations, 2021). After some time, the humiliation that Black South Africans felt turned to anger (Holland, 1988; Lynch, 1976; Nelson Mandela Foundation, 2022; South African History Online, n.d.; United Nations, 2021)

By 1927, the government determined that not only could they separate Blacks and Whites, but they could also regulate personal relationships (M. Wilcox, personal communication, September 21, 2022). The Act was named the Immorality Act (Holland 1988), which was also known as Act No. 5 of

1927. The immorality act indicated that mixed-race relationships were a crime with an emphasis on sexual interactions (Holland, 1988). By 1950, the law extended to sex between a White and any non-White person (Holland, 1988; South African History Online, n.d.). According to Trevor Noah (2019), there mere interaction of an Afrikaner and a Black was not only a crime but the birth of a mixed baby such as himself was a crime too. This law that many would perceive to be ridiculous now brought in 300,000+ convictions each year in South Africa (Holland, 1988).

In 1945, the Urban Areas Act was implemented (Holland, 1988). Basically, it stated that Blacks could only live with Whites if they were working for them (Holland, 1988; M. Wilcox, personal communication, September 21, 2022). Otherwise, there was to be no comingling (Holland, 1988; M. Wilcox, personal communication, September 21, 2022). Also, for Blacks to live or work in urban areas, they needed to "qualify" (Holland, 1988). If they did not "qualify" (Holland, 1988) they could only be in an urban area up to 72 hours (South African History Online, n.d.).

By 1948, an overreaching system of institutional racism was established known as apartheid (Golden, 2004; Holland, 1988; Lynch, 1976; Noah, 2019; van Vuuren, 2015; M. Wilcox, personal communication, September 21, 2022; M. Wilcox, personal communication, September 23, 2022; Willoughby-Herald, 2015). Under Apartheid, there was a caste system. Blacks were kept separate from Whites, Indians, etc. (Golden, 2004; Holland, 1988; Noah, 2019; van Vuuren, 2015; M. Wilcox, personal communication, September 21, 2022; M. Wilcox, personal communication, September 23, 2022; Willoughby-Herald, 2015). At the top of this caste system were the Whites (Noah, 2019). On November 19, 1948, the United National General Assembly censured the Union of South Africa because they failed to put themselves under UN trusteeship (Lynch, 1976). Ironically, the South African Citizen Act of 1949 was enacted as Act No. 44 of 1949, which set to make full provisions for anyone who was a South African Citizen (South African History Online, n.d.). In making this provision, the Apartheid government also under Malan passed the Mixed Marriages Act of 1949 (South African History Online, n.d.). This Act prohibited mixed marriages (South African History Online, n.d.).

By 1950, the Group Areas Act was implemented or Act No. 41 (Holland, 1988; Lynch, 1976). This act ensured that areas in the city or urbanized areas had zones and these zones were divided by race (Holland, 1988; South African History Online, n.d.). According to Holland (1988), White tenants were the only tenants who could stay in the city of even conduct business in the city (Holland, 1988). Blacks had to hold, rent or purchase offices in the rural areas (Holland, 1988). This law also affected the Indians (Lynch, 1976). At that time, most Indians were the descendants of indentured servants who had arrived in South Africa in the 1860s and therefore stayed in areas like Durban, which was for the Coloreds, which included the Indians at some point (Lynch, 1976). While Indians continued to have full citizenship, they were faced with various restrictions (Lynch, 1976). Thus, each classified race was kept separate (South African History Online, n.d.).

This was done to give Whites a chance to do better than the Blacks (Lynch, 1976). Some of these acts were influenced by the *Broederbond,* which existed to "promote the dominion of Afrikaners" (Lynch, 1976, p. 204). Already, the international community had been watching events unfold in Apartheid South Africa (Lynch, 1976). The United Nations continued to try to fight apartheid in South Africa and lost 8 to 7 in the International Court of Justice (July 12, 1950) (Lynch, 1976).

In the same vein, the government continued to implement controls on Black South Africans (Holland, 1988). In 1950, another Act was legislated, which was called the Suppression of Communism Act (Holland, 1988; Lynch, 1976). Act No. 44 of 1950, which was renamed the Internal Security Act in 1976 basically sought to banish communism from the borders of South Africa (Holland, 1988; Lynch, 1976). The law was so broad that activities such as that of the ANC or SOSA fell under its umbrella (Holland, 1988). In fact, Mandela was charged under this Act as well as the Treason Act and was imprisoned (Holland, 1988; Nelson Mandela Foundation, 2022; M. Wilcox, personal communication, September 21, 2022; M. Wilcox, personal communication, September 23, 2022;). In short, the Act was thought to be used to "stifl[e] opposition to [the] government's policies" (Lynch, 1976, p. 191). On December 6, 1956, 140 people were arrested including White males and females, Asians and "Negroes" including a Reverend Douglas Chadwick Thompson who was the superintendent minister of the Methodist Church (Lynch, 1976). Police busted into his home and ordered him out of his own bed at 4 A.M. (Lynch, 1976). A previous raid had led to an Anglican priest by the name of Reverend Trevor Huddleston being deemed an enemy of the state (Lynch, 1976).

The Separate Amenities Act of 1953 sought to separate people of different races (South African History Online, n.d.). This Act sought to separate classified races (South African History Online, n.d.). However, this separation was to be applied to public spaces and places (South African History Online, n.d.; M. Wilcox, personal communication, September 21, 2022; M. Wilcox, personal communication, September 23, 2022). This was one of the most devastating acts and it contributed to and created racial inequity (South African History Online, n.d.).

After banning interracial relationships and marriages, banning interactions between the races, forcing passes, etc.; the South African government passed yet another act called the Riotous Assemblies Act or Act No. 17 of 1956 (South African History Online, n.d.). This act noted that the public space was not only endangered by race mingling but also by having any gatherings in public (South African History Online, n.d.) where people could actually speak freely. Following this act, the Supreme Court of Appeals of the Union of South Africa passed made a constitutional decision and noted that if facilities were not equivalent then racial segregation would have to be made invalid (Lynch, 1976). The decision was passed down by Chief Justice A van de Sandt Centilvres (Lynch, 1976). This decision was in regard to and referenced Act CA of 1916 where people were not treated fairly on a railroad (Lynch, 1976).

Then the Natives (Prohibition of Interdicts) Act or Act No. 64 of 1956 was passed (South African History Online, n.d.). It ensured that Black Africans would not have a right to appeal to courts regarding forced removals (South African History Online, n.d.). In other words, when they were living on or moved to a homeland, the move was final (Lynch, 1976). Regardless, there was still an issue of carrying passes (Holland, 1988; Lynch, 1976; Nelson Mandela Foundation, 2022; South African History Online, n.d.; United Nations, 2021). In 1952, the Natives (Abolition of Passes and Co-ordination of Documents) Act of 1952 or the Pass Laws Act was passed (South African History Online, n.d.). While it seemed like the repealing of various regional pass laws was a move in the right direction; it just culminated into having to carry various documents in a passbook (South African History Online, n.d.). Thus, anyone who was 16 years or older, had to carry a passbook (Lynch, 1976; South African History Online, n.d.). The passbook contained birth certificate, photo, employment records, tax payments and any criminal record, which one may have had or has (South African History Online, n.d.; M. Wilcox, personal communication, September 21, 2022; M. Wilcox, personal communication, September 23, 2022).

Another bill was being considered circa May 26, 1957 (Lynch, 1976). If passed, Negroes would be classified as being a nuisance if found in a White neighborhood (Lynch, 1976). It would be an omnibus to a native law or an amendment bill (Lynch, 1976). The Minister of Native Affairs noted that if passed, Negroes would be banned or could be banned in White neighborhoods from going to bars, clubs, hospitals, schools and even churches (Lynch, 1976). Churches would have to review on a case-by-case basis if a Negro could go to service based on the availability of a Black church in the proximity, etc. (Lynch, 1976). Minister Dr. Hendrik F. Verwoerd stated the following regarding this possible bill, "[...] these powers are needed to insure that the relations between black and whites here be those of guardian and ward, consistent with the policy of rigid racial segregation" (Lynch, 1976, p. 192).

In 1958, the South African Constitutional Court of Appeal voted 10 to 1 (Lynch, 1976).

The vote was in regard to half-castes or coloreds (Lynch, 1976). There were 38,000 Coloreds in Cape Province and they were placed on a separate voting roll (Lynch, 1976). It was the first time within 100 years, that they would be able to vote in a segregated South Africa (Lynch, 1976). They could not be represented by Coloreds or Blacks and had to be represented by four (4) Whites (Lynch, 1976).

Another bill was to be passed (Lynch, 1976). The "Bill to Promote Self-Government among the Bantu," was passed in 1959 (Lynch, 1976). It was also known as the Promotion of Black Self-Government Act of 1959 and even as the Representation between the Republic of South Africa and Self-Governing Territories Act of 1959 (Lynch, 1976). This act allowed for traditional tribal lands to become Bantutstans or independent states (Lynch, 1976). It was thought that by creating a path of self-determination for eight tribal groups (Lynch, 1976). The eight ethnic groups that were represented were as follows: North Sotho, South Sotho, Swazi, Tsonga, Tswansa, Venda, Zhosa (Xhosa) and Zulu (Lynch, 1976).

By 1960, Albert Luthuli's name came up multiple times in the New York Times (Lynch, 1976). He refused to accept the slogan or policy of "Africa for the Africans" (Lynch, 1976). Rather, around March 19, 1960, Albert spoke publicly (Lynch, 1976). He stated the following:

We, the nonwhites, have come to hate white rule, but not the whites themselves. The whites are grinding us down with repressive measures but they will never destroy us spiritually. The nonwhite today are fighting against slavery. (Lynch, 1976, p. 194).

This was not to be the end of the matter.

In 1963, a strange development took place (Lynch, 1976). The Apartheid government no longer wanted to be associated with the term Apartheid (Lynch, 1976). They instead began to phase out the word Apartheid, which means "separateness" (Lynch, 1976, p. 209). And they began to utilize the term "separate development" (Lynch, 1976). However, this "separate development" worked both ways.

In the inverse, in 1964, the New York Times reported a side effect of Apartheid for the area of Soweto (Lynch, 1976). Ironically, Whites needed a pass to visit Soweto (Lynch, 1976). Soweto's land mass was 26 miles and there were 24 suburbs (Lynch, 1976). In fact, "[n]o Whites [were] allowed without a special permit and no Whites may own land or carry on any form of business" (Lynch, 1976, p. 213). Therefore, Whites were not only barred and banned from business, but they could not live in Soweto either (Lynch,

Figure 4. Selfie cast next to Nelson Mandela on August 26, 2021
Source: Janelle Christine Simmons, Ed.D.

Figure 5. (Myself) pictured in front of the Nelson Mandela house on August 26, 2021
Source: Unknown.

1976). According to a tour I took in 2021, this law still holds. Only Blacks can purchase land in Soweto.

The South African Publications Control Board even controlled what people watched (Lynch, 1976). After creating a movie titled "Zulu," the Apartheid government banned the film (Lynch, 1976). They believed the movie was not beneficial for the natives (Lynch, 1976). Thus, even the Zulus could not see their own history on the big screen (Lynch, 1976). Everything was controlled as was depicted in George Orwell's 1984. When one lives in

Figure 6. Depiction of Big Brother from George Orwell's 1984
Source: www.bing.com. May 9, 2022.

colonized nations, dictatorships, and the like, what is the correct response? Or what is the response that will garner a positive healthy outcome?

Comparing the Laws of Three Nations

This book sought to explore police brutality and to focus on three countries. These three countries are America, Australia, and South Africa. All countries were taken over and colonized by White Europeans who were mainly from Great Britain, which has been established throughout this book. The act of colonization extended the Commonwealth law of Great Britain (Gardbaum,

2013). Only two of the three aforementioned nations broke away from Britain, which was America in 1776 and South Africa in 1961. Regardless, the laws of the land framed the treatment of the Native people in each arena.

Several of the established acts, amendments bills, codes, laws, etc. were similar and served the same purpose – whether the purpose was negative or positive. That is what will be discussed here. It should be noted that in each country just as Europeans did throughout all colonized nations (Fanon, 2008), a caste system was created. For example, in Rwanda, a caste system was created between the Tutsi, which had been the warriors' caste and the Hutu who were the considered to be the commoners. These classifications often led to conflict, especially when the colonizers left. In the case of Rwanda, it led to the massacre known as the 1994 Rwandan genocide (BBC, 2019).

Massacres and genocides were the mark of the colonizer once he had stripped the country of its resources or could no longer control the masses (Fanon, 2008; Hilton, 2011). Nonetheless, before events like these occurred, he had control. He garnered much of this control through the imposition of laws and brute force. However, a similar pattern exists throughout some of these historical events. They all began with the story of an invader.

First, the colonizers arrived. The New World had its first colony from the beginning of the 1600s. Australia had its first settlers since 1788. South Africa had its first colony since the 17th century with the Dutch. Thus, all three countries had been colonized.

Second, after the land was taken piece by piece, reserves were set up or in the case of South Africa – homelands. Land acquisition was blocked in certain areas such as was the case with the Native Land Act of 1913 in South Africa (Lynch, 1976). Also, as in the case of the 1945 Urban Areas Act of South Africa (Lynch, 1976), Blacks were limited as to where they could live. This also was the unofficial case through housing laws whether official or unofficial under Jim Crow in America (Vrieland, 2022). The same was done to the next waves of immigrants such as the Chinese on the West Coast of America (Visit the Wing Luke Museum in Seattle). For Australia, Aborigines were forced to live where the British Commonwealth deemed, they should live and thus stole the rest of the land (Bringing Them Home, n.d.; Chang, 2019; Find and Connect, 2018).

Third, weapons were banned. In South Africa, weapons had been banned since 1840 (Gipps, 1840) even before institutionalized apartheid. In the New World/America, weapons were banned for slaves (Hansen, 2019; Spruill, 2016). Weapons were banned because the White man feared a rebellion. He also feared losing his life to his property. This is consistent throughout the globe (Fanon, 2008; Hilton, 2011) and throughout history.

Fourth, the State put itself in a patriarchal role. Throughout the laws that the reader had read, the State believed they were inherently better than their subjects. Conveniently, their subjects always had darker skin (Fanon, 2008; Hilton, 2011). The State told people where they could live in Australia (Bringing Them Home, n.d., 2019; Find and Connect, 2018).

Fifth, resources were controlled. Therefore, Blacks had a hard time garnering positions of power and wealth as in the case of Slaves and Freed Black men (Blight, 2018; Hughes & Meltzer, 1956; Khan Academy, 2022; Smith, 2021; South African History Online, n.d.). This was the same case for Australians (Bringing Them Home, n.d.; Chang, 2019). And it was the same case for South Africans (Biko, n.d., Holland, 1989; Lynch, 1976; Nelson Mandela Foundation, 2022; United Nations, 2021). Due to limited resources, people were often forced to work for low wages or for exchanged goods (Chang, 2009; Holland, 1989; Khan Academy, 2022). This also applied for lower educations and/or a lack of education (Chang, 2009; Holland, 1989; Khan Academy, 2022; Lynch, 1976).

Sixth, pass laws were established (Hansen, 2019; Holland, Karimi, 2013; Lynch, 1976; Miller, 2013; Spruill, 2016; United Nations, 2021). In South Africa, pass laws could mean the difference between free entrance and exit and a free stay in prison (Golden, 2014; Holland, 1989; Lynch, 1976; Nelson Mandela Foundation, 2022; Noah, 2019; South African History Online, n.d.; United Nations, 2021; van Vuuren, 2015). Pass laws required that Africans/Blacks carry passes to identify themselves (Chang, 2009; Golden, 2014; Hansen, 2019; Holland, 1989; Lynch, 1976; Nelson Mandela Foundation, 2022; Noah, 2019; Smith, 2021; South African History Online, n.d.; Spruill, 2016; Swift, 2022; United Nations, 2021; van Vuuren, 2015). Ironically, Australia did not have pass laws. Initially, Aborigines could go where they pleased (Chang, 2009). However, eventually, the Crown wanted Aborigines to live on certain lands, etc., which were often referred to as reservations.

Seventh, miscegenation laws were passed. Miscegenation meant that Whites slept with, procreated with and possibly married non-Whites (Browning, n.d.; Klamer, 1957; Martinez, 2017). In South Africa, the Immorality Act was passed in 1927 or Act No. 5 of 1927 (Lynch, 1976). In fact, from 1900 until the 1960s, the "Federation" restricted mixed-race relations by curbing courtship through the Aboriginal Protection Act(s), especially in Northern Australia (Bringing Them Home, n.d.; McGrath, 2016). And in America, there were 29 miscegenation laws across various states (Browning, n.d.) such as

Virginia where Whites and Blacks could not legally be married even through 1960 (IMDb, 2022) and on (Browning, n.d.). A case that finally came to the Supreme Court was decided in 1967 and it was known as Loving vs. Virginia, 388 U.S. 1 (1967). It should be noted that all the anti-miscegenation laws made loving someone of a different race a crime (Noah, 2019).

Ironically, there were consequences of miscegenation. In America, the one-drop rule prevailed (African American Registry, 2022; Bradt, 2010; Johnson, 2006; Library of Virginia, 1924; Pose, 2009; Smith, 2021; Snipp & Liebler, 2012). Depending on State laws, one's children could be enslaved (Snipp & Liebler, 2012). Also, children born from miscegenation were considered non-White and there for blemished (Smith, 2021). In addition, depending on

Figure 7. Picture of a scene from a true story called Loving, which depicts fighting anti miscegenation laws in the United States in the 1960s
Source: Bing (2022).

where one was located, they could be harassed or even be in danger of losing employment. Moreover, arrests were common (IMDb, 2022).

Eighth, various forms of laws were formed to separate the White and Black races such as Jim Crow laws in America (Belafonte & Shnayerson, 2011;

Blight, 2018; Haygood, 2013; Hughes & Meltzer, 1956; Khan Academy, 2022; National Park Service, 2018a; Obama, 2020) and Separate Amenities Act of 1953 which segregated all races in public spaces in South Africa (Lynch, 1976; South African History Online, n.d.). In Australia, Aborigines were mainly kept on reserves (Chang, 2009) or on reservations (Bringing them Home, n.d.). Ironically, Aboriginal children could be easily removed from their families, and they were placed in Caucasian families with the goal of assimilation and identifying as White, which would lead to an eventual breeding out of the races (Bringing Them Home, n.d.; Find & Connect, n.d.). The only time Aborigines were kept separate was a contradictory concept of them not being harangued by White men via miscegenation laws Bringing Them Home, n.d.; McGrath, 2016). However, the assimilation policy came thereafter.

Eventually, voting rights were established. Each country banned the voting rights of those they were subjugating at the time (Blight, 2018; Bringing Them Home, n.d.; Find and Connect, 2018; Haygood, 2013; Holland, 2013; Hughes & Meltzer, 1956; Lynch, 1976; Smith, 2021). After a long fight, African and Black and Aboriginal and Indian and Mixed-Race people were allowed to vote. A change had finally come but what would come of it – no one knew.

Solutions and Recommendations

Without sounding facetious, I think that solutions and recommendations are far spent at this point. The fact of the matter is, that each of these three countries that the author chose as cases, presented a myriad of issues and controversies. They also each presented an abundance of acts, amendments, bills, codes, laws, and the like, which were briefly introduced and examined. In the case of South Africa, the legislation was more extensive due to the nature of the South African Apartheid government. After all, a complete and total system had been created that had little flexibility at all.

First, rebellion, revolt and protest were always a response that garnered a response even if the response was unjustifiable. In this context, rebellion, revolt and protest are physical responses. According to Bayard Rustin, a gay Black man who was a Civil Rights Strategist and introduced the concept of civil disobedience and peaceful protest to Martin Luther King, Jr.; the second form of protest was to be physical if it were necessary (Smith, 2021). He also believed part of the principle of civil disobedience was to force a response whether that were to be an arrest or a physical attack and using one's body as a shield (Smith, 2021). They come in the form of fighting back physically such as throwing stones, etc. Now, while this is and should be the last response – when the government themselves becomes a dictatorship; it may be the only response. This often occurred in South Africa as Apartheid progressed due to the barbaric acts of some of the security council. It is the same response that the American settlers had to Britain after the Boston Tea Party. That response is simple: "Prepare for War!"

Second, running away to freedom was and is still a viable response. Every day, citizens of repressive regimes seek asylum all over the world. They seek freedom. This was the case for many Africans in America and Blacks in America who marooned or even made it North or to Canada as well as South Africans who crossed borders and sought help from partners with comparative worldviews.

Third, the law. Every country has laws. One way to change one's reality or at least the foundation of said reality is to change the law itself. Even when the law is passed, ratified, etc., and it is not followed; there is at least some form of instructional manual. One can refer to said law. One can chip away at said law. One can use said law to one's own benefit. The law has many functions.

The law is established to structure a government and tells one what type of country, province, state, etc. that they are living in at the time. For example, when the Constitution of the United States was written, each citizen knew that they were living in a democracy. For the Native and the Slave, that reality was more theoretical and yet it was something that they could gnaw at and work with at that time. The law is also a guide to knowing one's rights. For example, in Apartheid South Africa, the Black knew that they hardly had any rights. The protection they received was not a true form of protection but an isolationist tactic in order to use the Bantu for the White man's gain. The law also sets standards of conduct no matter how arbitrary they or it may seem. In Commonwealth Australia, the Aborigine was eventually forced to live where the White Australian told him/her or could be moved accordingly before and after the Constitution was established in 1900. The law is also supposed to bring about a form of orderly change. That change can be freeing or oppressive such as many of the Aboriginal Acts that were passed in Australia. There is also the issue of peaceably solving conflicts, garnering compensation such as in civil court and/or through mediations and punishment for wrongdoing. Regardless, the law is a powerful truth. It gives one a manual by which they can abide by or pick apart until true justice is served. Each group in each country discussed above, picked the law apart and/or held the White man accountable to said law. This was also a form of protest.

Fourth, record the history. Whether the history is recorded orally as in an oral tradition, or in written form or via video, it is imperative for minority groups and those groups who are being oppressed (i.e., in the case of South Africa it was the majority group) to know their history, record their history and ensure that that history is transmitted to future generations. If one does that, no one can come and try to change the rendering of the factual occurrences that have taken place in the past. It is also a buffer to one's future. If "we" do not forget, we can avoid a myriad of hardships, of one-handed or uneven deals, of trauma and war.

Fifth, it is imperative that "we" that is oppressed groups or descendants of oppressed groups build healthy and strong families. Just having generations is not enough as was learned in Chapter 12 regarding Aborigines and Torres Strait Islanders via the Healing Foundation (2022). Rather, "we" must seek to make ourselves healthy through diet, refraining from foreign substances, removing dependencies, exercising and allowing ourselves to be emotionally and spiritually healed and renewed. This can be done through traditions, through faith, etc. In knowing ourselves and forgiving ourselves, we can tend to the next generations and prepare them to be strong within the framework of their belief system while also transmitting the truth.

CONCLUSION

In conclusion, the act of colonization brings its own set of violence. It also brings its own set of laws. This chapter set out to introduce a myriad of laws across three cases known as case studies, which are as follows: America, Australia, and South Africa. In each of these countries, at some point - were under British rule. Eventually, America became a free country in 1776 as well as South Africa in 1961. They were no longer under British rule. In contrast, Australia is still a Commonwealth of Britain and Ireland as of 1900, but it became a Commonwealth with distinct democratic features.

Each country had implemented laws that encouraged the enslavement of a people. In the New World, the Native Americans or Indigenous people were maltreated in pursuit of their land. Africans were brought to America during the 17th century to work the land and were maltreated as well. Each law was passed to suppress a people group for economic gain and psychological and/ or physical pleasure. In Australia, a people who had lived there for 60,000 years – 80,000 years were almost annihilated. They were then debased and maltreated while facing an unfair division of land. They were also treated like infants. By 1844 and thereafter, Aboriginal children could be taken from their parents with virtually no reason. They were even considered wards of the state as the State was considered their official guardian.

A similar set of events occurred with Native Americans in America. This did not even account for the same circumstances that Aborigines and Native Americans had faced such as starvation, rape, being given poisoned goods, etc. The goal of Caucazoid people during this period was always to rid themselves of the burden of the Native. As far as the African who was kidnapped and had to survive only to come to America to work for a master who only wanted them for work and to rape them, and steal their work products, etc., there was almost no recourse. Tribes were split up, families were split up, new names were given, and people were forced not to speak their native tongue, etc. And yet, over time, progress was made.

While laws were passed to subjugate a people who the Whites had already subjugated, a common thread ran through them all. The message was clear. "You are not us!" As the New World became America in 1776, there was a promise of inalienable rights. However, those rights were for Whites only. These laws did not apply to the Native American Indian or to the African or Black or even the Mexican (i.e., at a certain point). They did not apply to the Asians who came to work the railroad, etc. Civil Rights became a movement where people did not beg for their rights but demanded them as citizens of the United States of America. The question is, where was the land of the brave and the home of the free? Did it exist.

As new Amendments were added, acts, bills, laws, etc.; each country tried to address their corruption. Yet, even when laws were passed that finally protected one's rights; other laws and unspoken practices occurred. For example, seeing how Apartheid was failing in South Africa, America still employed Jim Crow Laws to keep Blacks and Whites separate. By 1963, the first Civil Rights Act had been passed in the United States. In 1967, Aborigines were considered full citizens and could vote. By 1994, Black South Africans could finally vote and were seen as equals. However, look how long these dreams deferred took to come to pass as the White populace held on to the fleeting hope that because of the color of their skin and the aggressiveness of their missions to control others' lands that they were better than them. This inherent belief was not unlike that of Adolf Hitler and the proof of his thought was recorded in Mein Kampf. This delusional thinking led to the slaughter of over 6,000,000 Jews, Gypsies, Jehovah's Witnesses and homosexuals.

As the reader read the laws that the author proffered, I hope s/he considered their gravity and effect. As comparisons were made between each country, it is the author's hope that the reader will see the similarities. It is the author's hope that the reader will acknowledge that "…there is no new thing under the sun" (Ecclesiastes 1:9d). That statement then bears a question, "If there is no new thing under the sun, why do we keep repeating the same mistake?" History was never meant to repeat itself. No man is inherently better than another but different. No race is superior. This is a myth. No one has the same giftings but are called to work with what they have to the best of their ability. There was never meant to be a comparison. Rather, if we as a human race move forward to appreciate the differences in one another, without losing who we are and what we believe, not only will democracy not be a failing experiment; but we may be able to avoid World War III.

REFERENCES

African American Registry. (2022). *The 'one drop rule' in America, a story.* AAR. https://aaregistry.org/story/the-one-drop-rule-abriefstory/?msclkid=b7bcbe86cfa811ecb1 72602642076870.

Australian Law Reform Commission. (2022). *Australian law as applied to Aborigines.* ALRC. https://www.alrc.gov.au/publication/recognition-of-aborigina l-customary-laws-alrc-report-31/4-aboriginal-customary-laws-and-anglo-australian-law-after-1788/australian-law-as-applie d-to-aborigines/

Australians Together. (2022). *The stolen generations.* Australians Together. https://australianstogether.org.au/discover/australian-histo ry/stolen- generations#:~:text=First%20Nations%20people%20wh o%20were%20removed%20were%20left,children%2C%20their%20paren ts%20and%20families%2C%20and%20their%20descendants

BBC. (2019). *Rwanda genocide: 100 days of slaughter.* BBC. https://www.bbc.com/news/world-africa26875506?msclkid=9bdb22 55cfb111ecb557434b79b3261d

Belafonte, H., & Shnayerson, M. (2011). *My song: A memoir.* Knopf Publishers.

Biko, S. (n.d.). White racism and Black consciousness. *SA History*. FtFeb84.1683.7118.001.001.Feb1984.7.pdf (sahistory.org.za)

Blight, D. W. (2018). *Frederick Douglass: Prophet of freedom*. Simon & Schuster.

Bradt, S. (2010). *'One-drop rule' persists racial hierarchy*. Harvard Gazette. https://news.harvard.edu/gazette/story/2010/12/one-drop-rule-persists/

Bringing Them Home. (n.d.). *Historical context: The stolen generations*. BTH. https://bth.humanrights.gov.au/significance/historical-context-the-stolen-generations?msclkid=e1774539cf4711ec8c533f37dc49e321

Browning, J. (n.d.). *Anti-miscegenation laws in the United States*. Duke University. https://scholarship.law.duke.edu/cgi/viewcontent.cgi?article=1544&context=dlj&msclkid=17bb897bcfb411eca933b9a1cad5723c.

Chang, C. (2019, January 21). How early Australians treated Aboriginal people. *News.com*. https://www.news.com.au/national/politics/how-early-australians-treated-aboriginal-people/news-story/e984d3a453382c59a1d5d81f99a9ad8c

Commonwealth Consolidated Acts. (n.d.). *Racial discrimination act 1975*. CCA. http://www.austlii.edu.au/cgi-bin/viewdb/au/legis/cth/consol_act/rda1975202/

Constitution, U. S. com. (2022). *List of the 27 amendments*. Consitiutionus.com. https://constitutionus.com/constitution/amendments/constitutional-amendments/?msclkid=3272ff80cfa911ecab22099cf1237eab

Dahrendorf, R. (2003, October). A definition of democracy. *Journal of Democracy*, *14*(4), 101–114. doi:10.1353/jod.2003.0067

Digital Panopticon. (2020). *Convicts and the colonization of Australia, 1788-1868*. Digital Panopticon. https://www.digitalpanopticon.org/Convicts_and_the_Colonisation_of_Australia,_1788-1868

Fanon, F. (2008). *Black skin, White masks*. Grove Press.

Find and Connect. (2021). *The Aborigines protection act 1886 (1887-1890).* Find and Connect. https://www.findandconnect.gov.au/guide/vic/E000432?msclkid=ec9ee398cf4511ec9b478069421f9580

Gardbaum, S. (2013, February). *The new commonwealth model of constitutionalism.* Cambridge, UK: Cambridge University Press. doi:. doi:10.1017/CBO9780511920806

Gipps, G. (1840). *1840: 4 Victoria, No. 8. An act to prohibit the Aboriginal natives of New South Wales from having fire arms or ammunition in their possession, without the permission of a magistrate.* Kathy Stavrou. https://www.kathystavrou.net/caught-in-the-act/act5-1840.html?msclkid=86b2337bcf4711ecb557cec86ca930f3

Golden, M. (2014, Winter). *Carnegie corporation in South Africa: A difficult past leads to a commitment to change.* Carnegie Media. https://media.carnegie.org/filer_public/f3/54/f354cbf9-f86c-4681-8573-c697418ee786/ccny_cresults_2004_southafrica.pdf

Grobbelaar, P. (1987). *Reader's digest Afrikaans-Engelse Woordeboek English-Afrikaans.* Reader's Digest Association of South Africa.

Hansen, C. (2019, July 10). *Slave patrols: An early form of American policing.* NLEOMF. https://nleomf.org/slavhttpse-patrols-an-early-form-of-american-policing

Haygood, W. (2013). *The butler: A witness of history.* Atria Books.

Hillsdale College. (n.d.). *Political readings: From the Declaration of Independence.* Hillsdale College. https://www.hillsdale.edu/america/

Hilton, B. T. (2011). Frantz Fanon and Colonialism: A Psychology of Oppression. *Journal of Scientific Psychology*, 45–59.

Holland, H. (1989). *The struggle: A history of the African National Congress.* Toronto, CA: Grafton Paperback.

Hughes, L. & Meltzer, M. *A pictorial history of the negro in America.* New York, NY: Crown Publishers.

IMDb. (2022). *Loving (2016).* IMDb. https://www.imdb.com/title/tt4669986/?msclkid=4a10d795cfb411ec971d1432e11b4317

Johnson, A. G. (2006). *Privilege, power, and difference*. McGraw Hill Companies.

Klamer, M. (1995). Whitman, slavery, and the emergence of leaves of grass. University, PA: The Pennsylvania State University Press.

Laurence, P. (2010). *Race classification: Then and now*. Politics Web. https://www.politicsweb.co.za/news-and-analysis/race-classification-then-and-now

Library of Congress. (n.d.). *The Constitution of the United States*. Library of Congress. https://constitution.congress.gov/constitution/?msclkid=6ec01f36cff511ecbfcd5e5be68fe779

Library of Virginia. (1924). *The "one-drop" rule and racial identification by Whites, Blacks and Native Americans*. Library of Virginia. http://www.virginiaplaces.org/population/onedrop.html

Lockwood, L. (1970). *Conversation with Eldridge Cleaver (Algiers)*. Dell Publishing Co., Inc.

Lynch, H. (Ed.). (1976). *The great contemporary issues series – Set 1, Vol. 5: Black Africa*. New York, NY: The New York Times Arno Press.

Macabasco, L. W. (2022, March 8). Lynching postcards: A harrowing documentary about confronting history. *The Guardian*. https://www.theguardian.com/film/2022/mar/08/lynching-postcards-a-harrowing-documentary-about-confronting-history/

Martinez, M. M. (2017). Blackcreole: Too white to be black, too black to be white: Recollections of a mixed-race New Orleans colored creole. Wilmington, NC: DoorKnobFilms.Com.

McGrath, A. (2016, February 11). *Celebrating white men and their black lovers*. SMH. https://www.smh.com.au/opinion/love-and-living-in-early-australia-the-epitome-of-valentines-day-fervour-still-enflaming-a-big-divide-20160211-gmr23y.html#:~:text=Australia%27s%20anti-miscegenation%20laws%20came%20under%20the%20guise%20of,whose%20lacy%20gown%20ignited%20the%20%22white%20wedding%22%20trend%29.?msclkid=241ff2d0cfb611ec9cdc968b2b869935

Museum of Australian Democracy. (n.d.). *Commonwealth of Australia Constitution Act 1900 (UK)*. Museum of Australian Democracy. https://www.foundingdocs.gov.au/scan-sid-91.html

National Park Service. (2016a). *Voting Rights Act of 1965.* National Park Service. https://www.nps.gov/articles/votingrightsact.htm

National Park Service. (2018a). *Jim Crow laws.* National Park Service. https://www.nps.gov/malu/learn/education/jim_crow_laws.htm

Noah, T. (2019). *Born a crime: Stories from a South African childhood.* Spiegel and Grau.

Obama, B. (2020). *A promised land.* Crown.

Petersen, T.T. (2022, August 12). Military conquest of the prairie: Native American resistance, evasion and survival, 1865-1890. *Liverpool, UK: Liverpool University Press.*

Philpott, D. (2010). *A guide to federal terms and acronyms* (2nd ed.). The Scarecrow Press, Inc.

Pose, M. (2009). *Indigenous protest, Australian bicentenary, 1988 in museums Victoria collections.* Victoria Museums. https://collections.museumsvictoria.com.au/articles/2835

Potter, G. (n.d.). *The history of policing in the United States.* file:///C:/Users/janel/Desktop/Publications/Examining%20Black%20Deaths%20in%20Custody%20-%202022/The%20History%20of%20Policing%20in%20the%20United%20States.GaryPotter.8.22.2021.pdf.

Simmons, J. C. (2011). *Kept by Jesus.* Lu Lu Self-Publishing.

Smith, W. (2021, February 17). *Amend: The fight for America.* [Net Series]. Netflix.

Snipp, C. M., & Liebler, C. A. (2012). *The end of the "one-drop" rule?: Hypodescent in the early 21st century.* Princeton. https://paa2012.princeton.edu/papers/121933?msclkid=32762c9fd00211ec9876b854623994a5

South African History Online. (n.d.). *English settlement in South Africa.* SA History. https://www.sahistory.org.za/article/english-settlement-south-africa?msclkid=913ee8bfcdba11eca89fcce63fef6f72

South African History Online. (n.d.). *Pass laws in South Africa 1800-1994.* SA History. https://www.sahistory.org.za/article/pass-laws-south-africa-1800- 1994#:~:text=In%201866%20a%20Pass%20law%20was%20passed.%20Any,the%20Eureka%2C%20was%20found%20in%20Hopetown%20in%201867.?msclkid=7248423ecf6011eca7f20b2ad750dcf5.

Spruill, L. H. (2016). Slave patrols, "Pack of Negro dogs," and policing Black communities. *Phylon, 53*(1), 42–66.

Srividhya, S., Hutchings, K., & Wright, J. M. (2009). *Debating the slave trade: Rhetoric of British national identity, 1759-1815.* Taylor & Francis Group.

Swift, J. (2022). *The curious history of slavery in Africa.* Cornell. https://research.cornell.edu/news-features/curious-history-s lavery-west-africa

United Nations. (2021, July 17). *"The blood we sacrificed was worth it": Sharpeville Massacre.* UN. https://southafrica.un.org/en/135812-blood-we-sacrificed-was -worth-it-sharpeville- massacre?msclkid=9b9122c8ceea11ec9d5355ec4615bbe1.

University of Minnesota Human Rights Library. (n.d.). *All Amendments to the United States Constitution.* University of Minnesota. http://hrlibrary.umn.edu/education/all_amendments_usconst.ht m?msclkid=2ff06db1cff911eca379a664ac2ef6af

Van Vuuren, H. (2015). Apartheid, guns and money: A tale of profit. Auckland Park, South Africa: Jacana Media (Pty) Ltd.

Vrieland, D. (2022). *Dr. King comes to Grosse Pointe.* Academia Letters. *Article, 4541.* doi:10.20935/AL4541

Willoughby-Herald, T. (2015). *Waste of a White skin.* University of California Press. doi:10.1525/california/9780520280861.001.0001

KEY TERMS AND DEFINITIONS

Comparative Laws: Studying different legal systems between countries and comparing the differences and similarities of the laws and possibly the development of said laws.

Segregation: The byproduct of laws such as Jim Crow laws that made it illegal for races such as Blacks, Whites, Asians, and Mexicans to intermingle albeit for work purposes.

Study Abroad: Programs that allow a student to study in another country and possibly transfer credits.

Chapter 3
Case Study:
America

ABSTRACT

This chapter focuses on America as a case study. With the ratification of the 13th Amendment, which ended slavery, other forms of oppression were placed on the Black man and woman in America. This chapter also discusses events that led up to the major leg of the Civil Rights Movement such as lynchings, Black Codes, Jim Crow laws, etc. Continued slights, aggressions and even murders that took place are introduced and discussed. Due to the fact that some of the leaders themselves were Ku Klux Klan members, due justice was often denied. It took over 100 years after the ratification of the 13th Amendment and countless protests, imprisonments, and even assassinations, before true change started to truly emerge in America.

THE STAR SPANGLED BANNER

Oh, say! can you see by the dawn's early light

What so proudly we hailed at the twilight's last gleaming;

Whose broad stripes and bright stars, through the perilous fight,

DOI: 10.4018/978-1-7998-9304-2.ch003

O'er the ramparts we watched were so gallantly streaming?

And the rocket's red glare, the bombs bursting in air,

Gave proof through the night that our flag was still there:

Oh, say! does that star-spangled banner yet wave

O'er the land of the free and the home of the brave?

On the shore, dimly seen through the mists of the deep,

Where the foe's haughty host in dread silence reposes,

What is that which the breeze, o'er the towering steep,

As it fitfully blows, half conceals, half discloses?

Now it catches the gleam of the morning's first beam,

In fully glory reflected now shines in the stream:

'Tis the star-spangled banner! Oh, long may it wave

O'er the land of the free and the home of the brave!

And where is that band who so vauntingly swore

That the havoc of war and the battle's confusion

A home and a country should leave us no more?

Their blood has washed out their foul footsteps' pollution!

No refuge could save the hireling and slave

From the terror of flight or the gloom of the grave:

And the star-spangled banner in triumph doth wave

O'er the land of the free and the home of the brave.

Oh, thus be it ever, when freemen shall stand

Between their loved home and the war's desolation!

Blest with victory and peace, may the heav'n-rescued land

Praise the Power that hath made and preserved us a nation!

Then conquer we must, when our cause it is just,

And this be our motto: "In God is our trust":

And the star-spangled banner in triumph shall wave

O'er the land of the free and the home of the brave.

Figure 1. Wallpaper Cave (2022)
US Map Wallpapers: Wallpaper Cave

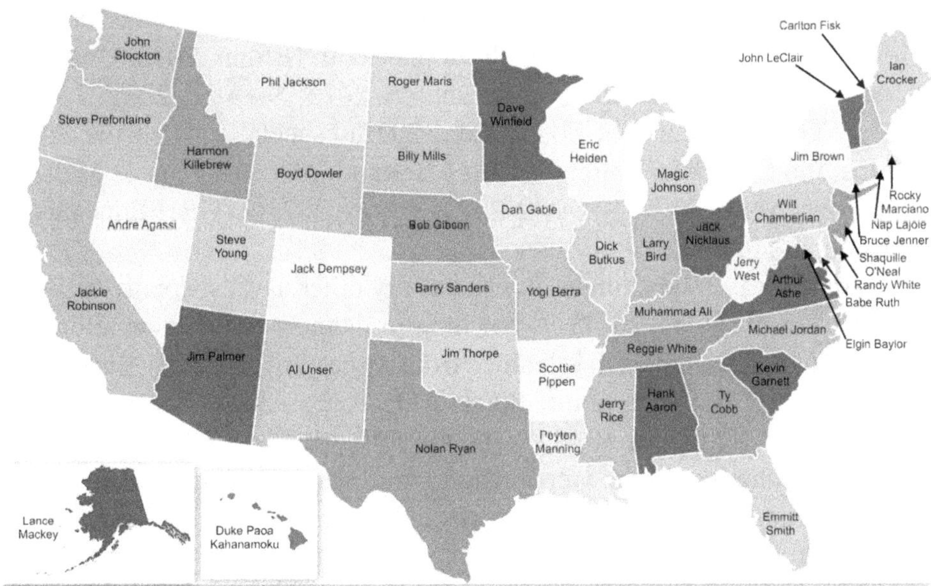

INTRODUCTION

There were a myriad of acts and transgressions that occurred before the Black populace as a whole began to fight the system and fight back hard. From their ancestors' travails and survival through the Middle Passage to being enslaved on a strange land. However, even with the hope that the end of the Civil War brought and the 13th Amendment, there was still progress that needed to be made. The author will introduce this chapter by discussing lynchings. Thereafter, organizations like the KKK or the Ku Klux Klan will be discussed as well as minor civil rights movements and the main Civil Rights Movement as well as their leaders.

Lynchings

The term lynching came from a Virginia Quaker by the name of Charles Lynch (Chestnut, 2008). Charles Lynch authorized "extralegal whippings" against those known as Tories who committed crimes during the American Revolutionary War and who harassed patriots (Chestnut, 2008). The act of lynching someone spread throughout the Western frontier and usually occurred to Whites although other races were not excluded such as African Americans, Asians, Mexicans and Native Americans or Indigenous persons (Chestnut, 2008; WGBH Educational Foundation, 2022). Lynchings[1] became a real concern for Blacks, especially in the South (Blight, 2018; Chestnut, 2008; Hughes & Meltzer, 1956; Macabasco, 2022; NAACP, 2022; Turner, 2021; WGBH Educational Foundation, 2022) especially when the South had lost the Civil War (Blight, 2018; Chestnut, 2008; Hughes & Meltzer, 1956; Macabasco, 2022; NAACP, 2022; Turner, 2021; WGBH Educational Foundation, 2022).

In some areas, a lynching took place every other day, especially between 1889 and 1899 (Jones, 2021). A lynching in its most basic association and form is when a Black person is hanged from a tree until s/he dies (Biography, 2022; Blight, 2018; Chestnut, 2008; Macabasco, 2022; Turner, 2021). Nonetheless, the full scope of the term is as follows; "[l]ynching is the killing of African Americans who were tortured, mutilated, burned, shot, dragged, or hung; accused of an alleged crime by a white mob; and deprived of their life without due process and equal protection of the law" (Chestnut, 2008, p. 2). The NAACP (2022) defines as lynching as follows; "A lynching is the public killing of an individual who has not received due process" (p.1).

Lynchings occurred for a myriad of reasons that were conjured up by the White man. For example, often, Black men were lynched for allegedly making sexual advances at the White man's White women (Jones, 2021; Macabasco, 2022; NAACP, 2022; Turner, 2021) as noted by Frederick Douglas (Blight, 2018), or for other offenses such as arson, murder, or vagrancy (NAACP, 2022). To be frank, any excuse could and would be made in order to kill another Black man and advance the White race (Jones, 2021, Macabasco, 2022; NAACP, 2022; Turner, 2021). Nonetheless, according to Ida B. Wells-Barnett, more of the truth is that those who were often lynched were of some prominence and were seen as a threat or as competition for the White man who wanted to continue to advance his own race at the expense of another (WGBH Educational Foundation, 2022). Approximately 28% of non-Black people were lynched for crimes such as helping a Black person, or being an immigrant (NAACP, 2022). According to the NAACP (2022). From 1882 to 1968, there were approximately 4,743 lynchings within the United States of America (NAACP, 2022). According to Ida B. Wells-Barnett who was an activist and an author (Chestnut, 2008) and an investigative journalist (Smith, 2021), from 1880 to 1941, approximately 4,179 people were lynched (Chestnut, 2008).

Figure 2. The family of Frazer Baker, a Postmaster – who was lynched along with his infant daughter (via bullets) and an angry White mob on February 22, 1898, for being an "uppity nigger."
Source: Library of Congress (2022)

The story of Frazier Baker was not an anomaly (Chestnut, 2008). While people like Ida B. Wells-Barnett fought for reparations for the Baker family, she was never able to acquire funding from the government unlike the family of the three Italians who had been lynched and were given $25,000 (Chestnut, 2008). Lynchings could be conducted by anyone or any mob of White people due to any criminal accusation that they decided to make at the time (Hughes & Macabasco, 2022; Meltzer, 1956; NAACP, 2022; Turner, 2021). Lynchings were used as forms of "wholesale intimidation" according to Dr. Jalane Schmidt (AARP Virginia, 2022). By January 20, 1900, Hughes & Meltzer (1956) noted that following: "George H. White introduced in-to the House of Representatives the first bill designed to make lynching a federal offense" (p. 232). It was a struggle indeed.

The fact is that lynchings took place in order to maintain the status quo (Hughes & Meltzer, 1956). Ida. B. Wells noted that [lynching as as] form of intimidation [was used to] preserve the plantation econ-omy and the white ballot box of the South" (Hughes & Meltzer, 1956, p. 233). Thus, lynchings were an indicator of "who belonged to the body of politic and who did not" (AARP Virginia, 2022). One organization that decided that Black people did not belong to the body of politic was the Ku Klux Klan.

MAIN FOCUS OF CHAPTER

The main focus of this chapter the causes of the Civil Rights Movement and some of the main incidents that left a subpopulation of the United States frustrated beyond belief is explored here. One organization that formed almost immediately after the Civil War ended was the Ku Klux Klan. The Klan included town, county, city, and state leaders such as police officers, which worked to terrorize the Black population. They were part of a massive resistance that worked to keep White America separate from Black America.

Ku Klux Klan

At the ending or after the end of the Civil War, an organization formed (Blight, 2018; Hughes & Meltzer, 1956; National Geographic Society, 2022; National Law Enforcement Museum, personal communication, March 12, 2022; Turner, 2021) that wanted to make it exceedingly clear that Blacks did not belong to the "body of politic" (AARP Virginia, 2022). This organization also wanted to make it clear that it would be in juxtaposition to the Republican Party, and any, and all Reconstruction-era policies (National Geographic Society, 2022a). That organization was known as the Ku Klux Klan (Blight, 2018; Hughes & Meltzer, 1956; Turner, 2021), and it was considered to be a terroristic group (National Geographic Society, 2022; National Law Enforcement Museums, personal communication, March 12, 2022) that was formed in Pulaski, Tennessee in 1865 (National Geographic Society, 2022a) in order to maintain a low status quo for newly freed slaves (Hughes & Meltzer, 1956; National Law Enforcement Museum, personal communication, March 12, 2022). By 1870, the Ku Klux Klan also known as the KKK had a chapter(s) in almost every Southern State (National Geographic Society, 2022a). By 1977, 7,000 Southerners had been arrested for violating the Civil Rights Laws of law-abiding African American citizens (National Law Enforcement Museum, personal communication, March 12, 2022).

This group is still considered to be an active domestic terroristic group specific to the United States of America (National Geographic Society, 2022). They were known for coming out in the white hoods to cause havoc on Black society (Hughes & Meltzer, 1056). As Billie Holiday sang it, they are responsible for the Black bodies that were continuing to swing in the breezes of the deep South (Biography, 2022).

"Southern trees bear a strange fruit, blood on the leaves and blood at the root. Black bodies swinging in the Southern breeze, strange fruit hanging from the poplar trees." – Billie Holiday (1939) – (Biography, 2022)

While it appears to be unheard of to see or read about a Black body hanging from a poplar tree these days, some may question whether certain acts of excessive force and police brutality are not modern forms of lynchings. Just as before some officers may be members of the KKK or organizations like it as well as prosecutors and judges.

Figure 3. Picture of a placard regarding the KKK at the National Law Enforcement Museum in Washington, D.C., March 12, 2022
Source: Janelle Christine Simmons, Ed.D. © 2022

Regardless, this organization still operates within the United States today and was quite active when I was a student at Michigan State University in various areas of Michigan such as Howell, MI, which known as the arena or home of the Grand Dragon Bob Miles (Michigan Radio, 2017). However, currently, there is no active KKK chapter in Howell, MI (Morehouse, 2018), and some disagree there ever was (Michigan Radio, 2017). Nonetheless, in a town like Howell, a lynching may have taken place if more Black people were there due to the fact that Howell is a racist town (History and Social Justice Website, 2022) just like many towns were down South.

While lynching(s) were still occurring, Black men were still being invited to the White House (Haygood, 2013). One such man was Booker T. Washington (Haygood, 2013). Such invitations continued to open avenues of dialogue to the future of the country and Civil Rights for Black Americans. These changes eventually led to a conversation that led for other minority groups well into the 21st century to also obtain "rights."

Another Great Man: Booker T. Washington

By October 16, 1901, another Black man who had been a slave known as Booker T. Washington was the first to dine at the White House (Haygood, 2013). He had been a born slave (Blight, 2018) and was born on April 5, 1856 (Hughes & Meltzer, 1956). President Theodore Roosevelt sat with Booker T. Washington and discussed issues of the South (Haygood, 2013). When the news leaked that a sitting president had actually invited and dined with a Black man, especially a Black man named Booker T. Washington – all hell broke loose (Haygood, 2013). The *Maryland Scimitar* indicted and charged the President with no trial, judge, or jury by stating the following:

The most damnable outrage which has ever been perpetrated by any citizen of the United States was committed yesterday by the president, when he invited a nigger to dine with him at the White House. [...] It is only recently that President Roosevelt boasted that his mother was a Southern woman, and that he is half Southern by reason of the fact. By inviting a nigger to his table he pays his mother small duty..." (Haygood, 2013, p. 50).

While men like Frederick Douglas and Booker T. Washington had been invited to the White House – a place that most Blacks could only dream of walking through, Black Americans were standing up for their rights. The "standing" or being a "standing man" took various forms and came in various expressions. Nonetheless, all the expressions and forms came in the form of defiance! That defiance grew as they were continuously denied their rights and basic dignity and respect by their White counterparts.

The Defiance of Denial

As pressures continued to keep Whites segregated from Blacks except for interactions when working, usually in positions of servitude for the Black man or woman, a righteous anger arose. Many Black people were part of the protest. Protests in all of their forms came in various ways and were accomplished through various means. One means of protest was to create "their own. This was the case in the case of the Negro Leagues and the Negro Leagues Baseball Museum (https://www.nlbm.com/).

Figure 4. Standing plaque commemorating the Negro leagues Baseball Museum, Kansas City, Missouri
Source: Janelle Christine Simmons, Ed.D. © 2019.

However, eventually many Black people began to fight against segregation completely. One of the main ways to fight against segregation was to acquire an equal education (Blight, 2018; Hughes & Meltzer, 1956; Haygood, 2013; Irons, 2002; Woodward, 1966). Regardless of the systematic battle, the form of nonviolent protest that had begun with Gandhi in India, Britain and South Africa was continued by Martin Luther King, Jr. in the United States of America (M. Jacobs, personal communication, August 27, 2021). "It became a beacon for other dispossessed, marginalized groups – including Black Americans in Jim Crow South – intent on securing their freedom" (Obama, 2020, p. 599).

Figure 5. Civil disobedience preparation meetings
Source: Howard Sochurek - Life Pictures (1960).
Civil Rights: Photos From Sit-ins and Protest Training Sessions, 1960 (life.com)

Figure 6. Civil rights protest in Petersburg, VA
Source: Howard Sochurek, Life Pictures (1960)

Figure 7. Picture of a protest placard, the Negro League Baseball Museum, Kansas City, Missouri
Source: Janelle Christine Simmons, Ed.D. © 2019.

Figure 8. Martin Luther King, Jr. speaking at a church in Virginia in 1960
Source: Howard Sochurek - Life Pictures © 1960.

Spotlight: Eugene Allen

Eugene Allen saw such defiance and he also saw prominent White men, such as the President of the United States stand up and fight for the freedoms listed in the Constitution and the Declaration of Independence that were not initially meant to apply to the Black race nor the Indigenous race, nor the Hispanic race; but that in the true spirit of the document were deemed to extend to all races of the human race. In The Butler: A Witness to History, Haygood (2013) states the following regarding a conversation between Eugene Allen and his wife Helene:

During the tense Little Rock school desegregation crisis, he watched President Eisenhower argue with Arkansas governor Orval Faubus over the phone. It made him mighty proud when Eisenhower sent in federal troops to protect black schoolchildren. He was there when President Kennedy had to protect James Meredith on the campus of the University of Mississippi in 1963 as the school, by court order, was forced to allow the first black student to enroll. (p. 11).

A flurry of dates passed by, and a flurry of events continued to take place (Hughes & Meltzer, 1956). On May 2, 1963, Martin Luther King, Jr. led a peaceful protest to Downtown Birmingham, Alabama (Irons, 2002; National Law Enforcement Museum, personal communication, March 12, 2022; Woodward, 1966). This peaceful protest turned into a violent series of altercations (National Law Enforcement Museum, personal communication, March 12, 2022). After taking legal action, the police arrested hundreds of protestors (National Law Enforcement Museum, personal communication, March 12, 2022; Irons, 2002; Smith, 2021; Woodward, 1966), and many of them were captured through a series of terroristic acts. Eugene "Bull" Connor utilized the police and the fire department with hoses to stop the progression of said peaceful protest (National Law Enforcement Museum, personal communication, March 12, 2022).

These dates and times and intersections of both physical and spiritual space eventually and finally led to the March on Washington (Bond-Nelms, 2018; Irons, 2002; McGovern Library and Dakota Wesleyan University, 2022; Smith, 2021; Woodward, 1966). On August 28, 1963 – a well-known event took place which had been organized by key civil rights leaders (Bond-Nelms, 2018; McGovern Library and Dakota Wesleyan University, 2022; Smith, 2021). A number of 200,000 (McGovern Library and Dakota Wesleyan University, 2022) to 300,000 (Bond-Nelms, 2018) has been given who were in attendance and congregated in Washington, D.C. to march peacefully (Bond-Nelms, 2018; McGovern Library and Dakota Wesleyan University, 2022). Their purpose and intent were to "force" new civil rights laws and ongoing legislation (McGovern Library and Dakota Wesleyan University, 2022; Smith, 2021). It was on this day that Martin Luther King, Jr. gave his "I Have a Dream" speech (Blight, 2018; Irons, 2002; McGovern Library and Dakota Wesleyan University, 2022; U.S. Embassy & Consulate in the Republic of Korea - Busan, n.d.; Smith, 2021).

It was often during peaceful demonstrations or even protests, that the police arrived (National Law Enforcement Museum, personal communication, March 12, 2022). In fact, law enforcement often arrived (National Law Enforcement Museum, personal communication, March 12, 2022; Smith, 2021), and sometimes they arrived ready to rumble. It was due to instances like these in the sixties that police began to search for a better way to interact with the public, especially the Black community (National Law Enforcement Museum, personal communication, March 12, 2022). Thus, community policing began to change (National Law Enforcement Museum, personal communication,

March 12, 2022). It appears that the "dream" (Blight, 2018; Irons, 2002) was slowly being realized. This topic will be discussed further later in this book.

The Loss of a Great Man

One of the greatest proponents for civil rights and for the Civil Rights Movement was an Irishman and a Catholic by the name of John Fitzgerald Kennedy (Irons, 2002; Woodward, 1966). John F. Kennedy was born on May 19, 1917, in Brookline, MA (IMDb, 2022). He became the youngest president of the United States when he became the 35th president of the United States (Friedel & Sidey, 2006). He was a registered Democrat (Haygood, 2013). He also was fighting within his own Democratic party against the "intransigent Southern Democrats [...] over the issue of civil rights" (Haygood, 2013, p. 12).

He also hosted more Black people at the White House than any other president until that point (Haygood, 2013) – both to discuss civil rights but also to model behavior and build bridges of peace, hope and love. He had been a president that everyone would remember. On November 22, 1963, he was gunned down by Lee Harvey Oswald in Dallas Texas (Friedel & Sidey, 2006; National Law Enforcement Museum, personal communication, March 12, 2022; Smith, 2021). His death was to bring a blow to the nation and the world.

Less than a year after John F. Kennedy's death (IMDb, 2022), the 24th Amendment was passed on June 23, 1964 (National Park Service, 2016a). The amendment was passed to bar unfair voting practices such as poll taxes (National Park Service, 2016a). The amendment states the following in Section 1: "The right of citizens of the United States to vote in any primary or other election for President or Vice President, for electors for President or Vice President, or for Senator or Representative in Congress, shall not be denied or abridged by the United States or any State by reason of failure to pay any poll tax or other tax" (Library of Congress, n.d., p. 1). Section 2 continues and reads as follows: "The Congress shall have power to enforce this article by appropriate legislation" (Library of Congress, n.d., p. 1). Yet, even once this Amendment was passed, illegal practices continued. This may account for why only two (2) percent of African Americans were even registered to vote (National Park Service, 2016a).

In the mist of this apparent victory, a lynching took place (Federal Bureau of Investigation, 2006; Woodward, 1966). A young boy by the name of Emmett Till, a 14-year-old boy (Federal Bureau of Investigation, 2006;

Hughes & Meltzer, 1956; WGBH Educational Foundation, 2022; Woodward, 1966) traveled from Chicago to Money, Mississippi to visit family members (Federal Bureau of Investigation, 2006). He was chatting up White people at a store he stopped at and showing pictures of his White friends. He was accused of flirting with one Mrs. Bryant, one of the owners of the shop by whistling at her (Federal Bureau of Investigation, 2006; Hughes & Meltzer, 1956), and even whistling at her (Hughes & Meltzer, 1956). And just like that, Emmett Till was to be no more (Hughes & Meltzer, 1956; Smith, 2021; WGBH Educational Foundation, 2022). He was kidnapped, beaten and then he was shot in the head (i.e., lynched) (Hughes & Meltzer, 1956) on August 28, 1964 (Federal Bureau of Investigation, 2022). His body was thrown into the Tallahatchie River with a large metal fan that had been tied to his neck via barbed wire (Hughes & Meltzer, 1956; Federal Bureau of Investigation, 2006). According to the Federal Bureau of Investigation (2006), "[a]though justice ha[d] not been served [...], the tragic murder helped galvanize the growing civil rights movement in [the United States from] the 1950s and beyond" (p. 1). Mass resistance continued (Hughes & Meltzer, 1956; Smith, 2021).

Figure 9. Emmett Till's mother mourns for her dead son, 1964
Source: Bing Images. (2022).

It was in the midst of this dark night, that Black people were still working for greater Civil Rights and making sure that the Civil Rights Act was being upheld. Even after this Act was passed, President Johnson met with Martin who had just received the Nobel Peace Prize in Norway and noted that the country needed to rest from the dissension that the Civil Rights Movement and civil rights had caused (Belafonte & Shnayerson, 2011). The statement is shocking and the apparent inuendo and throwback to slavery is compelling. In other words, for a sitting president to tell one of the most famous Civil Rights proponents in American history to stop making a fuss reeks of master without the ability to utilize a whip, This is especially the case considering every Amendment of the Constitution speaks to a civil right and a right of engagement as a United States citizen; King still went on to lead the march to Selma (Belafonte & Shnayerson, 2011; Irons, 2002) from the Edmund Pettus Bridge (Haygood, 2013; National Park Service, 2018). On March 7, 1965, Martin Luther King, Jr., and other peaceful protesters marched in honor of Jimmie Lee Jackson (National Park Service, 2018) who was a civil rights activist in Marion, Alabama and who was also a deacon in his Baptist Church (Smith, 2021). The march started in Selma and went to Montgomery, Alabama (McGovern Library, Dakota Wesleyan University, 2022; Smith, 2021). The day was called "Bloody Sunday" Alabama (McGovern Library, Dakota Wesleyan University, 2022; Smith, 2021) and on that day, King marched on to address issues such as civil unrest, racism, inequality, the Klan, police brutality, et al.

The Dangers That They Faced: Martin Luther King, Jr.

Martin Luther King, Jr. was/is known worldwide (Hughes & Meltzer, 1956; Smith, 2021; Vrieland, 2022). He was a prolific leader during the Civil Rights Movement (Belafonte & Shnayerson, 2011; Hughes & Meltzer, 1956; Irons, 2002; National Park Service, 2018; Smith, 2021; Vrieland, 2022; Woodward, 1966). He practiced principles of Mohandas Karamchand Gandhi known as nonviolent protest (M. Jacobs, personal communication, August 27, 2021; Obama 2020; M. Wilcox, personal communication, September 21, 2022). For many, he did not just fight for justice but "he nourished [their] soul" (Belafonte & Shnayerson, 2011, p. 297).

And yet, Martin was surveilled by government agencies (Belafonte & Shnayerson, 2011) as were many Civil Rights Leaders such as Malcolm X (TRT World, 2021). Specific to Martin Luther King, Jr., Belafonte & Shnayerson (2011) state the following: "The pressures Martin felt were not just political. Death threats came with unnerving frequency. Often enough he heard about them from the FBI. Yet this was the same FBI that under J.

Edgar Hoover was wiretapping his conversations in motel rooms" (p. 297). He was also arrested repeatedly (Hughes & Meltzer, 1956).

During March of 1965, Martin Luther King Jr. led marches in Selma, Alabama to dramatize the voting issue. Selma had a record of using violence to prevent African Americans from voting (National Park Service, 2016a; Smith, 2021). Some de-segregationists and African Americans who voted were even fired from their jobs or positions (Woodward, 1966). Shortly after the marches, President Johnson sent a voting rights bill to Congress to remove race-based restrictions. This bill was quickly adopted by Congress and signed into law (National Park Service, 2016a). The Voting Rights Act of 1965 made discriminatory voting practices illegal (Woodward, 1966). It is still considered to be one of the most far-reaching pieces of Civil Rights legislation.

It should be noted that before the March on Selma took place, another great Civil Rights Leader had fallen. His name was Malcolm X (Ali, 2016; Lee, 1992; Peck 2017; Smith, 2021; TRT World, 2021), formerly known as Malcolm Little (Lee, 1992). He died at the age of 39 in February 1965 – gunned down while speaking at a Nation of Islam event (Ali, 2016; Belafonte & Shnayerson, 2011; Bridgewater State University, 2007; Lee, 1992; Smith, 2021; WorldHistory.edu, 2019). Due to his resistance to White oppression, he had been vilified. However, it was not until he turned to true "Islam" and called for peace that he became a threat to both the Nation of Islam and continued to be a threat to the government of the United States of America (Bridgewater State University, 2007; Lee, 1992; Phorn, et al., 2017; WorldHistory.edu, 2019). Before his death, he faced a myriad of dangers.

The Dangers That They Faced: Malcolm X

Malcolm Little was born in Omaha, Nebraska in May of 1925 (Bridgewater State University, 2017; Lee, 1992; WorldHistory.edu, 2019) on the 19th (Bridgewater State University, 2007). He was born to Louise Little (Phorn, Price, Moralic & Roonemaa, 2017) or Louise Norton (Bridgewater State University, 2007), and Earl Little (Bridgewater State University, 2007; Phorn, Price, Moralic & Roonemaa, 2017). His father was a Baptist preacher (Bridgewater State University, 2017; Lee, 1992; Phorn, et al., 2017) who was also a Black Nationalist and supported leaders like Marcus Garvey (WorldHistory.edu, 2019). His father often received death threats and eventually their home was burned down in Lansing, MI (Phorn, et al., 2017) in 1929 (Bridgewater State University, 2007). Sometime later, his father's body was found on the railroad tracks (Lee, 1992; Phorn, etc., 2017). Malcolm was only five (5) years old (Phorn, etc., 2017). Eventually, his mother had a nervous breakdown, and all eight (8) kids were split up and put in orphanages (Bridgewater State University, 2007).

Malcolm began to "run the streets" after he became truant (Lee, 1992; WorldHistory.edu, 2019) and began selling drugs, burglarizing homes and was even known to dabble in the prostitution ring (Bridgewater State University, 2007; Phorn, et al., 2017; WorldHistory.edu, 2019) all throughout Boston (Bridgewater State University, 2007). By 1946, Malcolm had been arrested and jailed, which led to a ten-year bid (Bridgewater State University, 2007; Lee, 1992; Phorn, et al., 2017; WorldHistory.edu, 2019). He met a man named Baines (Lee, 1992; Phorn, et al., 2017) who taught him about the Nation of Islam, and he became a star pupil and eventually converted to the Nation of Islam (Bridgewater State University, 2007; Lee, 1992; Phorn, et al., 2017; WorldHistory.edu, 2019). Malcolm dropped his slave name "Little" and replaced it with an X for the unknown quantity of his origin (Lee, 1992; Phorn, et al., 2017). By 1952, he was paroled early, and he became one of the most outspoken speakers for the NOI or Nation of Islam (Bridgewater State University, 2007; Lee, 1992; Phorn, et al., 2017; WorldHistory.edu, 2019).

By 1958, he had met and married Betty Shabbaz (Lee, 1992; WorldHistory.edu, 2019). He had four daughters and they lived in a home in East Elmhurst, Queens (Bridgewater State University, 2007) and everything seemed to be progressing. However, five years later in 1963, Malcolm X found out that his mentor and leader, Elijah Muhammad had had several affairs and illegitimate children (Bridgewater State University, 2007; Lee, 1992). He was greatly disappointed and split from the NOI and founded his own Muslim organization and began to explore Islam from its roots (Bridgewater State University, 2007; Lee, 1992; WorldHistory.edu, 2019). He went to Saudi Arabia and did *Hajj* and became a changed man (Bridgewater State University, 2007; Lee, 1992). Upon his return in 1964, he was not only a threat to the White establishment, but he was also a threat to the Nation of Islam (Bridgewater State University, 2007; Lee, 1992; TRT World, 2021; WorldHistory.edu, 2019).

While Malcolm X was initially standing against the tyranny of the White men in America and the treatment of himself and his people, he did not only face the general dangers of racism. Malcolm X was a "marked man." According to Bridgewater State University (2007), the "FBI informants working in the NOI warned officials that Malcolm had been marked for assassination" (Bridgewater State University, 2007). On February 14, 1965,

Betty and Malcolm's home was firebombed (Bridgewater State University, 2007). One week later, on February 21, 1965, Malcolm went to speak in front of 400 people at the Manhattan Audubon Ballroom, Malcolm was gunned down by three gunmen/shooters (Bridgewater State University, 2007; Lee, 1992; Phorn, et al., 2017; WorldHistory.edu, 2019). Suspicions of government involvement in Malcolm's death was confirmed during the next century. In 2011, a confession letter was found that outlined how the NYPD and the FBI conspired to kill Malcolm X (TRT World, 2021). He dealt with endless threats (WorldHistory.edu, 2019). Some of the same dangers that Malcolm X had, other Civil Rights activists like Muhammad Ali endured albeit differently.

The Dangers That They Faced: Muhammad Ali

Another unsuspecting activist during the Civil Rights Movement was Muhammad Ali, formerly known as Cassius Clay or Cassius Marcellus Clay, Jr. who was born on January 17, 1942 (The History of Us, 2022). By the age of twelve (12), Cassius was an angry boy and he cross paths with a police officer named Joe E. Martin (The History of Us, 2022). Joe encouraged Cassius to channel his anger through boxing and became his coach (The History of Us, 2022). He was to become a world champion (Ali, 2016; Cission US, Inc., 2022; Lee, 1992; The History of Us, 2022).

Cassius crossed paths with the NOI and the Honorable Elijah Muhammad and became a member of the Nation in 1964 (Ali, 2016; Cission US, Inc., 2022; Lee, 1992; The History of Us, 2022). In the same year, he married Sonji Roi (The History of Us, 2022). Eventually, there was an attempt to draft him into the U.S. Army (Ali, 2016; Lee, 1992; The History of Us, 2022). On April 28, 1967, Muhammad Ali refuses his US Army induction (Lee, 1992; The History of Us, 2022). His transition to an activist outside of defending Islam was during the 1960s when he refused to fight in the Vietnam War (Ali, 2016; Cission US, Inc., 2022; Lee, 1992; The History of Us, 2022).

He was not only an athlete, but he was also an activist, and he was a great orator (Cission US, Inc., 2022; Lee, 1992). When Ali refused to be drafted, he had this to say: "I have said it once and I will say it again. The real enemy of my people is right here [in America]. I will not disgrace my religion, my people or myself by becoming a tool to enslave those who are fighting for their own justice, freedom and equality…If I thought the war was going to bring freedom and equality to 22 million of my people they wouldn't have to draft me, I'd join tomorrow. I have nothing to lose by standing up for my beliefs. So I'll go to jail, so what? We've been in jail for 400 years" (Ali, 2016, p. 5).

His punishment was a five-year sentence and being stripped of his title in 1967 (Ali, 2016). Finally, on June 28, 1971, the Supreme Court reversed Muhammad Ali's conviction in Clay v. US, 403 U.S. 698 (1971) (Lee, 1992; The History of Us, 2022). Thus, his fighting career and his fight to evolve continued (Lee, 1992; The History of Us, 2022). By 1975, like Malcolm X, Muhammad Ali parted ways with the Elijah Muhammad and converted to Sunni Islam (Lee, 1992; The History of Us, 2022). In 1984, he was diagnosed with Parkinson's Disease (The History of Us, 2022). On January 8, 2005, he was awarded the Presidential Citizen's Medal by President George W. Bush, Jr. in honor of his protest to injustice from the United States government and his service of his country despite of said treatment (The History of Us, 2022).

Figure 10. Picture of the entry point of a pop-up exhibit in lower Manhattan, New York, 2019
Source: Janelle Christine Simmons, Ed.D. © 2019.

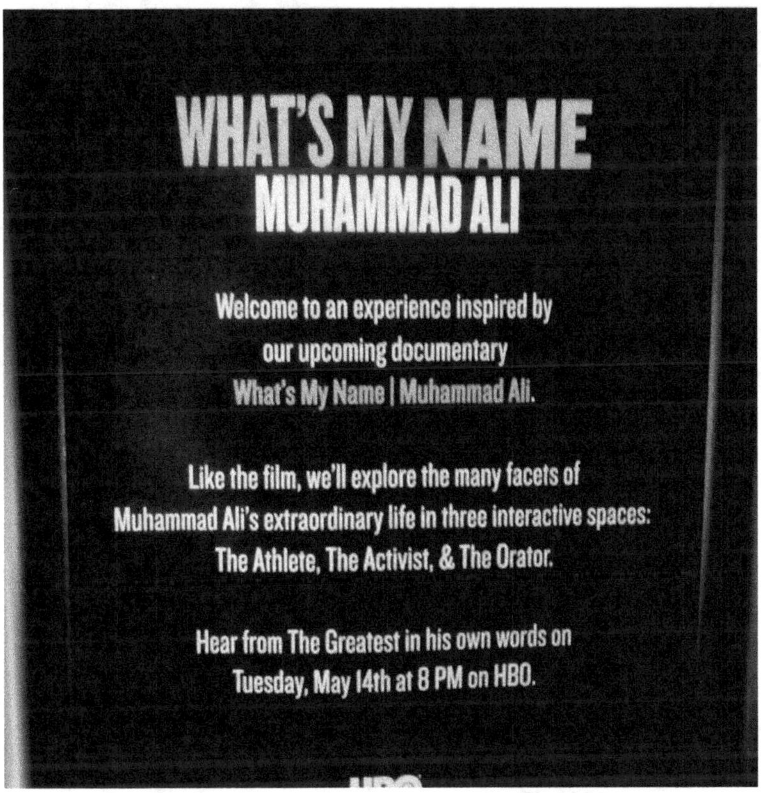

Figure 11. Picture of author at the Muhammad Ali: What's My Name Pop-Up Exhibit, 2019
Source: Janelle Christine Simmons, Ed.D. © 2019.

Issues, Controversies, Problems

Throughout this chapter, the issues, controversies, and problems that occurred are some of the same deterrents that some Blacks in certain regions of the United States face today. This is especially the case if they are a political leader. First, there is usually a "massive resistance" to the Black man or woman's request (Hughes & Meltzer, 1956; Lee, 1992; National Geographic Society, 2022; National Law Enforcement Museum, personal communication, March 12, 2022; Smith, 2021). That resistance may not necessarily have involved or involves lynching(s) (AARP Virginia, 2022; Chestnut, 2008; NAACP, 2022; Equal Justice Initiative, 2022). Second, Black Americans pushed back through protest and the road was never easy and it was never a short journey (Hughes & Meltzer, 1956; Irons, 2002; Lee, 1992; National Law Enforcement Museum, personal communication, March 12, 2022; Woodward, 1966). Third, leaders were assassinated such as John F. Kennedy, Martin Luther King, Jr., and Malcolm X (Ali, 2016; Belafonte & Shnayerson, 2011; Bridgewater State University, 2007; Bridgewater State University, 2007; Lee, 1992; Phorn, et al., 2017; Smith, 2021; WorldHistory.edu, 2019) to name a few. Fourth, even when the laws were established that granted certain rights like the 13th Amendment (Blight, 2018; Hughes & Meltzer, 1956, Irons, 2002; Smith, 2021; Woodward, 1966) locally other laws and practices were established that undermined said federal statutes and laws (Potter, n.d.; Smith, 2021). While these laws and amendments were already put into place, the author has several solutions and recommendations to suggest.

Solutions and Recommendations

First, as discussed previously, part of the solution was in identifying the problem and forming strategies of action. While some were more militant such as the Black Panthers and Malcolm X (Lee, 1992), at least initially, other movements and leaders such as Martin Luther King, Jr. proposed nonviolence (Hughes & Meltzer, 1956; Irons, 2002; Lee, 1992; Woodward, 1966; Smith, 2021). The same protests we see in response to excessive force cases such as Michael Brown (Smith, 2021) and even George Floyd (American Federation of Teachers, 2021; April 21; Anti-Defamation League, 2021; Arango, 2021), are the cry of the unheard (60 Minutes - Overtime, 2018). Until the populace is heard, they must cry out in protest.

Second, documenting and publicizing civil rights injustices are necessary in the delivery of an accurate narrative and a call for a public outcry such as in the case of Emmett Till (FBI, 2006; Hughes & Meltzer, 1956; WGBH Educational Foundation, 2022; Woodward, 1966). Part of that documentation involves going to the proper authorities (i.e., even when you know that it may appear to be useless) and reporting any and every crime (FBI, 2006). In modern times, that documentation also comes in newsrooms, through journalists, et al. Nonetheless, a problem cannot be fixed if a problem is not addressed.

Third, creating organizations that fight for justice is a necessary component (Equal Justice Initiative, 2022). It is impossible for individuals to do it alone.

One of the great successes of the Civil Rights Movements was the organization of the protest and the centralization of the command centers (Blight, 2018; Equal Justice Initiative, 2022; Hughes & Meltzer, 1956; Lee, 1992). This is necessary. If one considers continuous injustice as an intermittent war (Irons, 2002; Lee, 1992; Woodward, 1966), one can create command posts that denounce that act(s) of disrespect and possibly - considered acts of injustice.

Fourth, creating a legacy is a necessity. One thing that Bryan Stephenson did was two-fold: he created an organization to address injustice related to incarceration and he created an organization of remembrance (Equal Justice Initiative, 2022). The first addressed mass incarceration and excessive forms of punishment (Equal Justice Initiative, 2022). The latter addressed the telling of the stories of African Americans who have suffered a multitude of injustices through the National Memorial for Peace and Justice (Equal Justice Initiative, 2022). This list is by no means extensive. Moreover, some of the solutions and recommendations will repeat thematically due to the material that has already been reviewed.

Fifth, the author recommends that there be a focus on training new Black attorneys who are not focused necessarily in business or entertainment law but in Civil Rights Law, Native American Law, Holocaust Law, and the like. The focus on justice and addressing issues of justice do not only fall in social protest but also in water rights, land use rights, etc. Moreover, partnerships with the United States and the Hague will empower Black people to take the fight within an international space and not just in a national space as they form partnerships with other people who have been disrespected, grieved, and denied justice.

CONCLUSION

In conclusion, America as a case study is an interesting case indeed. America, previously known as the New World, has had a checkered past and a colored history. Nonetheless, it is important to consider how Black Deaths in custody occurred and continue to occur as well as other acts of Police Brutality. The history of America sheds light on this reality. With that being said, America has come a long way from the slaughter of many Native American tribes to slavery, the Civil War and its end, the forming of the Ku Klux Klan and Blacks Codes as well as Jim Crow Laws, etc. Today, many of these laws have been eradicated. They have been replaced with the 13th, 14th, 15th, etc. Amendments, and changes to local, state, and federal laws.

The average citizen has stood up to protest through various means such as writing, protests, sit-ins, et al. One of the greatest tools in the fight for justice has not been the invention of a story, but the telling and re-telling and the documentation of the actual and factual occurrences. From 1865 until the present-day, the journey of the African American in America has traversed space and time to continue the public outcry for freedoms in a country that claims to be the "land of the free and the home of the brave." However, even within its borders, various human rights abuses continue. Nonetheless, through their own boldness and acts of bravery they, i.e., African Americans have garnered more freedoms. And people of other cultures and religions have travailed with them to attempt to make America great again!

REFERENCES

A&E Network Television, LLC. (2022). Jim Crow laws. *History.com.* https://www.history.com/topics/early-20th-century-us/jim-crow-laws

A&E Network Television, LLC. (2022a). Ku Klux Klan. *History.com.* https://www.history.com/topics/reconstruction/ku-klux-klan

Ali, K. (2016, July 1). Muhammad Ali: Boxing, legend, human rights activist. *Crescent.* https://crescent.icit-digital.org/articles/muhammad-ali-boxing-legend-human-rights-activist#:~:text=Muhammad%20Ali%20was%20not%20only%20a%20world-class%20boxer%2C,him%20because%20he%20had%20become%20an%20international%20icon

American Federation of Teachers. (2021, April 21). George Floyd's family vows to 'keep fighting' for just policing after Chauvin verdict. *Share My Lesson.* https://sharemylesson.com/todays-news-tomorrows-lesson/derek-chauvin-verdict

Anti-Defamation League. (2021, April 21). The verdict is in: How to talk with young people about the Derek Chauvin murder trial verdict. *Share My Lesson.* https://sharemylesson.com/blog/derek-chauvin-murder-trial-verdict

Arango, T. (2021, June 25). Derek Chauvin is sentenced to 22 and a half years for the murder of George Floyd. *New York Times.* https://www.nytimes.com/2021/06/25/us/derek-chauvin-22-and-a-half-years-george-floyd.html

Biography. (2022). *The tragic story behind Billie Holiday's strange fruit.* Biography.com. https://www.biography.com/news/billie-holiday-strange-fruit#:~:text=The%20Tragic%20Story%20Behind%20Billie%20Holiday%27s%20%22Strange%20Fruit%22,the%20world%20of%20jazz%20and%20pop%20music.%20

Blight, D. W. (2018). *Frederick Douglass: Prophet of freedom.* Simon & Schuster Paperbacks.

Bridgewater State University. (2007). In Massachusetts hall of Black achievement: *Malcolm X (Item 13).* BSU. https://vc.bridgew.edu/hoba/13

Chestnut, T. (2008). *Lynching: Ida B. Wells-Barnett and the Outrage over the Frazier Baker Murder.* Archives. https://www.archives.gov/files/publications/prologue/2008/fall/lynching.pdf

Cission, U. S. Inc. (2022). HBO sports to celebrate 'What's my name: Muhammad Ali.' *PR News Wire.* https://www.prnewswire.com/news-releases/hbo-sports-to-celebrate-whats-my-name--muhammad-ali-documentary-with-nyc-pop-up-experience-300842993.htm

Equal Justice Initiative. (2023). *Equal justice initiative.* EJI. https://eji.org/

Federal Bureau of Investigation. (2006). *Emmett Till.* FBI. https://www.fbi.gov/history/famous-cases/emmett-till

History, W. edu. (2019, March 16). How Malcolm X died. *World History.* https://www.worldhistoryedu.com/how-malcolm-x-died/

History and Social Justice Website. (2022). *Howell, MI.* Howell - History and Social Justice (tougaloo.edu).

Hughes, L., & Meltzer, M. (1956). *A pictorial history of the negro in America.* Crown Publishers.

IMDb. (2022). *John F. Kennedy: Biography.* IMBd. https://www.imdb.com/name/nm0448123/bio

Irons, P. (2002). *Jim Crow's children: The broken promise of the Brown decision.* Strand Books.

Jones, J. (2021). Frazier Baker: Black postmaster and infant daughter lynched in Lake City, South Carolina '1898.' *Black Then.* https://blackthen.com/frazier-baker-black-postmaster-and-infant-daughter-lynched-in-lake-city-south-carolina-1898/

Lee, S. (1992). *Malcolm X.* [Video file]. Amazon. https://www.amazon.com/Malcolm-X-Denzel-Washington/dp/B0097JUG86/ref=sr_1_2?crid=2FGRH3CVPI161&keywords=malcolm+x&qid=1680501278&s=instant-video&sprefix=malcolm+x%2Cinstant-video%2C141&sr=1-2

Macabasco, L. W. (2022, March 8). Lynching postcards: A harrowing documentary about confronting history. *The Guardian*. https://www.theguardian.com/film/2022/mar/08/lynching-postcards-a-harrowing-documentary-about-confronting-history

Moorehouse, B. (2018, February 21). Still no KKK in Howell: Updated "hate map" shows all the groups in Michigan. *The Livingston Post*. https://thelivingstonpost.com/still-no-kkk-in-howell-updated-hate-map-shows-all-the-groups-in-michigan./

NAACP. (2022). *History of lynching in America*. NAACP. https://naacp.org/find-resources/history-explained/history-lynching-america/

National Geographic Society. (2022). *Ku Klux Klan*. National Geographic Society. https://www.nationalgeographic.org/article/ku-klux-klan/

Potter, G. (n.d.). *The history of policing in the United States*. file:///C:/Users/janel/Desktop/Publications/Examining%20Black%20Deaths%20in%20Custody%20-%202022/The%20History%20of%20Policing%20in%20the%20United%20States.GaryPotter.8.22.2021.pdf.

Radio, M. (2017, September 12). *Why is Howell Considered the KKK capitol of the klan?* Michigan Radio. https://www.michiganradio.org/arts-culture/2017-09-12/why-is-howell-considered-the-kkk-capital-of-klan/

Turner, C. (2021). *Lynching postcards: A harrowing documentary about confronting history*. [Video file]. Paramount Plus. https://www.paramountplus.com/movies/video/hselCM7fYyRK6mazd5ooDmdhlYiMrNYH/

Woodward, C. V. (1966). *The strange career of Jim Crow*. Oxford University Press.

World, T. R. T. (2021, February 22). *New evidence: NYPD and FBI allegedly conspired in the murder of Malcolm X*. Bing. https://www.bing.com/videos/search?q=malcom+x+and+surveillance&docid=608038232636278311&mid=E7F121B84F99E605B75BE7F121B84F99E605B75B&view=detail&FORM=VIRE/

KEY TERMS AND DEFINITIONS

Black Codes: codes that were instituted as law in order to restrict Black people from owning land and being able to move as they wished – freely. Vagrancy laws were also instituted.

Jim Crow Laws: laws, both state and local that were implemented in order to enforce segregation of the Black, Indigenous and White population, etc. These laws were enacted after the South lost the Civil War.

Lynching: the act of killing a person, via a mob and usually by hanging them from a rope until they are dead.

ENDNOTES

1 Frederick Douglas published a work titled "Lynch Law in the South" in the *North American Review* during July of 1892 where he explained the commonplace of lynching mobs in the South. He notated that lynching a man without a judge or jury was the real crime (Blight, 2018).

Chapter 4
Case Study:
Australia

ABSTRACT

This chapter focuses on discussing the "founding" of Australia and the events that took place thereafter. Once Australia was "found," the Aborigines were eventually raped, some were killed, and others subdued. The original people of the land became strangers on said land. Outside of a form of genocide, the creation of a prison colony and the forming of reservations, there were other implications. Policies established by the colonizers caused a myriad of issues for the Aborigines - the most damning being the policy for "Lost Children." Many changes have occurred since the 1950s and 1960s. An overview of the most pressing developments and issues will be discussed.

AUSTRALIAN NATIONAL ANTHEM

Australians all let us rejoice,

For we are one and free;

We've golden soil and wealth for toil;

Our home is girt by sea;

Our land abounds in nature's gifts

DOI: 10.4018/978-1-7998-9304-2.ch004

Of beauty rich and rare;

In history's page, let every stage

Advance Australia Fair.

In joyful strains then let us sing,

Advance Australia Fair.

Beneath our radiant Southern Cross

We'll toil with hearts and hands;

To make this Commonwealth of ours Renowned of all the lands;

For those who've come across the seas

We've boundless plains to share;

With courage let us all combine

To Advance Australia Fair.

In joyful strains then let us sing,

Advance Australia Fair.

Figure 1. Australia map
Source: Thinglink (2022)

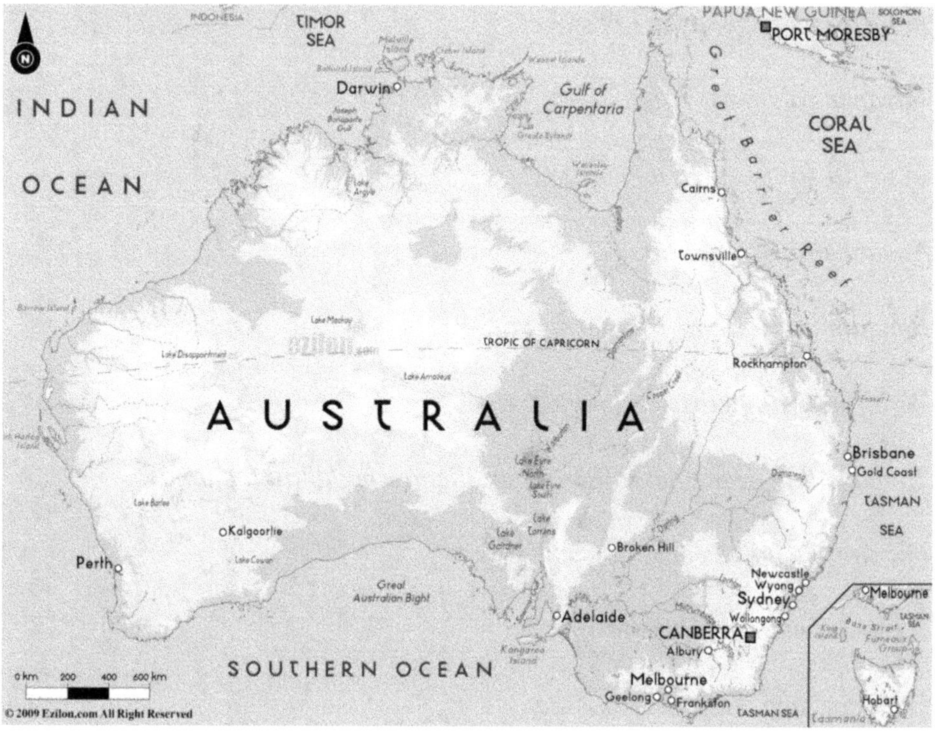

INTRODUCTION

Aborigines are tied or linked to the original land of Australia (Nettelback, 2015; Oldfield, 1865; Trigger, 1985), and that tie goes back approximately 60,000 years (Healing Foundation, 2022). Australia was colonized (Chang, 2019; Harrison, 2020; Healing Foundation, 2022; Nettelback, 2015; Oldfield, 1865; Trigger, 1985) in 1788 (Australian Law Reform Commission, 2022; International Work Group in Indigenous Affairs, n.d.; Maxwell-Stewart & Oxley, 2020) on January 26 (Chang, 2019). At that time, there could have been as many as 1.5 million Aborigines inhabiting Australia (International Work Group in Indigenous Affairs, n.d.). From 1788, New South Wales had been established as a convict or penal colony and stayed that way until 1840 (Maxwell-Stewart & Oxley, 2020). Along the same vein, "Van Diemen's Land" better known as Tasmania was also a convict colony from 1803 to 1853 (Maxwell-Stewart & Oxley, 2020).

Some of the consequences of colonization for the Aborigines was cultural obliteration, disease, famine, wars, etc. (Healing Foundation, 2022; Nettelback, 2015). Due to the violence that Aboriginals continued to endure such as being beaten, raped and killed, reserves were created to try to protect the Aborigines from 1824-1834 in Tasmania by Lieutenant Governor George Arthur (Chang, 2019). Due to the fact that the Aborigines did not wish to stay on reserves (i.e., in general), martial law was finally established in November of 1828 and if caught off their reservations or trespassing, they were to be shot on sight (Chang, 2019). While settlements were spread out (Trigger, 1985), the Aboriginal population had been declining (Oldfield, 1865). In fact, some like Oldfield (1865) noted that the Aboriginal population was declining, and Aboriginal women would soon not be able to have children, however, there was no need to waste resources in order to save the Aboriginal population. Additionally, the Whites were uncertain as to how many Aborigines from different regions still existed at that point (Oldfield, 1865). It was a natural consequence of colonization (Oldfield, 1865).

Britain established British law better known as a form of Common Law in the colonized country (Australian Law Reform Commission, 2022) from the moment they arrived. The British described the country as a "[…] a settled colony, that is, one uninhabited by a recognized sovereign or by a people with recognizable institutions and laws" (p. 1). In other words, the land was stolen and then Britain imposed their way of life. In many ways, the law and its interpretation expressed in multiple ways that it was better than the original inhabitants of the land and their customary laws.

British Law: A Conundrum

As expressed already, British law was established in Australia (Australian Law Reform Commission, 2022, Chang, 2019; Maxwell-Stewart & Oxley, 2020; Trigger, 1985). One of the main issues that arose was that the British colonizers of Australia had agreed that British law ruled the land without initially involving the Aborigine (Australian Law Reform Commission, 2022). Thus, there was no clear way to administer said law (Australian Law Reform Commission, 2022). For example, there is the case of the King v. Jack Congo Murrell who had killed another Aborigine in 1836 (Australian Law Reform Commission, 2022). Since the British had no way to determine how to try most Aboriginal crimes, they decided that murder would be the crime they would address, especially if it involved an Aboriginal and a settler (Australian

Law Reform Commission, 2022). Thus, the New South Wales Court "held unanimously that it had jurisdiction to try one Aborigine for the murder of another" (Australian Law Reform Commission, 2022, p.). Ironically, before and after 1836, this law was not even really applied since for a while Aboriginal customary law was still given "administrative flexibility" (Australian Law Reform Commission, 2022).

In 1835, the Aboriginal Protection Society was established in Great Britain and by 1837, it was considered an absurdity to try to apply British law to Aborigines (Australian Law Reform Commission, 2022). By 1840, Captain Grey or Sir George Grey stood against allowing Aboriginal Customary Law and noted that English law or Common law should be the law of the land since the land was theirs (Australian Law Reform Commission, 2022; Nettelback, 2015). However, he did note that since Aborigines did not know their law, they really should not be punished for what they are unaware of regarding British law (Australian Law Reform Commission, 2022). By 1850, this mood of hospitality changed as Britain decided that no Aboriginal Customary Law should be allowed or followed (Australian Law Reform Commission, 2022). And while it was claimed that Aborigines should be protected, colonial expansion became the focus and the utmost goal (Nettelback, 2015). Therefore, for an extended period of time, the Aboriginal and their needs were usurped for the White man's goal of domination (Nettelback, 2015).

Another application of the law and to do with civil law and land rights (Australian Law Reform Commission, 2022). First, Aboriginal marriages were not recognized by British Common Law (Australian Law Reform Commission, 2022). Second, there were no rights that could be determined when it came to the children of Aborigines as they were non-existent (Australian Law Reform Commission, 2022). Third, regarding trespassing, Aborigines were not considered to be trespassing when they were on "Crown Land" (Australian Law Reform Commission, 2022), which was a strange law since it had been their land in the first place.

There was also another application of the law, **which had to do with** civil law and land rights (Australian Law Reform Commission, 2022). First, Aboriginal marriages were not recognized by British Common Law (Australian Law Reform Commission, 2022). Second, there were no rights that could be determined when it came to the children of Aborigines as they were non-existent (Australian Law Reform Commission, 2022). Third, regarding trespassing, Aborigines were not considered to be trespassing when they were on "Crown Land" (Australian Law Reform Commission, 2022), which was a strange law since it had been their land in the first place. **WorldHistory.**

edu. (2019, March 16). How Malcolm X died. *World History.* https://www.worldhistoryedu.com/how-malcolm-x-died/

Figure 2. White settlers killing Aborigines in massacres
Source: Chang (2019) https://www.news.com.au/national/politics/how-early-australians-treated-aboriginal-people/news-story/e984d3a453382c59a1d5d81f99a9ad8c.

Thus, this chapter will flesh out some of the aforementioned historical facts and issues that proceeded from the colonization of Australia. The main focus will be the treatment of the Aborigine and what that meant for Australia in future generations and what it may mean for the years to come. In retrospect, although there have been many attempts at reconciliation, there are still deep wounds. Much of this history only spans over 200 years. Only 60 to 70 years ago were 33% of Aboriginal children ripped from their parents, their families, their homes as the government tried to force assimilation (O'Loughlin, 2022).

MAIN FOCUS OF CHAPTER

This chapter's main focus is on introducing the history of Australia. In doing so, the reader will be able to understand the setting in which Australia became a colonized nation. The reader will also be able to understand how Great

Britain established their law in the land and the issues that this caused and still does in some ways today (Nettelback, 2015; Trigger, 1985). Part of that colonization involved the brutalization of the Aboriginal people (Chang, 2019; Hilton, 2011; Maxwell-Stewart & Oxley, 2020; Nettelback, 2015; Oldfield, 1865) as well as their neglect (Nettelback, 2015; Oldfield, 1865; Trigger, 1985). Concurrently, outside of the physical brutalization was a systematic disregard (i.e., for the most part) of their cultures or a blatant ignorance (Australian Law Reform Commission, 2022; Chang, 2019; Hilton, 2011; Maxwell-Stewart & Oxley, 2020; Nettelback, 2015), or even a blatant disregard for the preservation of Aboriginal life (Oldfield, 1865), which included the land (Trigger, 1985). These *faux paxes* led to a continuous tension between Aboriginals and their "White" counterparts.

Issues, Controversies, Problems

There are so many issues, controversies and problems to unpack. Quite frankly, the author cannot focus on them all. The reality is that the process of colonization in and of itself is an egregious act upon the colonized. As Frantz Fanon noted, the colonizer looks at the native or indigenous people of the country as being "savage" (Hilton, 2011). It is even expressed as follows regarding the Australian Aboriginal; "Treachery is a characteristic of all savages, but this quality is merely a phase of the instinct of self-preservation leading me to endeavour to do the greatest possible mishap to their enemy at the least possible risk to themselves […]" (Oldfield, 1865, p. 225). This savagery was expressed in order to take control of their land and other resources. The only way to justify taking their land was/is to dehumanize them (Hilton, 2011). It (i.e., the idea that the native group is savage) creates in a people an insecurity but also ignites a flame. Eventually, Aborigines identified themselves tribally and identified themselves by their homeland, their language and their 'Bora' or initiation ceremony (Trigger, 1985). This helped in being able to identify themselves as groups to fight for their land against the White people (Trigger, 1985). However, the issue of patriarchy continued.

First, the patriarchal attitude that the British had regarding Aborigines was laudable. For example, according to Chang (2019), January 26 as a Day of Remembrance angers Aborigines. Chang (2019) states the following:

Some argue that Aboriginal people should be grateful about the modernization of the country and all the benefits this has them. That they should just get on with things and let the past go (p. 1).

It is obtuse to not understand why the Aborigine would be angry about having their land stolen, their heritage highjacked, their culture disrespected and that is not to mention the emotional and physical violence that they endured as a people. This attitude extended further into a whole day on May 26, 1998 from Prime Minister Kevin Rudd, which became an annual remembrance called 'Sorry Day' (AIATSIS, n.d.; Al-Jazeera Media Network, 2019; Australians Together, 2022).

Second, colonization requires a certain amount of disrespect and hatred for a people in the author's opinion. This is especially the case since to colonize a nation you have already told the nation that their way of life, their rights, their culture is insignificant (Bird-Hutchinson, 2020; Oldfield, 1865). This disrespect for Aborigines and Torres Straight people was made known from the moment of colonization (Nettelback, 2015; Oldfield, 1865; Trigger, 1985), which had included various massacres (Chang, 2019, Maxwell-Stewart & Oxley, 2020; O'Loughlin, 2022; Healing Foundation, 2022). However, other acts made it clear that there was a lack of respect for the Aborigines. For example, Aboriginal Customary Law was at first allowed until it interfered with the White Australian's goal and that it was ceremoniously outlawed (Australian Law Reform Commission, 2022). This disrespect was communicated in other ways as well. For example, as Fanon had mentioned regarding Algerian women (Hilton, 2011), Aboriginal women were mocked by the British for their chastity and told that their custom of staying pure was preposterous (Chang, 2019). They were also often preyed upon (Chang, 2019). Once raped when an Aboriginal woman became pregnant, the European men despised their offspring (Chang, 2019). Regarding this topic, Oldfield (1865) stated the following: "The half-castes breed indiscriminately `with Europeans and aborigines" (p. 222). At a certain point, when Aboriginal women were deemed almost barren, the White populace had the expressed opinion that they would just die out and that it was not worth addressing as their numbers were dwindling (Oldfield, 1865).

Figure 3. Aboriginal woman and child in photo titled "A Gin & Picaninny" taken in Queensland (1868-1872)
Source: C.H. Allen © 1870, PIC/8277/119 LOC Album 280D, https://nla.gov.au/nla.obj-140700080/view

Third, there were so many "crimes" committed against the Aboriginal people of Australia as well as the Torres Straight people of Australia (Chang, 2019; Maxwell-Stewart & Oxley, 2020; O'Loughlin, 2022). Aborigines were often beaten, raped and killed (Al-Jazeera Media Network, 2019; AIATSIS, n.d.; Australians Together, 2022; Chang, 2019; Healing Foundation, 2022). The term "dispersing the natives,' which would imply moving a group of people from one place to another was a joke amongst Europeans (Chang, 2019). What it really meant was that the Europeans were killing more Aborigines (Chang, 2019). During the earliest points of contact with settlers, 20,000 Aborigines had already been killed (Chang, 2019). In Eastern Australia, there had been 170+ massacres between 1794 and 1872 with only six settlers being killed (Chang, 2019). It was not unheard of for settlers to put arsenic in damper, flour or sugar that had been given to the natives as a gift (Chang, 2019). Moreover, waterholes were often poisoned (Chang, 2019). In Northern Australia, Aborigines were segregated and often flogged (Chang, 2019), worked for free (Chang, 2019; Trigger, 1985) or for rations (Trigger, 1985), and given little education (Chang, 2019). These are only a few examples. However, these examples impacted this community profoundly in unaccountable ways. However, a greater controversy and loss to the Aboriginal and Torres Strait people was the reality of having their children stolen from them.

Fourth, the controversy of the Stolen Generation continues (O'Loughlin, 2022). For all intents and purposes, the First Nation peoples had their children stolen from them or kidnapped by the Australian government (Al-Jazeera Media Network, 2019; AIATSIS, 2022; Australians Together, 2022; O'Loughlin, 2022). Dates vary. For example, in Victoria, this practice began in the 1860s (Healing Foundation, 2022). The federal policy was extended to the whole country by the 1900s (Healing Foundation, 2022). Most people consider this period to have occurred from 1910 to the 1970s (Al-Jazeera Media Network, 2019; AIATSIS, n.d., Australians Together, 2022; O'Loughlin, 2022; VanKrieken, 1999).

When Patrick Henry cried "Give me liberty of give me death!" in 1775– the act was an act of war. When Australia basically communicated to the Aborigines that they should assimilate or die – it was also an act of war. This policy led to a form of cultural disconnection (Healing Foundation, 2022) or a 'cultural genocide' (VanKrieken, 2019). No to mention, it led to other issues for Aboriginal peoples overall.

Basically, the policy was to remove Aboriginal and Torres Straight children or First Nation children from their families by force (Al-Jazeera Media Network, 2019; AIATSIS, n.d.; Australians Together, 2022; Healing

Foundation, 2022; O'Loughlin, 2022; VanKrieken, 1999). The Australian government's policy was to assume "legal guardianship," remove said children and put them in adoptive families and/or institutions (VanKrieken, 1999). The goal was to force assimilation (Al-Jazeera Media Network, 2019; AIATSIS, n.d.; Australians Together, 2022; Healing Foundation, 2022; O'Loughlin, 2022; VanKrieken, 1999) and had been introduced by both the authorities of the church and the state and was to be considered a cornucopia remedy for Aboriginal children (VanKrieken, 1999). Brian Morley, a stolen child who was taken in 1960 at the age of two from his mother Mary stated the following regarding the Australian government's policy: "that wasn't the object of the exercise. It was to divide and conquer, split them up and throw them to the wind" (Al-Jazeera Media Network, 2019, p. 6). According to Australians Together (2022), the Australian government had a "[…] misguided assumption that the lives of First Nations people would be improved if they became part of White society" (p. 2). The real goal and hope were that First Nations people would 'fie out' through the theory of natural elimination or assimilate (Australians Together, 2022). It was a continuation of the original policy of colonization (Chang, 2019), which was to eradicate the original culture and by proxy the "Original Inhabitants."

The policy included forcing name changes, forcing the "Original Inhabitants" to reject their heritage by not speaking their original native tongue, being abused, neglected and institutionalized (Australians Together, 2022). This forced separation led to trauma, which then became generational amongst their next generations (Al-Jazeera Media Network, 2019; Australians Together, 2022; Healing Foundation, 2022; VanKrieken, 1999). According to the AIATSIS (n.d.), "the removal of children broke important cultural, spiritual and family ties and has left a lasting and intergenerational impact in the lives and well being of Aboriginal and Torres Strait Island people" (p. 2). The exact number of how many stolen children there are and still is still unknown (AIATSIS, n.d.).

While being within adoptive families and/or institutionalized, many of the stolen generation dealt with being disconnected from their families, being emotionally, physically, and sexually abused, etc. (Al-Jazeera Media Network, 2019; AIATSIS, n.d., Australians Together, 2022; Healing Foundation, 2022; VanKrieken, 1999). They also have lower levels of education overall and higher rates of unemployment (Al-Jazeera Media Network, 2019; Australians Together, 2022; VanKrieken, 1999). Stolen children or the stolen generation also deal with higher rates of incarceration (Al-Jazeera Media Network, 2019), which obviously places them at a higher risk for being killed or dying while in custody in the first place. Some of the issues that stolen children suffer from may also be causational factors for being incarcerated such as alcoholism and drug abuse or having a lower level of education (Al-Jazeera Media Network, 2019; Australians Together, 2022; Healing Foundation, 2022). Also, having lower levels of education and higher rates of unemployment may lead to or being correlated with higher rates of incarceration. While causation may not have been proved, there is most likely a correlational relationship.

Many stolen children have suffered from alcohol abuse, broken relationships, depression, drug abuse, high rates of suicide, various forms of violence including domestic abuse (Al-Jazeera Media Network, 2019; AIATSIS, n.d., Australians Together, 2022; Healing Foundation, 2022; VanKrieken, 1999) as well as higher rates of anxiety and PTSD as well as increased rates of poverty (Australians Together, 2022) that led to intergenerational economic hardship and losses. Tied to economic hardship may have been the fact that Aborigines who were stolen had lower levels of education (Australians Together, 2022), which again seems to be a continuation of the colonizer's original policy (Chang, 2019). They wanted Aborigines to work for free (Chang, 2019; Trigger, 1985). Stolen children were also often punished very harshly and grew up cold and hungry (Australians Together, 2022). Another consequence of that was that parents were not able to assist their children with their homework even when they did have children of their own (Australians Together, 2022), which may have also led to a continuation of struggling with studies and being at a lower economic echelon for their own children since positive parental involvement is often linked to higher academic achievement in one's children (Simmons, 1997).

Some of the other general and main consequences have been as follows; never locating their parents or other family members, feeling disconnected from the Aboriginal community, suffering from high stress levels and being traumatized (Healing Foundation, 2022) and retraumatized (Harrison, 2020). They were forced to not only deal with the trauma of colonization but also the trauma of being part of the stolen generation (Healing Foundation, 2022). This trauma has never ceased. In fact, this trauma has continued to be passed on to future generations (AIATSIS, n.d.; Australians Together, 2022; Healing Foundation, 2022).

As of 2022, 17,000 stolen children were identified as survivors within Australia (Healing Foundation, 2022). One-third of all Australians and Torres Strait Islanders are their descendants (Healing Foundation, 2022). While many of these issues have been perpetuated throughout their generations, they don't have to be forever. There is a place and time for healing (Healing

Foundation, 2022). Aborigines can live again and again and be healthier in the future forever (Healing Foundation, 2022).

Figure 4. Copy of Brian Morley's adoption record (1988)
Source: Al-Jazeera Media Network (2019)

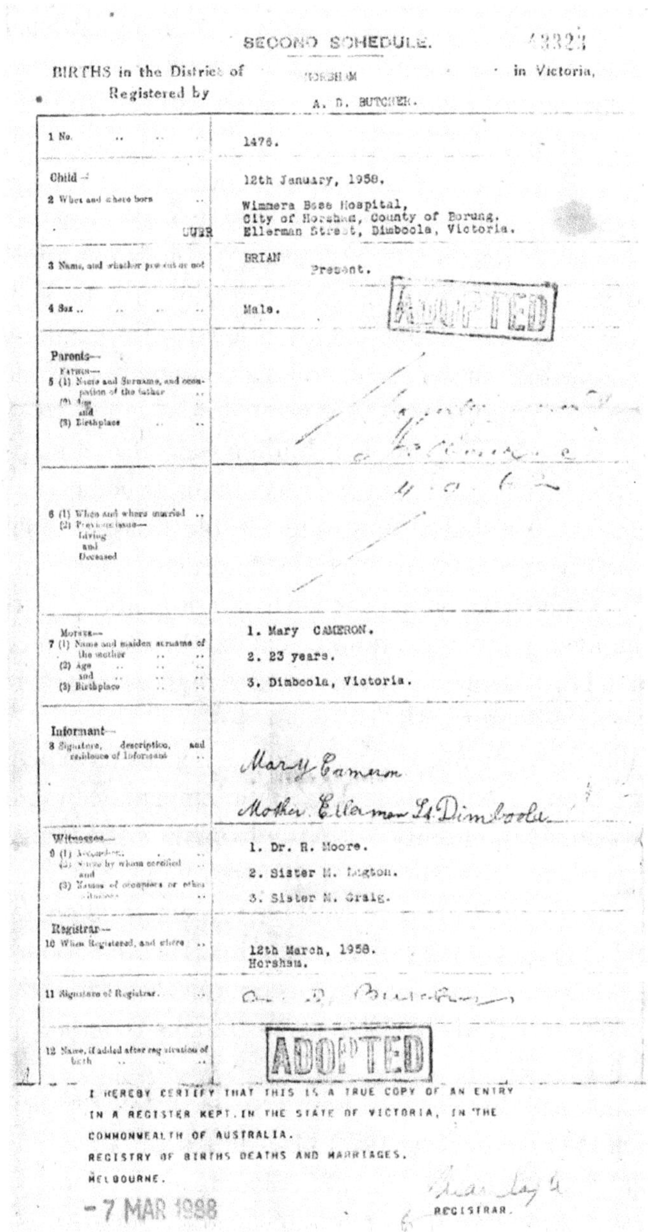

SECOND SCHEDULE.

BIRTHS in the District of HORSHAM in Victoria,
Registered by A. D. BUTCHER.

1 No.	1476.
Child— 2 When and where born	12th January, 1958. Wimmera Base Hospital, City of Horsham, County of Borung. Ellerman Street, Dimboola, Victoria.
3 Name, and whether present or not	BRIAN Present. ADOPTED
4 Sex	Male.
Parents— Father— 5 (1) Name and Surname, and occupation of the father (2) Age and (3) Birthplace	
6 (1) When and where married (2) Previous issue— Living and Deceased	
Mother— 7 (1) Name and maiden surname of the mother (2) Age and (3) Birthplace	1. Mary CAMERON. 2. 23 years. 3. Dimboola, Victoria.
Informant— 8 Signature, description, and residence of Informant	Mary Cameron Mother. Ellerman St. Dimboola
Witnesses— 9 (1) Accoucheur, (2) Nurse by whom certified and (3) Names of occupiers or other witnesses	1. Dr. R. Moore. 2. Sister M. Lugton. 3. Sister M. Craig.
Registrar— 10 When Registered, and where	12th March, 1958. Horsham.
11 Signature of Registrar.	A. D. Butcher
12 Name, if added after registration of birth	ADOPTED

I HEREBY CERTIFY THAT THIS IS A TRUE COPY OF AN ENTRY IN A REGISTER KEPT IN THE STATE OF VICTORIA, IN THE COMMONWEALTH OF AUSTRALIA.
REGISTRY OF BIRTHS DEATHS AND MARRIAGES.
MELBOURNE.
- 7 MAR 1988
REGISTRAR.

Fifth, another major issue/problem was that of segregation (Chang, 2019). Aboriginals were segregated from White Australians until the 1960s (Chang, 2019; Oldfield, 1865; Trigger, 1985) on settlements or other forms of reservations (Oldfield, 1865), and the settlers had arrived since 1788 (Chang, 2019). That is a span of 170+ years. Segregation had led to lower pay for Aborigines as well as less education (Chang, 2019; Al-Jazeera Media Network, 2019; AIATSIS, n.d., Australians Together, 2022; Healing Foundation, 2022) or an exchange system (Trigger, 1985). In 1965, Aborigines were finally given the right to vote in their own land (Chang, 2019). On May 27, 1967, Aborigines were considered Australian citizens and were finally included in the census (Chang, 2019). The journey had taken almost 200 years.

Sixth, aside from stolen children, one of the most compelling calls for change is the issue surrounding "Black Deaths in Custody" (Doherty, 2021; Harrison, 2020; Hinman, 2021; Marchetti, 2012; Mitchell, 2018; Qasem, 2019). While Black Deaths in Custody (i.e., police custody, prison custody and the like) has appeared to decrease, there is still a call for a change (Doherty, 2021). At approximately March 23, 2022, there was documentation that three more Aborigines from the First Nations had died (Hinman, 2021). That brought the number of Black Deaths in Custody to 440 by March 2021 over a period of 30 years (Hinman, 2021). In other words, every year, an average of approximately 14.67 Aborigines were being killed while in some form of custody

For example, in 2015, David Dungay who was in prison custody was moved from Cell 71 to 77 (Mitchell, 2018), because he wouldn't stop eating biscuits (Harrison, 2020; Mitchell, 2018). Since he had been examined and found to be diabetic, the guards took alarm (Mitchell, 2018). The guards repeatedly told him to stop eating the biscuits and he refused (Mitchell, 2018). While five prison guards held him down, he repeatedly said that he could not breathe (i.e., "I can't breathe!") (Harrison, 2020; Mitchell, 2018). After being restrained, he lost consciousness (Harrison, 2020; Mitchell, 2018). On December 29, 2015, David Dungay died at Sydney's Long Bay Jail (i.e., at the prison hospital) (Harrison, 2020; Mitchell, 2018), and passed on to the next realm.

Nearly four years later in November of 2019, Derek Kee, the NSW deputy coroner made a finding that David had not posed a "security risk" (Harrison, 2020). Moreover, the guards had no right to conduct themselves in said manner (Harrison, 2020). He chalked it up to "systematic efficiencies in training" and a "product of misunderstanding" (Harrison, 2020). Therefore, the prison guards received no disciplinary action (Harrison, 2020). Yet, a man is dead from a cardia arrythmia and had no pre-existing health conditions prior to being diagnosed with diabetes in the prison (Harrison, 2020; Mitchell, 2018).

Figure 5. David Dungay who was killed in 2015 while in custody as seen in the Sydney Morning Herald – date unknown
Source: Mitchell (2018), https://www.smh.com.au/national/nsw/officer-thought-david-dungay-may-have-been-tricking-them-on-breathing-20180717-p4zs0n.html.

Seventh, there are a multitude of health issues for Aborigines compared to the rest of the population (Al-Jazeera Media Network, 2019; Healing Foundation, 2022; IWGIA, n.d.). Aborigines have a 1.7 higher mortality rate than other Australians (IWGIA, n.d.). Additionally, another issue that confounds Black Deaths in Custody as a cause solely by the police or prison guard is that of suicide. Aborigines tend to have a high suicide rate (AIATSIS, n.d.; Australians Together, 20221 Healing Foundation, 2022; IWGIA, n.d.). This controversial phenomenon most likely finds it roots from the colonization of their country. These issues are often correlated with higher incarceration rates and Black Deaths in Custody overall.

For those who are incarcerated, other issues such as drugs and alcohol are usually detected in their blood streams (Blue, 2017). Specific to women, an underlining issue or controversy, at least for women who have been incarcerated (Blue, 2017; Marchetti, 2012) is that of alcohol or drug dependency and being in abusive relationships (Blue, 2017). More specifically, Aboriginal women are usually abused by family, etc. 37x more than non-Aboriginal women (Blue, 2017). Moreover, the fact is that Aborigines are incarcerated at a higher rate to begin with (Al-Jazeera Media Network, 2019; Australians Together, 2022).

Eighth, the last issue and controversy is that of accountability (Harrison, 2020; Healing Foundation, 2022). Thirty-two years ago, the Royal Commission into Indigenous Deaths in Custody was launched or established (Qasem, 2019). Twenty-one years after that Kevin Rudd made a national apology and yet hundreds more Aborigines have died since then (Al-Jazeera Media Network, 2019; Hinman, 2021; Qasem, 2019). This is a major issue but beyond that it is a great injustice. It points to systemic and structural issues. These issues are more than challenges and they are not unlike the issues in the United States. As previously discussed, in America, the slave trader, the overseer, etc. instituted the slave patrol and some of those who had been part of the slave patrol became the first police officers.

In Australia, the police officers were the fruits of the first colonial powers or colonialists (Qasem, 2019). Some of the roots are the same, they are racism, and in a report out of New South Wales, one of the complaints was that of racist policing – case in point is the case of Mr. Ward who had been taken into police custody, was arrested for drunk driving, was refused bail and then he was forced to be held in a police cell (Qasem, 2019). When he was being transported to the Kalgoorlie Court, he collapsed and it was reported that he died from being "cooked to death" (Qasem, 2019, p. 1). Regardless, the times are changing. Another subsidiary issue is that of suppressing evidence (Harrison, 2020).

Unlike in colonial times (Oldfield, 1865), there is footage now from various sources that document police brutality (Blue, 2017). Now, previous accusations are no longer accusations (Blue, 2017). In the case of David Dungay, they was/were camera footage from (Harrison, 2020; Mitchell, 2018) Cell 77 of the events that led to his death (Mitchell, 2018). In some of these cases, footage was shown. It should continue to be shown as previously often evidence was suppressed (Harrison, 2018). Nor should they be allowed to stay silent (Longman, 2020). In other words, this is a new era and soon police officers who have truly brutalized those in custody will no longer be able to hide behind a wall of blue. This is a reckoning, and the reckoning of accountability is not only for Australia or Britain or America or South Africa but for the world.

The cases of Ms. Dhu, which has not been mentioned here, Mr. Dungay, or even Mr. Ward are only a few of many. Unlike in previous years, women are now dying in custody just like men, and these cases are often overlooked (Blue, 2017; Marchetti, 2012). It should also be noted that Aborigines have just increased their population to 745,000 as of 2021 or so (IWGIA, n.d.). In other words, they only make up about 3.3% of the total population, which is approximately 24,220,200 inhabitants (IWGIA, n.d.). Outside of Australia lives 62% of the Indigenous people who originally came from Australia (IWGIA, n.d.). With that being said, whether they are male or female, Aborigines have suffered long and those who live are walking miracles. It is time that the Australian police force looks at their neighbor, the original inhabitant and not consider him or her to be "too black" (Qasem, 2019), but consider themselves to be newer inhabitants who should respect the older ones.

Ninth, another major controversy is length of time that it takes to get a trial done and media coverage (Harrison, 2020). Often trials take years, and the families are not supported by the media, etc. (Harrison, 2020). For example, David Dungay's case took four years (Harrison, 2020), and had no seeming resolve (Harrison, 2020; Mitchell, 2018). Many Australians knew more about the Black Deaths in Custody cases in America than in their own country of Australia (Harrison, 2020). According to Harrison (2020), Alexis Daish, a Today US Correspondent thanked American protestors for their input since most Australians know little about killings by police that occur within their own country (Harrison, 2020).

Solutions and Recommendations

When it comes to Black Deaths in Custody and the case of Australia, it may be even seemingly harder to comprehend than that of the United States of

America. The author says that because the land was originally taken care of by the Aborigines. They were dispossessed of their land and then European colonialists – mostly from Britain began to chip away at their identity and being. Everything the Aborigine knew was minimalized and deemed preposterous or barbaric. Some of the same strategies that we saw with Africans in America took place with Aborigines in Australia. With that being said, there are several recommendations if not solutions.

First, an open dialogue needs to occur. While there are commissions and hearings that occur in Australia, it is hard to say that dialogue with transparency always takes place. In fact, many police officers and/or prison officers remain silent, which leads to a lack of evidence for Black Deaths in Custody cases (Harrison, 2020; Longman, 2020). The wounds of the Aboriginal and Torres Strait people are deep and wide (Healing Foundation, 2020; Trigger, 1985). The amount or number of "Natives" now compared to the time before the British arrived is minimal. In other words, with the best estimates, there is only half the population of Aboriginals and Torres Straight Islanders as in 1788. The reserves that were created to protect were often given as a forced option (Chang, 2019). When that option was ignored, the British treated the Aborigines like infantile buffoons (Chang, 2019; Oldfield, 1865; Trigger, 1985). At first, they were segregated (Chang, 2019; Oldfield, 1865; Trigger, 1985), then some were stolen (Al-Jazeera Media Network, 2019; AIATSIS, n.d.; Australians Together, 2022; Healing Foundation, 2022; VanKrieken, 1999) then voting rights were deemed to a people and they were finally titled Australian when they had almost always been Australian. What can be more Australian than the first people of the land? Without the acknowledgment of who these people are, where they were "found," how they were treated and true repentance and reconciliation, not only will Black Deaths in custody continue to occur, but the divide between the "original" people of the land and mostly Caucasian Europeans will continue to cause a division within the country.

Open dialogue can be tribunals, but it can also be town halls, festivals, circle talks, and real conversations. These conversations must be brutally honest. No more can political correctness, which is often not correct be a substitute for vulnerability and transparency. Without these steps towards truth, nothing will change. If nothing changes, and everything remains the same, the country of Australia and the government of Australia will suffer one of its greatest losses ever.

Second, Britain and the leaders of Australia need to shy away from apologies that are often seen as empty words. While Prime Minister Rudd made apologies repeatedly, these apologies were not always met with action or actions that always seemed to matter to the Aboriginal and Torres Strait people. This is especially the case, when one apologizes for their ancestors' brutal behavior towards to the Aborigines and Torres Strait people and then celebrates holidays like January 26th. It is a contradiction pointed to the previous point. How can you be sorry and then celebrate conquering the same people you claim to be sorry to have almost eradicated from the earth? This in and of itself is dishonest. However, on May 26, you are sorry again.

Third, while the cases of Black Deaths in custody may seem minute or minimal, the patterns continue to cause questions and concerns. The fact is, that Aborigines have been killed repeatedly and semi-regularly since 1788 (Chang, 2019; Nettelback, 2015; Oldfield, 1865; Trigger, 1985). Let that sink into your brain for a moment! To say that White Australians or other racialized Australians now die at a higher rate or number while in custody does not address the aforementioned issue. Case in point, there are less Aborigines in comparison in the country according to the International Work Group for Indigenous Affairs (n.d.) or IWGIA. Therefore, Aborigines must hold the Australian government accountability for their actions while in the commission of their duties (Harrison, 2020; Healing Foundation, 2020; Trigger, 1985), and not be pacified with false apologies.

Fourth, Aborigines and Torres Strait people must continue to hold the government accountable for their actions through activities like protest (Goldsmith, 2021; Harrison, 2020; Longman, 2020). Goldsmith (2021) notes that as of March 2021, Black deaths in custody had increased to 474 and had already passed 400 by 2020 (Longman, 2020). This finding is unacceptable. Especially, when many cases have no logical explanation when it comes to the death of the person such as the cases of Mr. Ward (Qasem, 2019) and Mr. Dungay (Doherty, 2011; Goldsmith, 2021; Harrison, 2020; Mitchell, 2018). According to Longman (2020), it is preposterous "to allow prison or police officers to avoid admitting to serious breaches of policy in order to protect them from disciplinary proceedings does little to instil[1] confidence that the State is serious about tack-ling First Nation deaths in custody" (p. 3). Perhaps, the real issue is that to address First Nations deaths in custody, would be used as evidence or precedent for a civil case with "forced" compensation that the State is not ready to afford. Moreover, it would cost the State millions if not billions of dollars in additional training for their police and prison officers.

Fifth, in 1980, New South Wales created a Link-up service, which by 1995 was extended to all Australian states and territories (Australians Together, 2022). This service allowed stolen children to locate their loved ones and was called "Bringing Them Home" (Al-Jazeera Media Network, 2019; Australians Together, 2022). Parliament also continued to address this issue on Mar 26, 1997 (Australians Together, 2022). While this program is much appreciated, other forms of assistance should be extended. For example, financial and education assistance should be encouraged and offered. At some point, New South Wales did extend paid compensation to stolen children in the amount of 75,000 AUD or $53,000 (Al-Jazeera Media Network, 2019). However, the state of Victoria refused to compensate Aboriginals at all (Al-Jazeera Media Network, 2019). The idea of compensation at this point should be a requirement across the board throughout all states as these were literally the "Original Inhabitants" of the land. The fact is the land was theirs. Since then, they have suffered emotional, physical and spiritual loss and traumatization due to this loss (Al-Jazeera Media Network, 2019; AIATSIS, n.d.; Australians Together, 2022; Blue, 2017; Chang, 2019; Doherty, 2011; Goldsmith, 2021; Harrison, 2020; International Work Group for Indigenous Affairs, n.d.; Longman, 2020; Mitchell, 2018; Nettelback, 2015; O'Loughlin, 2022;Oldfield, 1865; Qasem, 2019; Trigger, 1985; VanKrieken, 1999).

CONCLUSION

In conclusion, it is hard to consider the effects and consequences of over 200 years of abuse to a people and a nation. Australia is a case study that is one of the hardest to fathom. A people who lived on its land for over 60,000 years were nearly wiped out by their British colonizers over 200 years ago to make the country a prison colony. Consider that notion for a moment!

In an ironic twist, the creation of a prison colony, led to the imprisonment of Aborigines. Moreover, even today, they are incarcerated at a higher rate than their non-Aboriginal counterparts. The consequences that led to that reality and that reality are astounding. Even the policy of creating a stolen generation led to a different form of imprisonment. Many stolen children were robbed of their culture, their identity, their family, their childhood, their health and possible future wealth, etc. The trauma that they endured through emotional, physical and spiritual abuses including sexual abuse often led to intergenerational trauma as well. At every turn, the average Aborigine is faced with the reality of their oppressor telling them it is okay and trying to pacify them with an apology. Where if the tables were turned, it would most likely be an outright war.

While some Australians may cringe at the idea that Aborigines are angry about remembrances like January 26, they should be reminded that most likely they shouldn't have been there in the first place. However, they are. For Australia to be a healthy nation and promote a healthy society, they should consider making sure that the Aborigines and the Torres Strait Islanders become healthier too. This population should not be laden with the abuses that White Australians wish to avoid. The author is clear that her words appear to be strong, but as one who traveled through Australia and studied in Australia over twenty years ago and was even taught by a stolen child; she cannot ignore the injustices that continue to occur to and amongst the Aboriginal peoples of the land.

As far as the roll that Aborigines play in the matter, she implores Aborigines to embrace their culture, to fight for the health and wealth of their families and to "remember." Through silence, through letters, through other forms of protest, it is important for Aborigines to make sure their stories make it to the media far and wide. As the Healing Foundation (2022) had noted it is important to remember that the healing process has begun. In 60,000 years, it is the author's hope that her future generations will see the future generations of the Aborigines healed and in a better light.

REFERENCES

Al-Jazeera Media Network. (2019, February 13). *'It never ends': Trauma of Australia's 'stolen' children.* Al Jazeera Media Network. https://www.aljazeera.com/news/2019/2/13/it-never-ends-trauma-of-australias-stolen-children

Australian Institute of Aboriginal and Torres Strait Islander Studies. (n.d.). *The stolen generations.* Aiatsis. https://aiatsis.gov.au/explore/stolen-generations

Australian Law Reform Commission. (2022). *Australian law as applied to Aborigines: August 28, 2010.* ALRC. https://www.alrc.gov.au/publication/recognition-of-aboriginal-customary-laws-alrc-report-31/4-aboriginal-customary-laws-and-anglo-australian-law-after-1788/australian-law-as-applied-to-aborigines/

Australians Together. (2022). The stolen generations. *Australians Together.* https://australianstogether.org.au/discover/australian-history/stolen- generations#:~:text=First%20Nations%20people%20who%20were%20removed%20were%20left,children%2C%20their%20parents%20and%20families%2C%20and%20their%20descendants

Bird-Hutchinson, S. (2020, December 2). *Assimilation vs. acculturation.* COE. https://coe.ksu.edu/about/publications/journey-to-refuge/refugee-experience.html

Blue, E. (2017). Seeing Ms. Dhu: Inquest, conquest, and (in)visibility in black women's deaths in custody. *Settler Colonial Studies*, *7*(3), 299–320. doi:10.1080/2201473X.2016.1229294

Chang, C. (2019, January 21). How early Australians treated Aboriginal people. *News.com.* https://www.news.com.au/national/politics/how-early-australians-treated-aboriginal-people/news-story/e984d3a453382c59a1d5d81f99a9ad8c

Doherty, L. (2021). *Deaths in custody in Australia 2020-2021. Statistical report 37.* Canberra: Australian Institute of Criminology. https://www.aic.gov.au/sites/default/files/2021-12/sr37_deaths_in_custody_in australia_2020-21.pdf. doi:10.52922/sr78436

Fanon, F. (2008). *Black skin, White masks.* Grove Press.

Goldsmith, J. (2021, April 10). Protests around Australia to stop indigenous deaths in custody. *9 News.* https://www.9news.com.au/national/stop-deaths-in-custody-protest-sydney-aboriginal-deaths-in-custody/128b0da7-e6ac-485b-9fcf-c656942ab852

Harrison, K. (2020, June 10). I can't breathe: The suffocating truth of Australia's race relations. *Newsroom.* https://newsroom.unsw.edu.au/news/social-affairs/i-cant-breathe-suffocating-truth-australia%E2%80%99s-race-relations

Healing Foundation. (2022). *Who are the stolen generations?* Healing Foundation. https://healingfoundation.org.au/who-are-the-stolen-generations/#:~:text=The%20Stolen%20Generations%20refers%20to%20a%20period%20in,Aboriginal%20children%20to%20be%20removed%20from%20their%20parents

Hilton, B. T. (2011). Frantz Fanon and Colonialism: A Psychology of Oppression. *Journal of Scientific Psychology*, 45–59.

Hinman, P. (2021, March 23). Anger over three more black deaths in custody. *Green Left Weekly, 1301,* p. 10. https://searchinformitorg.ezproxy.liberty.edu/doi/10.3316/INFORMIT.703562380364826

International Work Group for Indigenous Affairs. (n.d.). *Indigenous peoples of Australia.* IWGIA. https://iwgia.org/en/australia#:~:text=The%20Indigenous%20World%202022%3A%20Australia%20Written%20on%2001,Australians%20in%202021%20was%20estimated%20to%20be%20881%2C600

Longman, C. (2020, July). Police silence and Aboriginal deaths in custody. *LSJ, 68,* pgs. 1-3.

Marchetti, E. (2012, June 14). Victim or offenders: Who were the 11 indigenous female prisoners who died in custody and were investigated by the Australian Royal Commission into Aboriginal deaths in custody. *International Review of Victimology, 19*(1), 37-49. . doi:10.1177/0269758012447218

Maxwell-Stewart, H., & Oxley, D. (2020). Convicts and the colonization of Australia, 1788-1868. *Digital Panopticon.* https://www.digitalpanopticon.org/Convicts_and_the_Colonisation_of_Australia,_1788-1868

Mitchell, G. (2018, July 17). *Officer thought David Dungay may have been tricking them on breathing.* SMH. https://www.smh.com.au/national/nsw/officer-thought-david-dungay-may-have-been-tricking-them-on-breathing-20180717-p4zs0n.html

Nettelback, A. (2015, February 18). Colonization and the origins of humanitarian governance: Protecting aborigines across the nineteenth-century British empire. [Review of the book Colonization and the origins of humanitarian governance: Protecting aborigines across the nineteenth-century British empire, by A. Lester and F. Dussart]. *Australian Historical Studies, 46*(1), 149–150. doi:10.1080/1031461X.2015.992845

O'Loughlin, M. (2022, June 20). *The stolen generation.* Australian Museum. https://australian.museum/learn/first-nations/stolen-generation/

Oldfield, A. (1865). On the Aborigines of Australia. *Transaction of the Ethological Society of London, 3*, 215–298. doi:10.2307/3014165

Qasem, D. A. H. (2019, August 22). *Black deaths in custody – Where did we go wrong?* Sydney Criminal Lawyers. https://www.sydneycriminallawyers.com.au/blog/black-deaths-in-custody-where-did-we-go-wrong/?utm_source=Mondaq&utm_medium=syndication&utm_campaign=LinkedIn-integration

Simmons, J. C. (1997). *The relationship between parent involvement, head start, the head start transition program and academic achievement.* [Thesis, Michigan State University]. https://waldenu.academia.edu/DrJanelleSimmons

Trigger, D.S. (1985, June). *Doomadgee: A study of power relations and social action in North Australian Aboriginal settlement.* [Doctoral dissertation, University of Queensland].

Van Krieken, R. (1999, August 1). The 'stolen generations and cultural genocide: The forced removal of Australian indigenous children from their families and its implications for the sociology of childhood. *Childhood, 6*(3), 297-311.

KEY TERMS AND DEFINITIONS

Aborigine: One of the first people of the land of Australia. Translates as "Original Inhabitants."

Aboriginal Customary Law: The Aborigines' original law and customary ways of dealing with conflicts, etc.

Acculturation: The ability to preserve one's main culture while interacting with and respecting other people's cultures.

Assimilation: The process of losing who you are to be accepted by the dominant culture. Sometimes, this process is forced by others such as colonizers.

Dispersing the Natives: euphemism for the genocide or mass killing of Aborigines native to Australia.

Stolen Child: An Aboriginal child or a Torres Straight child who was forcibly removed from their home and family of origin to be placed in a "White Australian" family usually through foster care to be assimilated and "whitened" up.

Stolen Generation: A term used for the process of assimilation during the period of the 1910s to the 1970s where Aboriginal and Torres Straight children were taken from their home of origin by the government of Australia.

Chapter 5
Case Study:
South Africa

ABSTRACT

This chapter focuses on a brief history of South Africa from slavery until modern-day South Africa. The main focus of this chapter will be the period of Apartheid, which translates as 'separateness.' After a further definition of apartheid is explored, the history of Apartheid will be explored and discussed along with Apartheid's policies and its impact on South Africa as well as the world and its politics. An analysis of the issues that led to Apartheid and that led to the end of Apartheid will take place. Additionally, key opponents to Apartheid will be introduced with their philosophies introduced/introduced further, such as Steve Biko and Nelson Mandela.

NKOSI SIKELEL'IAFRIKA

Nkosi sikelel' iAfrika (Xhosa)

Maluphakanyisw' uphondo lwayo, (Xhosa)

Yizwa imithandazo yethu, (Zulu)

Nkosi sikelela, thina lusapho lwayo.(Zulu)

Morena boloka setjhaba sa heso,

DOI: 10.4018/978-1-7998-9304-2.ch005

O fedise dintwa le matshwenyeho,

O se boloke, O se boloke setjhaba sa heso, Setjhaba sa, South Afrika.

(Entire verse is performed in Sesotho)

South Afrika!

Uit die blou van onse hemel,

Uit die diepte van ons see,

Oor ons ewige gebergtes,

Waar die kranse antwoord gee,

(Entire verse is performed in Afrikaans)

Sounds the call to come together,

And united we shall stand,

Let us live and strive for freedom,

In South Africa our land.

(Entire verse is performed in English)

"You do not own the thing that you love." - Trevor Noah (Born a Crime)

"During my lifetime ... I have cherished [loved] the ideal of a democratic and free society in which all persons live together in harmony and with equal opportunities. It is an ideal which I hope to live for and to achieve. But if needs be, it is an ideal for which I am prepared to die." – Nelson Mandela, April 20, 1964 (Spielvogel, 2014)

Figure 1. Centers for Disease Control and Prevention
South Africa - Chapter 10 - 2020 Yellow Book | Travelers' Health | CDC

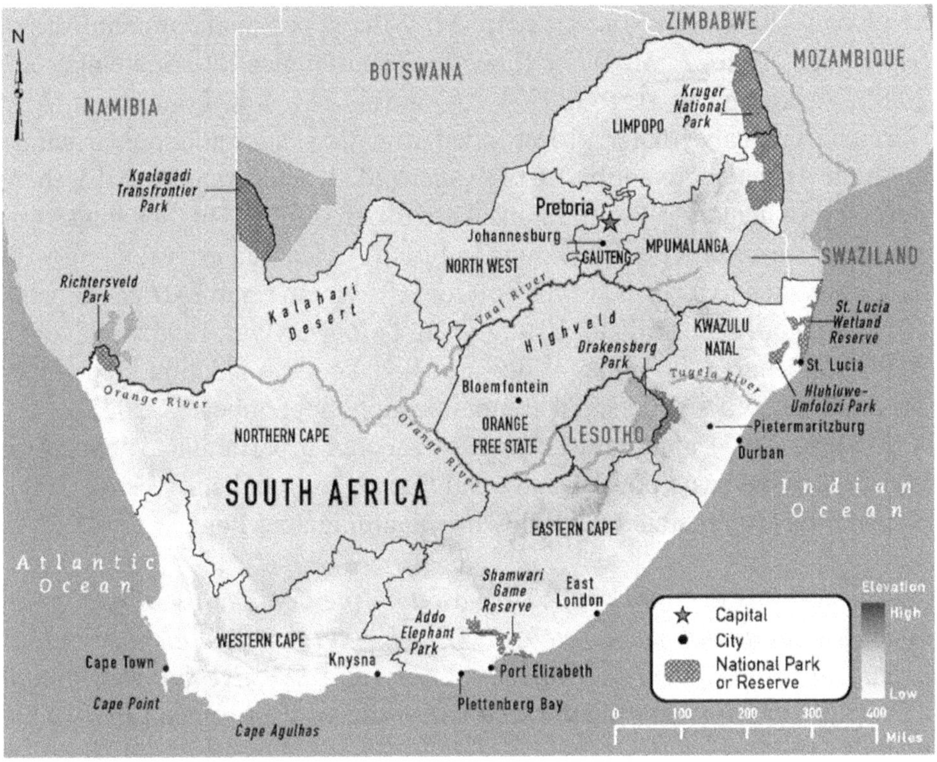

INTRODUCTION

My first introduction to the plight of South Africa regarding Apartheid was on Broadway in New York City. Although I cannot find the tickets nor an advert for this play, I took one Constance Louise Adams Simmons to see an Off-Broadway show about Steve Biko and the Uprising. It was in the nose-bleed section. I was mesmerized. I began to consider – as a young adult – what it means to be separate. How is South Africa different than the United States or countries like Australia? Personally, I had studied in Australia in 1997-1998 and faced discrimination. Within the past two years (2021) I visited South Africa to do research for a chapter I submitted and that is now in print along with this book titled Ubuntu Through the Lens of Tikkun Olam that was printed in Understanding Ubuntu for Enhancing Intercultural Communications (2021); and I started to understand the complexities of the Boer invasion, the policy of Apartheid, tribal wars, et al.

Apartheid or 'separateness' or 'apartness' is a word derived from Afrikaans (Gibson, 2011; Kihato, 2014; Lynch, 1977; Maylam, 1995; Noah, 2019; Spielvogel, 2014; Van Vuuren, 2015; M. Wilcox, personal communication, September 21, 2022; M. Wilcox, personal communication, September 23, 2022). According to Ager (2022), "Afrikaans is a low Franconian West Germanic language [that was] descended from [the] Dutch and spoken mainly in South Africa and Namibia" (p.1). Ager (2022) notes that by 2013, there were approximately 17 million speakers of Afrikaans. This language was only later spoken by the Black man in South Africa. It's arrival along with its speakers led to a period of turmoil for Africans in South Africa (Gibson, 2011; Holland, 1988; Kihato, 2014; Lynch, 1976; Maylam, 1995; Spielvogel, 2014; Van Vuuren, 2015; M. Wilcox, personal communication, September 21, 2022; M. Wilcox, personal communication, September 23, 2022).

In short, "[...] apartheid may be considered a particular extension or variation of the basic politics and conditions of colonialism" (Hook, 2004, p. 88). Ellis (2019) stated the following regarding apartheid:

Apartheid in its original context is based on the domination of one group (Whites) over an indigenous majority (Blacks). It is a racial identity with its origins in South Africa. [...] Apartheid was an exhaustive system of racial discrimination that restricted education, political engagement, and social contact" (p. 63).

From May 20, 1948, apartheid was instituted as a policy in South Africa (TimeToast, 2022). It was instituted for Whites to progress over Blacks (Biko, n.d.; Golden, 2004; Spielvogel, 2014; Van Vuuren, 2015). White Afrikaners put themselves in the position of being "god" (Biko, n.d.).

Figure 2. Picture of a sign depicting the segregation or "separateness" that began due to apartheid
Source: TimeToast (2022)

Apartheid was just the beginning of a list of events that became known as some of the greatest human rights violations in the world. These and other matters will be the focus of this chapter.

MAIN FOCUS OF CHAPTER

South Africa met with its first "invaders" during the 1600 and 1700s (South African History Online, n.d.; Spieglvogel, 2014). In 1652, Whites arrived and were met by the Xhosa[1] (Holland, 1988). The Dutch East Indian Company also arrived, which was the first multinational corporation (Van Vuuren, 2015) and began bringing slaves from Madagascar to the Cape (Lafranier, 2005) in 1658 (Boshoff, 2018). This indispensable commodity was worth a lot to the British (Boshoff, 2018). 63,000 slaves had made their way to the Cape (Public Broadcasting Service, 2019). The British continued to trade on the East with the Khoikhoi (South African History Online, n.d.).

Robben Island was also used as a prison colony by the British (South African History Online, n.d.; M. Wilcox, personal communication, September 21, 2022). They continued to visit through the 1700s to areas like the Cape and Table Bay (South African History Online, n.d.). The British began to falsify documents to prevent the French from acquiring the land (South African

History Online, n.d.). An armed conflict began, and the British defeated the Dutch and they proceeded to Cape Town in the late 18th century circa 1775 (South African History Online, n.d.; M. Wilcox, personal communication, September 21, 2022; M. Wilcox, personal communication, September 23, 2022).

In 1803, the British signed a treaty known as the Treaty of Amiens and the Cape was returned to the Dutch Batavian government (South African History Online, n.d.). However, when the Napoleonic wars began, the British again attacked the Cape to keep the French from advancing in 1806, and finally acquired the Cape in 1806 and permanently as a British protectorate (Holland, 1988; M. Wilcox, personal communication, September 21, 2022; M. Wilcox, personal communication, September 23, 2022) and in 1814 via the Treaty of Vienna (South African History Online, n.d.). The Cape had finally been colonized by Britain and they paid royally in the amount of six (6) million pounds to the Dutch (South African History Online, n.d.).

Cape Town became the capital of British control throughout South Africa (South African History Online, n.d.). By the 1820s, English became an official language (South African History Online, n.d.). The British came and established themselves in various careers (e.g., 1790s as merchants, in 1817 forming the Commercial Exchange, etc.) (South African History Online, n.d.). Brits were brought to work as indentured servants including children (South African History Online, n.d.). Eventually, the descendants of Dutch settlers left the Cape between the 1830s and the 1840s and headed north eastward and further eastward to complete the "Great Trek" (South African History Online, n.d.). They left in order to escape the colonial law of the British and the native population (Golden, 2004; M. Wilcox, personal communication, September 21, 2022; M. Wilcox, personal communication, September 23, 2022). They believed themselves to be a White nation within a Black African country who deeply believed in Jesus Christ (Golden, 2004). Due to the Great Trek, Afrikaner Republics were finally established such as the Natal Republic (1839), the Transvaal (1852) and the Orange Free State (1854) (South African History Online, n.d.).

Figure 3. Picture of the 1st Anglo Boer War (1880-1881) taken at the War Store in Johannesburg, South Africa on August 20, 2021
Source: Janelle Christine Simmons, Ed.D. © 2021

Eventually, the British and the Afrikaner republics came to blows as diamonds and gold were discovered in the 1860s and the 1880s respectively (Golden, 2004; South African History Online, n.d.). By 1890, Britain annexed the remaining of the former Orange Free State (Holland, 1988). The South African War or the Boer War lasted from 1899 to 1902 (A. Coleman, personal communication, August 20, 2021; Golden, 2004; Holland, 1988; South African History Online, n.d; M. Wilcox, personal communication, September 21, 2022; M. Wilcox, personal communication, September 23, 2022; Willoughby-Herald, 2015). By May 31, 1910, the four colonies became the Union of South Africa and were a self-governing colony under British control (South African History Online, n.d.). Overall, the British government housed in London had determined that the country should become a self-governing domain (Holland, 1988).

In 1912, the White Union of South Africa continued to allow Blacks to make laws, but they were not allowed to administer such laws (Holland, 1988). The African National Conference was formed in 1912 (Spielvogel, 2014) on January 8th (South African History Online, n.d.; M. Wilcox, personal communication, September 21, 2023). By 1913, the Native Land Act had been instituted (Van Vuuren, 2015; Willoughby-Herald, 2015). This act further alienated black people from their own ancestral lands (Van Vuuren, 2015). Additionally, this act forced men to seek and garner employment in dangerous positions at mines earning small salaries (Van Vuuren, 2015).

In 1916, the Craddock Congress had determined that there were 105,518 poor Whites in rural South Africa (Willoughby-Herald, 2015). What came to be an invisible force behind the NP or National Party (Willoughby-Herald, 2015) began in 1918 and was known as the *Broederbond* or the Brotherhood (Van Vuuren, 2015). The "Brotherhood" was an all-white, patriarchal society that was formed and operated in secret and sought to increase the position of the White Afrikaner after the South African War had ceased (Van Vuuren, 2015). In 1923, the number of poor Whites had increased to approximately 120,000 to 160,000 (Willoughby-Herald, 2015). After the Trek and the war, several Afrikaners found themselves to be of low means (Golden, 2004; Willoughby-Herald, 2015). According to Willoughby-Herald (2015), research members of the Carnegie Commission and Columbia University blamed this plight on the native Blacks. They were blamed because the Whites had to depend on them and compete with them and this was a root of the White man's poverty (Willoughby-Herald, 2015). Only Ernest Gideon Malherbe (1895-1982) noted the plight of Blacks as being greater (Golden, 2004; Willoughby-Herald, 2015).

Several other events happened (M. Wilcox, personal communication, September 21, 2022; M. Wilcox, personal communication, September 23, 2022). However, a conference was held due to the dire needs of Black Africans in Apartheid South Africa, and the African Native National Congress (ANNC) was formed in the 1960s (South African History Online, n.d.; M. Wilcox, personal communication, September 21, 2022). This was Black South Africa's response to being colonized and introduced to further measures of Apartheid (South African History Online, n.d.; M. Wilcox, personal communication, September 21, 2022). It was not to be the last known solution.

Figure 4. Picture of the Voortrekker Monument, Pretoria, South Africa (August 24, 2021)
Source: Janelle Christine Simmons, Ed.D. © 2021

Figure 5. Picture of the myself at the Voortrekker Monument, Pretoria, South Africa (August 24, 2021)
Source: Janelle Christine Simmons, Ed.D. © 2021

Issues, Controversies, Problems

The issues, controversies and problems with Apartheid appeared to be endless (Gibson, 2011; Kihato, 2014; Maylam, 1995; Noah, 2019; Spielvogel, 2014; M. Wilcox, personal communication, September 21, 2022; M. Wilcox, personal communication, September 23, 2022), which is most likely why it has ended. Outside of the issue of colonization, one of the real roots of the policy that was to become known as Apartheid was the "Poor White Study" (Golden, 2004; Willoughby-Herald, 2015). This study was to be carried out by the Carnegie Commission of Investigation, which was under the auspices of the Carnegie Corporation of New York (Golden, 2004; Willoughy-Herald, 2015). This study was to have lasting effects on both the Whites and the Blacks of South Africa (Golden, 2004; Willoughby-Herald, 2015).

The Carnegie Corporation of New York (2022) is an organization that was founded in 1911 and it "works to promote democracy, education, and peace across the globe, advancing knowledge and understanding in these areas of central importance" (p. 1). Perhaps, it was not inconsequential that right before this trip, Adolf Hitler had begun to write a work that would be known as *Mein Kampf* or "My Struggle" while being imprisoned in Landsberg for his crime of high treason (United States Holocaust Memorial Museum, n.d.) By 1925, copies were being sold worldwide (United States Holocaust Memorial Museum, n.d.). Then the Carnegie Corporation began to further establish itself financially (Golden, 2004).

Two years later, the founder of the Carnegie Corporation, Frederick Keppel and his Corporation secretary James Bertram sought to explore grant possibilities in South Africa and visited said country in 1927 (Golden, 2004). They saw a country that was diverse and rich in natural resources (Golden, 2004) as had the British (South African History Online, n.d.). However, there were racial segregation laws (Dubow, 2000; Gibson, 2022; Holland, 1988; Kihato, 2014; Maylam, 1995; Niefragodie, 2014; Spielvogel, 2014; M. Wilcox, personal communication, September 21, 2022; Van Vuuren, 2015; M. Wilcox, personal communication, September 23, 2022; Willoughby-Herald, 2015), and only Whites (i.e., 20%) of the population could even vote or acquire the highest paying jobs (Golden, 2004). Even when seeing the racism and inequities, Keppel returned and asked to grant South Africa with educational funding that would only go to Whites in the amount of $500,000 (i.e., $5,000,000 in today's currency) (Golden, 2004).

Through "race relations technicians" race relations scholars sought to endorse segregation (Willoughby-Herald, 2015). By creating the largest and by far the most complex social science study ever conducted in Africa as a whole, the question was addressed (Golden, 2004). The Poor White Question was then answered by the report that was generated in 1929 known as the "Carnegie Poor White Study"[1] (Golden, 2004). The question was only posed because the supposition was that Whites should be smarter, faster, stronger and more advanced than the Black man from the beginning (Golden, 2004).

Thus, the question of racism existing was in effect a non-question. That fact did not need to be studied.

The poor White had been identified (Golden, 2004). They were mainly descendants of those who were trekkers during the Voortrekker Boers (Golden, 2004). Various members of the Poor White Commission sought to assist these Afrikaans speakers (Golden, 2004). The commission itself included academics, clergy, and political as well as welfare activists who wanted to assist the 300,000 Afrikaners who they found were impoverished in the farming areas (Golden, 2004). They had little thought for the poor Black South African whose land had been robbed in the first place (Golden, 2004). The fact was that "race was believed to determine which rights and which quality of life one ought to have" (Kihato, 2014; Willoughby-Herald, 2015, p. 6) as it was linked to privileges and rights overall (Noah, 2019).

In 1924, the Pact government instituted a policy called the "civilized labor policy" which guaranteed "employment, wages and hiring preferences for White men" (Willoughby-Herald, 2015, p. 5). By 1932, a push was made to create a Unified Afrikaans Nationalistic Party (Willoughby-Herald, 2015). By the 1940s, the British control of the Cape and other parts of South Africa had been significantly weakened (South African History Online, n.d.; M. Wilcox, personal communication, September 21, 2022; M. Wilcox, personal communication, September 23, 2022). At the same time, the Poor White Study was being used to move for the establishment of a full Apartheid state (Dubow, 2000; Holland, 1988; Niefragodie, 2014; Van Vuuren, 2015; Willoughby-Herald, 2015) as well as the Party (Van Vuuren, 2015). By this point, the Brotherhood was 12,000 or more members and they were to place every NP PM and president from 1948 to 1994 from DF Malan to F.W. de Klerk (Van Vuuren, 2015). During this period, more apartheid laws were put into place.

Apartheid Begins

To fight the 'black peril,' a vote was taken on May 26, 1948 (Holland, 1988). Slogans accompanied the campaign and the vote such as *'Kaffir op sy plek'* and *'Koelies uut die land uit,'* which mean "Kaffir in his place" and "Coolies out of the country" (Holland, 1988). Jan Smut's United Party was ousted by Dr. Daniel Malan's National Party (Holland, 1988; M. Wilcox, personal communication, September 21, 2022; M. Wilcox, personal communication, September 23, 2022). Smuts in "describing the National Party's new policy of apartheid as 'a crazy concept, born of prejudice and fear' he warned that it 'may create and inflame Native communism and even end in a totally black South Africa'" (Holland, 1988, p. 68). Nonetheless, it was instituted. According to Trevor Noah (2019), "the genius of apartheid was convincing people who were the overwhelming majority to turn on each other. Apart hate, is what it was. You separate people into groups and make them hate one another so you can run them all" (p. 1). Thus, the goal had always been that they be a separated people (Golden, 2004; Holland, 1988; Noah, 2019; Van Vuuren, 2015; Willoughby-Herald, 2015). At first the practice was just one of separateness but eventually as it was implemented as a policy, which became law, apartheid became an ever-increasing, complex, intricate "network of laws" that set barriers for Blacks (Golden, 2004; M. Wilcox, personal communication, September 21, 2022; M. Wilcox, personal communication, September 23, 2022). They could not live in certain areas or live in certain areas without "permission" (Golden, 2004; Kihato, 2014; Spielvogel, 2014; M. Wilson, personal communication, September 21, 2022; M. Wilson, personal communication, September 23, 2022). Blacks were forced from their homes (Kihato, 2014; Maylam 1995), some even after 50 years such as the case of Sophiatown (Lynch, 1976) and "banished" to *Bantustans* (Golden, 2004) or homelands (Spielvogel, 2014), which were impoverished territories that were usually far from the cities (Golden, 2004). The policy also had other issues. For example, the laws created crime.

The fact is/was that the "South African apartheid laws turn[ed] innumerable innocent people into 'criminals'" (Holland, 1988, p. 85). Everything was a crime (Holland, 1988; Van Vuuren, 2015). Being in a mixed-race relationship was a crime (Holland, 1988; Noah, 2019). In fact, due to this law, 300,000+ people per year became criminals for being in a relationship with someone who was not of their race classification (Holland, 1988). Even unemployment was a crime and having a passbook without a stamp with approved employment could lead to being arrested (Holland, 1988) or being without a passbook could lead to an arrest (Gibson, 2011; Lynch, 1976). As each act was passed, there was more police harassment (Holland, 1988). Much of this harassment took place at night (Holland, 1988).

On August 22, 1949, the New York Times noted that the White policy was to "divide and rule" (Lynch, 1976) and they did through 1994 (Golden, 2004; Karimi, 2013; Kihato, 2014; Miller, 2013; Nelson Mandela Foundation, 2022; Noah, 2019; Spielvogel, 2014; Van Vuuren, 2015). On June 21, 1950, a bill to suppress communists was being passed (Lynch, 1976). Riots continued to take place every month for six months as of February 19, 1950 (Lynch, 1976).

Blacks outnumbered Whites by 3-2 and as policies increased, Blacks were said to have become more impudent at that time (Lynch, 1976). A separation between English speakers and Afrikaans speakers had taken place as well (Gibson, 2011; Lynch, 1976).

As of April 15, 1950, there were 2,6000,000 Whites and 8,500,000 Blacks (Lynch, 1976). Blacks and Whites were always divided physically in public (Gibson, 2011; Kihato, 2014; Maylam, 1995; Lynch, 1976). Another separation was that of duties. The capital was Pretoria, and it was administrative, but the parliament was in Cape Town (Lynch, 1976; M. Wilcox, personal communication, September 21, 2022; M. Wilcox, personal communication, September 23, 2022). Various bills, laws and decisions continued to take place and were passed (See Chapter 10).

By June 1951, figures like Mandela and Tambo and Sisulu began to make a campaign plan, which came to be known as the Defiance Campaign (Holland, 1988) by 1952 (Nelson Mandela Foundation, 2022). They established a resistance based in civil disobedience (Holland, 1988; Spielvogel, 2014). Defiance leaders had to follow strict rules. For example, no one could be drunk, disorderly, rowdy, and the police had to be informed by the leader beforehand that they were going to demonstrate (Holland, 1988). Mandela and Yusuf Cachalia had come up with the procedures (Holland, 1988). Defiers as they were called even included people like Mahatmas Gandhi's son Manilal (Holland, 1988).

Figure 6. Picture of the ANC office in Gauteng, Johannesburg, South Africa taken on August 27, 2021
Source: Janelle Christine Simmons, Ed.D. © 2021

"The White volunteers were led by Patrick Duncan, an Oxford graduate whose father had been governor-general in South Africa" (Holland, 1988, p. 83). Seven Whites joined the group of 30 defiers (Holland, 1988).

On February 21, 1953, there was still a surge of Africans trying to enter South Africa to make it their home even though Apartheid had been in position for six years (Lynch, 1976). Prime Minister Daniel Malan noted that 255,000 Negro or Black immigrants were known to have entered illegally and were forced to work in farms that were located outside of the city (Lynch, 1976). And out of 245,000 who were legally here, 195,000 Blacks garnered positions in the coal and gold mines (Lynch, 1976). According to Alan Paton, to address this issue, a new liberal party was led that sought full citizenship for "all civilized people irrespective of race, color or creed" (Lynch, 1976, p. 182). While it may sound like everything was going well, it was not.

By August 9, 1954, Pretoria had ordered separation by tribal confines (Lynch, 1976). Dr. Hendrik Verwoerd, the Minister of Native Affairs stated the following: "new residential cities and settlements for Negroes are to be subdivided according to tribal allegiance" (p. 186). Moreover, "negro children are [to be] educated on the basis of ten major tribal language groups and the schools are to be situated to fit the tribal subdivision pattern" (Lynch, 1976, p. 1986). This was allegedly done in order to respect the minorities and their original way of life. Therefore, 9,000,000 Negro South Africans should practice their own cultures and beliefs (Lynch, 1976). However, it appears to have been a different strategy of "divide and conquer." This is especially the case because the government could continue to keep people separate based on tribe (Noah, 2019).

By November 30, 1954, Johannes Gerhardus N. Strydom becomes the New Prime Minister (See Figure 1). As an extreme nationalist, and leader of the UP (United Party) opposition, he sought to divorce the "republic" from any British interference (Lynch, 1976). He also separated the Indians from Blacks and Whites (Lynch, 1976), especially when it came to residential segregation (Maylam, 1995), and ensured that they had no political rights whatsoever (Lynch, 1976). During February of 1955, forced moves continued. 130 Negro families were forced out of Johannesburg on the 9th (Lynch, 1976). In fact, there were 2,000 heavily armed policemen who came and made sure that these families moved from Sophiatown to the Meadowsland where rent for a new development was \$3-\$13 a month (Lynch, 1976).

With increasing limitations, Mandela pushed the struggle ahead (Holland, 1988; Spielvogel, 2014). "Mandela's new forms of political struggle centered on a drive to politicize the masses, using the 'M'; (for Mandela) Plan" (Holland, 1988, p. 91; Nelson Mandela Foundation, 2022). This plan worked to combat bans, created zones (i.e., a zone consisted of 7 streets) with "chief stewards" and to politicize the masses (Holland, 1988). According to Holland (1988), "three months later, in the early hours of 27 September 1955, over 1,000 officers launched the biggest police raid in the country's history" (p. 101). There were hundreds of search warrants issues and over 500 body searches (Holland, 1988).

In order to maintain power Strijdom (i.e., also spelled Strydom) made sure that the Supreme Court was increased from five to eleven persons and the Senate was increased from 48 to 89 senators where approximately 67% of them were nationalists (Lynch, 1976). Soon, Kimbereley was classifying the races (Lynch, 1976; M. Wilcox, personal communication, September 21, 2022; M. Wilcox, personal communication, September 23, 2022). The classifications were White, Colored and Negro where Negros were at the bottom of the socially stratified race ladder (Lynch, 1976; M. Wilcox, personal communication, September 21, 2022; M. Wilcox, personal communication, September 23, 2022). Suddenly, 7,000 people were reclassified (Lynch, 1976). 260 people sent a notice to appeal (Lynch, 1976). Many people sought to stay classified as colored or White because they had more opportunities (Noah, 2019). Depending on one's classification, they had access to different privileges and rights (Noah, 2019).

The Sharpeville Massacre

By 1960, another watershed event took place in South Africa. The event was known as the Sharpeville Massacre (Gibson, 2011; Holland, 1988; Karimi, 2013; Nelson Mandela Foundation, 2022; United Nations, 2021; M. Wilcox, personal communication, September 21, 2022). On March 21, 1960, four years after Mandela's treason charge (Karimi, 2013), 69 unarmed protestors were killed (Holland, 1988; Karimi, 2013; Lynch, 1976; Miller, 2013; United Nations, 2021). They were killed outside of the police station (United Nations, 2021) while they protested peacefully (Miller, 2013). They were killed because they were demonstrating against pass laws (Gibson, 2011; United Nations, 2021). Pass laws were restrictive laws meant to control the comings and goings of Blacks (Gibson, 2011; Lynch, 1976; Miller, 2013; United Nations, 2021). Even a visitor in one's home had to be reported to the police (Miller, 2013). Moreover, the police would tell the host how long the visitor could stay (Miller, 2013).

The demonstration began with thousands of Black South Africans protesting pass laws, (Holland, 1988; Karimi, 2013; Miller, 2013; United Nations, 2021; M. Wilcox, personal communication, September 21, 2022; M. Wilcox, personal communication, September 23, 2022). The object of this exercise was to be arrested (Miller, 2013), thus, filling the jails and creating a hardship for the police and detention centers. They may also may have been able to communicate with one another more freely. However, what ensued was a shooting (Holland, 1988; Karimi, 2013; Lynch, 1976; Miller, 2013; Nelson Mandela Foundation, 2022; United Nations, 2021; M. Wilson, personal communication, September 21, 2022; M. Wilson, personal communication, September 23, 2022).

In fact, due to this massacre, hundreds of protests took place (United Nations, 2021). More importantly, Mandela's anger grew (Karimi, 2013). In fact, he took a more militant tone and began to train to fight physically against apartheid (Karimi, 2013). However, he was imprisoned (Karimi, 2013; Nelson

Mandela Foundation, 2022). Within two minutes, 1,300 bullets had been fired (Miller, 2013). The martyrs were the seeds that began a further process of change. Not only did it spark international outrage and protest, but it set off three decades of protest within South Africa (Miller, 2013). This protest also led to Mandela's freedom after 27 years of imprisonment (Miller, 2013; M. Wilson, personal communication, September 21, 2022; M. Wilcox, personal communication, September 23, 2022), 18 of which had been spent at Robben Island (Karimi, 2013; M. Wilson, personal communication, September 21, 2022; M. Wilson, personal communication, September, 23, 2022).

Figure 7. Picture of the aftermath of the Sharpeville Massacre on March 21, 1960
Source: Google Cultural Institute (2015).

Within ten years, a new issue arose. The issue was that of classifications that had begun in 1955 (Laurence, 2010). This push for race classifications would eventually affect a little girl known as Sandra Laing (Fabian, 2008; Laurence, 2010; Journeyman Pictures, 2000).

Spotlight: Sandra Laing

A national and worldwide example of how classifications affected people's lives is depicted in the story of Sandra Laing (Fabian, 2008; Journeyman Pictures, 2000; Laurence, 2010). She was born in 1955 (Fabian, 2008; Journeyman Pictures, 2000) to two White Afrikaner parents (Fabian, 2008; Journeyman Pictures, 2000) who supported apartheid and supported the National party (Laurence, 2010). She had a darker complexion than her siblings, but they looked alike (Fabian, 2008; Journeyman Pictures, 2000); Laurence, 2010). Nonetheless, all was well until she went to boarding school at the age of 11 (Fabian, 2008; Journeyman Pictures, 2000; Laurence, 2010).

Eventually, she was expelled (Laurence, 2010), and the government via the Commission of Home Affairs classified her as "Black" (Fabian, 2008; Journeyman Pictures, 2000). Her father fought for reclassification, and they all had to take blood tests, and Sandra Laing's bones were measured, etc. and two years later she was considered "White" again (Fabian, 2008; Journeyman Pictures, 2000), which was the best position. According to the classification, the categories were as follows with White being the best and Black being the worst: White, Coloured, Asian and Black (Laurence, 2010). Indians were considered Coloured (Laurence, 2010).

Due to the expelling, she was behind in school as well and struggled academically (Fabian, 2008; Journeyman Pictures, 2000). By the age of 15, she ran away with a Black man (Laurence, 2010) named Petrus and had two children where she raised them in a homeland (Fabian, 2008; Journeyman Pictures, 2000). Her family disowned her, and she remained "White" (Fabian, 2008; Journeyman Pictures, 2000). Eventually, Sandra had herself reclassified as Coloured person so she would not lose custody of her children from her first husband (Fabian, 2008). Before she had reached the age of eleven, South Africa had gained its freedom.

Figure 8. Picture of Sandra Laing and her parents when she was a child
Source: Face2Face Africa (2018). https://face2faceafrica.com/article/the-interesting-case-of-the-black-south-african-girl-born-to-conservative-white-pare nts-during-apartheid.

By 1961, South Africa had obtained freedom from the British Commission and/or Britain and was deemed independent (Van Vuuren, 2015; M. Wilson, personal communication, September 21, 2022) as did other African nations broke free from their colonial oppressors (Golden, 2004). Now, apartheid had fuller reign and the country was becoming more isolated (Golden, 2004). In April of 1961, Nelson Mandela wrote a letter of ultimatum to the NP Prime Minister Hendrik Verwoerd for or on behalf of the ANC calling for a democratic nation (Van Vuuren, 2015). Eventually, Mandela and his people went on strike, and were imprisoned (Van Vuuren, 2015). By 1963, the United Nations placed a voluntary arms embargo on South Africa (Van Vuuren, 2015). In 1964, Mandela and the ANC leaders were sentenced to life in prison (Van Vuuren, 2015). And due to internal resistance and fury among the masses, in 1966, the PM Hendrik Voewoerd was assassinated (Van Vuuren, 2015). The protests continued, and partially due to the Sharpeville Massacre, the International Convention on the Elimination of All Forms of Racial Discrimination was formed on January 4, 1969 (United Nations, 2021).

From the 1970s to the mid-1990s, apartheid led to a 20-year period of substantial abuses of power that were unparalleled in the past (Van Vuuren, 2015). In 1973, the United Nations General Assembly declared that apartheid was a crime against humanity (Van Vuuren, 2015). By the time Steve Biko was murdered in 1977, the United Nations Security Council began to starve

South Africa's "war" economy and placed or imposed mandatory arms sanctions (Van Vuuren, 2015).

"Let me say, no attempt to overthrow our country or revolution will succeed. Out security forces are trained to withstand revolution." – PW Botha, Minister of Defence, August 23, 1977

By 1978, PW Botha was elected as the Prime Minister (Van Vuuren, 2015). During the 1980s, there internal resistance continued within South Africa and could not be ceased as people were calling for change (Van Vuuren, 2015). However, one leader whose name continues to repeat during this time was that of Nelson Mandela. He also followed some principles of Gandhi and worked with him against an Apartheid state (M. Jacobs, personal communication, August 27, 2021). He deserves the Spotlight. (See below!)

Figure 9. Picture of myself at Gandhi Square in Johannesburg, South Africa on August 27, 2021
Source: Merle Jacobs, Tour Guide. © 2021

Figure 10. Picture of myself at Gandhi's House – August 27, 2021
Source: Merle Jacobs, Tour Guide. © 2021

Spotlight: Nelson Rolihlahla Mandela

Nelson Mandela or Rolihlahla, which means "one who brings trouble on himself" was one of the staunch opponents of Apartheid (Gibson, 2011; Holland, 1989; Spielvogel, 2014). He was born in the Transkei village of Qunu (Holland, 1989, p. 13) or noted as being born in Mvezo in the Transkei on July 18, 1918 (Nelson Mandela Foundation, 2022). He did however attend primary school in Qunu in 1925 (Nelson Mandela Foundation, 2022). When he was only a child, he was the only one of his family and possibly his tribe to speak English which he had spoken since 1928 without any formal education. He recalls an incident with the Xhosa chiefs and the White men who had come (Holland, 1988). One of the chiefs was his grandfather. The White men had told the chiefs to bend over and kiss their feet (Holland, 1988). They were outraged (Holland, 1988). From the Xhosas' view, "the white men thought themselves superior and viewed the Xhosas as savages" (Holland, 1988; p. 16). The chiefs went home and told their tribes stories of the insult and how previous chiefs had "dealt" with the White man (Holland, 1988).

In 1930, his father passed away (Nelson Mandela Foundation, 2022). In 1934, he attended Clarkebury Boarding Institute in Engcobo followed by Healdtown, the Wesleyan College at Fort Beaufort in 1937 (Nelson Mandela Foundation, 2022). Finally, he enrolls at the University College of Fort Hare in Alice in 1939, and was expelled in 1940 (Nelson Mandela Foundation, 2022). In 1941, he became a mine security officer, started working at a law firm called Witkin, Sidelsky and Eidelman and avoided an arranged marriage (Nelson Mandela Foundation, 2022). By 1942, he finally completed his BA via the University of South Africa (UNISA) (Nelson Mandela Foundation, 2022). Concurrently, he became involved with the ANC (Holland, 1988; Nelson Mandela Foundation, 2022). In 1943, he graduated with a BA from Fort Hare and enrolled at Wits University in the LLB program (Nelson Mandela Foundation, 2022). In 1944, he co-founded the ANCYL (ANC Youth League), married Evelyn Ntoko Mase and she gave birth to four children eventually (Nelson Mandela Foundation, 2022). By 1948, he was elected as the national secretary of ANCYL and then the President in 1951 (Nelson Mandela Foundation, 2022), and he left law school at Wits without finishing (Karimi, 2013). By 1952, he began the Defiance Campaign (Holland, 1988; Nelson Mandela Foundation, 2022). He was arrested for violating the Suppression Communism Act and was also elected the ANC President of Transvaal (Nelson Mandela Foundation, 2022).

On December 5, 1956, Mandela was arrested and was put on trial with 155 others for treason (Karimi, 2013; Nelson Mandela Foundation, 2022). He was acquitted by March 29, 1961 (Nelson Mandela Foundation, 2022). After divorcing Evelyn in 1958, he marries Winnie, and they have two children in 1959 and 1960 (Nelson Mandela Foundation, 2022). The year that Zindzi was born (Nelson Mandela Foundation, 2022), the Sharpeville Massacre took place (Gibson, 2011; Nelson Mandela Foundation, 2022). On March 30th, a State of Emergency is called, and thousands are detained (Nelson Mandela Foundation, 2022). On April 8, 1960, the ANC is banned (Karimi, 2013; Nelson Mandela Foundation, 2022). Thus, Nelson Mandela went underground (Holland, 1988; Jacobs, M., personal communication, August 27, 2021; Karimi, 2013; Nelson Mandela Foundation, 2022), and *Umkhonto weSizwe* (MK was formed (Nelson Mandela Foundation, 2022).

On January 11, 1962, Mandela left and performed military training (Karimi, 2013), and he further communicated with the outside world to garner support for the ANC and returned by July 23rd (Nelson Mandela Foundation, 2022). His training led him to Morocco and Ethiopia (Karimi, 2013). Within two weeks, Mandela was arrested on August 5 near Howick in KwaZulu-Natal, and he was sentenced for five years for incitement and leaving the country without a passport on November 7th (Nelson Mandela Foundation, 2022). By May 27, 1963, Mandela was sent to Robben Island (Nelson Mandela Foundation, 2022; M. Wilcox, personal communication, September 21, 2022; M. Wilcox, personal communication, September 23, 2022). On June 12, he was returned to a local prison in Pretoria (Nelson Mandela Foundation, 2022). On October 9, he appeared in court and became a participant in the Rivonia Trial along with his comrades (Karimi, 2013) Sisulu, Lionel 'Rusty' Bernstein, Denis Goldberg, James Kantor, Ahmed Kathrada, Govan Mbeki, Raymond Mhlaba, Andrew Mlanfeni and Elias Motsoaledi (Nelson Mandela Foundation, 2022). Nelson Mandela pled not guilty to sabotage on December 3rd (Nelson Mandela Foundation, 2022). In 1969, Thembekile dies in a car accident (Holland, 1988; Nelson Mandela Foundation, 2022).

On February 10, 1985, Mandela refused to be released (Nelson Mandela Foundation, 2022). He rejected Botha's offer because it would have required him to renounce violence (Nelson Mandela Foundation, 2022), and his protest was one of civil disobedience like Gandhi and not violence (M. Jacobs, personal communication, August 27, 2021; Spielvogel, 2014; M. Wilcox, personal communication, September 21, 2022; M. Wilcox, personal communication, September 23, 2022). After being admitted to various hospitals for prostate surgery, tuberculosis, etc. from 1985 to 1990, ANC was finally unbanned on February 2, 1990 (Nelson Mandela Foundation, 2022). On February 11, 1990, Nelson Mandela was released from prison (Golden, 2004; Karimi, 2013; Nelson Mandela Foundation, 2022; Van Vuuren, 2015; Willoughby-Herald, 2015). Nelson Mandela stated the following regarding being freed in 1990: "As I walked out the door toward the gate that would lead to my freedom, I knew if I didn't leave my bitterness and hatred behind, I'd still be in prison" (Karimi, 2013).

In 1990 (Golden, 2004; Kihato, 2014; Kirami, 2013; Miller, 2013; Nelson Mandela Foundation, 2022; Spielvogel, 2014), on March 2, Mandela was elected as the ANC Deputy President (Nelson Mandela Foundation, 2022). On December 10, 1993, President FW de Klerk and on April 27, 1994, Mandela voted for the first time in his life (Karimi, 2013; Nelson Mandela Foundation, 2022) in a non-apartheid South Africa. By 1994 (Gibson, 2011; Maylam,

1995; Spielvogel, 2014), on May 9, 1994, Nelson Mandela was elected by Parliament as the first President of a free South Africa (Golden, 2004; Karimi, 2013; Miller, 2013; Nelson Mandela Foundation, 2022; Van Vuuren, 2015). It had taken over 75 years to reach freedom from when he was born. He served as the president until 1999 when he stepped down (Karimi, 2013; Nelson Mandela Foundation, 2022) after one term and formed the Nelson Mandela Foundation (Nelson Mandela Foundation, 2022). Ironically, until 2008, the Unites States still had former President Nelson Mandela on their terrorist watch list (Karimi, 2013). For almost over a decade more, Mandela wrote books, gave lectures, divorced and remarried, etc. and suffered with various health issues (Nelson Mandela Foundation, 2022). He finally died on December 5, 2013, at the age of 95 (Karimi, 2013; Nelson Mandela Foundation, 2022).

However, during his time he saw many events take place. He watched the events of the Sharpeville Massacre unfold. He was imprisoned. And eventually in 1976, he heard of the Soweto Uprisings. This eventually all culminated to him becoming the 1st president of South Africa.

Figure 11. Picture of myself with a message board of Winnie Mandela at the Mandela House in Johannesburg, South Africa (August 26, 2021)
Source: Unknown, Tour Guide. © 2021

Figure 12. Picture of myself with a portrait of Nelson Mandela at the Mandela House in Johannesburg, South Africa (August 26, 2021)
Source: Janelle Christine Simmons, Ed.D. © 2021

Figure 13. Picture of a message from Nelson Mandela to Winnie Mandela at the Mandela House in Johannesburg, South Africa (August 26, 2021)
Source: Janelle Christine Simmons, Ed.D. © 2021

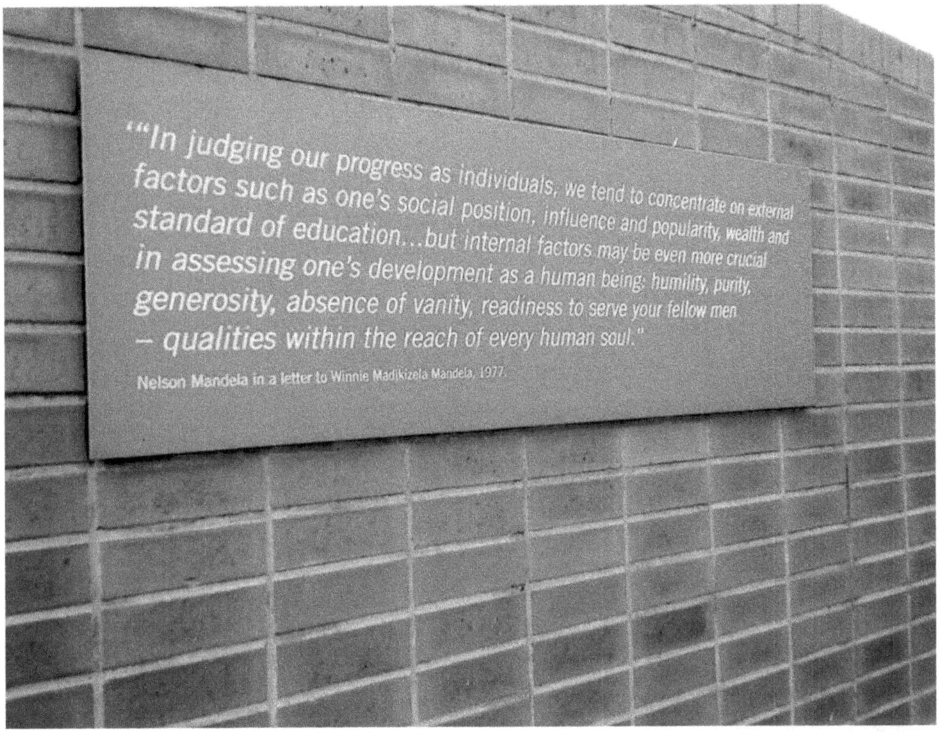

The Soweto Uprising (1976)

On June 16, 1976 (See Photo of the Hector Peterson Monument below!), Blacks planned demonstrations across various townships (Golden, 2004). These uprisings were known as the Soweto uprisings named after where they took place (Gibson, 2011; Golden, 2004; Holland, 1988). By the time the Soweto Uprising(s) occurred, there had been dissent amongst various tribes in South Africa. Nonetheless, the uprisings were well-organized (Holland, 1988), and in many cases led by children (Golden, 2004). The protest started due to the new compulsory educational policy that all South Africans had to learn Afrikaans (Golden, 2004; Holland, 1988). This posed a great issue as many teachers were not trained in Afrikaans and the students, grades were affected by the compulsory class (Holland, 1988). Thus, thousands of high school students protested and many of their parents were unaware of the protest that was to ensue (Holland, 1988).

At a certain point, the police converged on the crowds. Tear gas was thrown, protestors were beaten and eventually the police shot into the crowd (Holland, 1988). At least four students were killed and one of them was a thirteen-year-old boy named Hector Petersen (Golden, 2004: Holland, 1988). By the end of this police procedure/debacle and as protests broke out countrywide, over 1,000 people lay dead most of whom had been killed by the police (Golden, 2004) over something as simple as a curriculum change (Holland, 1988). It was at this point, that the Carnegie Corporation of New York and the Ford Foundation used their resources to support "public interest law" projects to challenge the polices of apartheid (Golden, 2004). These challenges were brought up and went through the Centre for Applied Legal Studies at the University of the Witwatersrand, and the Legal Resources Centre with locations throughout South Africa (Golden, 2004). Arrests and bannings were countered and cases began to be won (Golden, 2004).

Figure 14. Picture of a Map in Orlando West – Soweto, August 26, 2021
Source: Janelle Christine Simmons, Ed.D. © 2021

Figure 15. Monument in memorial for Hector Peterson in remembrance of June 16, 1976. (August 26, 2021)
Source: Janelle Christine Simmons, Ed.D. © 2021

The Loss of a Black Consciousness Leader: Steve Biko

Steve "Bantu" Biko born on December 18, 1946, in the King William's Town of South Africa (Encyclopedia Britannica, 2022). He was the Founder of the Black Consciousness Movement in South Africa (Encyclopedia Britannica, 2022; Gibson, 2011; Hilton, 2011; Michigan State University, n.d.), which was founded on Fanon's philosophy and praxis (Gibson, 2011; Hilton, 2011). Biko was angered by Apartheid for a myriad of reasons (Gibson, 2011; Hilton, 2011). However, he also noted how the Black man, or the African was always limited. For example, the Afrikaners tried to limit Blacks to the "homelands" (Biko, n.d., p. 6; Golden, 2004; Lynch, 1976). He was angered by the fact that Radio Bantu was used as the government's propaganda tool to brainwash the Bantu, who hardly listened to it now believed in it anymore (Biko, n.d.). He also pointed to other issues such as constant police harassment whether one was in the towns or in the townships (Biko, n.d.; Holland, 1988), which was also noted by the ANC Leaders (Holland, 1988). He was quoted as saying that "the most important possession for any South African over 16 years of age is his pass-book. Without it on his person, he can be arrested and charged for failing to produce it on demand" (Lynch, 1976, p. 175).

In 1955, Biko noted the importance of the "People's Charter" in Kliptown, which was a statement of Blacks for the future of the country such as a land where Blacks and Whites live together in harmony (Biko, n.d.). At the same time, Nelson Mandela was also watching the events in Kliptown (Nelson Mandela Foundation, 2022). Biko was expelled from high school due to his political activism and eventually enrolled at St. Francis College in 1966 and went to boarding school in Natal (Encyclopedia Britannica, 2022). He then attended the University of Natal Medical School and became a campus leader (Encyclopedia Britannica, 2022). By 1968, he had basically implemented his philosophy at SASO[3] as its president at his campus and that philosophy spread to university campuses throughout South Africa (Encyclopedia Britannica, 2022) and known for creating the Black Consciousness Movement in 1969 (Gibson, 2011; Michigan State University, n.d.; M. Wilson, personal communication, September 21, 2022). As a Black Consciousness Leader, he believed that knowing who "we," i.e., Black people as a people are/were and what they could accomplish was beautiful (Biko, n.d.). He believed that the Black person is not called to hate the White man but to love him/herself (Biko, n.d.). During this movement of enlightenment, Biko also helped to continue to increase group pride and determination for the lives of Black people by Black people (Biko, n.d.; Gibson, 2011). He also believed that the Black wo/man should not merely be a participant in a White South Africa but be the leaders of their original homeland (Biko, n.d., Britannica Encyclopedia, 2022).

Figure 16. Picture of Steve Biko
Source: Encyclopedia Britannica (2022).

In 1972, Steve created the Black People's Convention (Britannica Encyclopedia, 2022). By 1973, he had already been banned and censured and his movements were limited by the government (Britannica Encyclopedia, 2022; Gibson, 2011). He continued to move around in secret (Britannica Encyclopedia, 2022). In 1975, he established the Zimele Trust Fund to assist the families of political prisoners and the political prisoners (Britannica Encyclopedia, 2022) if they survived. After being arrested four times in two years and being held for months without a trial; Steve Biko and an activist mate (Britannica Encyclopedia, 2022) known as Peter Jones were seized at a roadblock by Grahamstown, and jailed in Port Elizabeth (Michigan State University, n.d.) on August 18, 1977 (Britannica Encyclopedia, 2022). They had violated a banning order and Biko and Jones had gone to meet other liberation movement organization members and leaders (Michigan State University, n.d.). Due to their prominence and the fact that the police had recognized both of them, they were arrested and held indefinitely under Section 6 of the 1967 Terrorism Act (Michigan State University, n.d.; Phillips, 2001).

Biko was examined a number of times and by September 7, 1977, at 10:10 a.m., Dr. Lang noted that he had not found any evidence of him having any abnormality although he could no longer speak (Phillips, 2001). After being tortured for possessing pamphlets as many had been in Pretoria, Biko was found chained outside of a hospital – naked on September 11 (Encyclopedia Britannica, 2022; Michigan State University, n.d.; Phillips, 2001). He died of a brain hemorrhage the next day (Encyclopedia Britannica, 2022; Phillips, 2001) and other injuries he had sustained while in custody (Encyclopedia Britannica, 2022; Michigan State University, n.d.; Phillips, 2001). His death was noted as being a murder while in detention (Van Vuuren, 2015). The day right after his death, protests broke out all over the world (Michigan State University, n.d.; Phillips, 2001). His death was an alert to the international community of the extremism that the Apartheid government had engaged in, and he became an international martyr (Encyclopedia Britannica, 2022; Phillips, 2001). His story was depicted in multiple plays and in a movie starring Denzel Washington titled 'Cry Freedom' (Encyclopedia Britannica, 2022).

After his death, the world mourned (Burns, 1977; Phillips, 2001). The five (5) police officers claimed they had treated Biko well and that he had not been maltreated (Burns, 1977; Encyclopedia Britannica, 2022; Phillips, 2001; M. Wilcox, personal communication, September 21, 2022). The Minister of Police, J. Kruger claimed Biko died from a hunger strike (Burns, 1977; Michigan State University, n.d.). However, it was established that he died of brain damage (Burns, 1977; Michigan State University, n.d.; Phillips, 2001). After an autopsy, it was noted that he was most likely severely beaten (Encyclopedia Britannica, 2022; Phillips, 2001), and it was noted that he had been punched by an officer and beaten with a pipe and chained without any real medical care (Michigan State University, n.d.). By the time he was transferred naked in a police van to Pretoria for medical care, it was too late (Michigan State University, n.d.' Phillips, 2001). The police officers were cleared of any wrongdoing but finally confessed later that they had in fact killed Biko in 1977 and applied to the Truth and Reconciliation Commission for amnesty (Encyclopedia Britannica, 2022). In 1999, amnesty was denied (Encyclopedia Britannica, 2022).

Figure 17. Screenshot of a newspaper clipping regarding Steve Biko's death
Source: New York Times, September 14, 1977.

Due to this reality and the abhorrent acts of the politic, they drew attention to themselves. Biko (n.d.) had stated the following before his death: "Then again the progressively sterner legislation that has lately filled the South African Statute books has a great effect in convincing the people of the evil inherent in the system of apartheid" (p. 6). And now the people had evidence that apartheid was an evil game of "us" versus "them. The international community continued to question the death of Steve Biko (Burns, 1977; Michigan State University, n.d.), and they were angered by it (Burns, 1977). Moreover, a final international battle cry ensued that led to the eventual toppling of apartheid as a system in South Africa. That journey took 17 years.

Figure 18. Newspaper clipping absolving the security council of Steve Biko's death
Source: John F. Burns, NY times, December 3, 1977.

Five years after Biko's death, the Carnegie Corporation revisited the poverty study (Golden, 1982). In 1982, another study of poverty ensued. It was known as the Second Carnegie Inquiry into Poverty and Development in Southern Africa (Golden, 2004). This study was broader and included everybody – not just poor Whites (Golden, 2004). Approximately, 300 academics, humanities specialists, and political and social activists were hired as consultants for the study (Golden, 2004). Not only was South Africa studied but so was Botswana, Lesotho and Namibia (Golden, 2004). They found that in some black homelands, that the people did not even have food in their cupboards to eat at all and lived in filthy conditions (Golden, 2004). Other townships had to share facilities such as limited toilets, which eventually led to infectious diseases such as in Orange Free State (Golden, 2004). In 1989, a final report was submitted titled "Uprooting Poverty: The South African Challenge (W.W. Norton and Company), which summarized findings and as well as conference recommendations (Golden, 2004). They noted that the first report had failed to acknowledge Blacks and their humanity (Golden, 2004). Thus, some of the dire effects of Apartheid had been discovered and documented. This truth may be linked to the actual secret reality of apartheid and its institution.

The Secret Reality of Apartheid

The reality of Apartheid was two-fold. The policy was driving racism (Burns, 1977; Gibson, 2011; Golden, 2004; Kihato, 2014; Maylam, 1995; Phillips, 2001; Van Vuuren, 2015; M. Wilcox, personal communication, September 21, 2022; M. Wilcox, personal communication, September 23, 2022; Willoughby-Herald, 2015), and it was driven by greed (Van Vuuren, 2015; M. Wilcox, personal communication, September 21, 2022; M. Wilcox, personal communication, September 23, 2022). Over a period of forty (40) years, there was a legacy of various economic crimes during apartheid that led to 'state capture' (Van Vuuren, 2015). There had been 42+ million rand that was donated to the National Party (Van Vuuren, 2015). There were 844 bank accounts that were used to move money through twenty-seven (27) countries (van Vuuren, 2015). While the Big Five was identified as sponsoring and supporting Apartheid in some form (i.e., China, France, Russia, the United Kingdom, and the United States) (Van Vuuren, 2015). Eventually 47 countries had been identified in collaborating with South Africa to defy the arms, oil and even the trade sanctions for Apartheid South Africa (Van Vuuren, 2015). By the time Apartheid was coming to an end, the National Intelligence Agency (NIA) had destroyed 44 tonnes of documents (Van Vuuren, 2015).

Apartheid Finally Ends

In February of 1990, de Klerk finally has an epiphany (Van Vuuren, 2015). He decides to release Mandela from Robben Island (Gibson, 2011; Spielvogel, 2014; Van Vuuren, 2015; M. Wilcox, personal communication, September 21, 2022; M. Wilcox, personal communication, September 23, 2022). As he began to start the negotiations (Van Vuuren, 2015), it would become the beginning of the end (Willoughby-Herald, 2015). In 1994, the first democratic elections were held in South Africa (Gibson, 2011; Golden, 2004; Michigan State University, n.d.; Phillips. 2001; Spielvogel, 2014; Van Vuuren, 2015). And by 1996, the constitution had been finalized (M. Jacobs, personal communication, August 27, 2021; Van Vuuren, 2015; M. Wilcox, personal communication, September 21, 2022; M. Wilcox, personal communication, September 23, 2022). For decades, White South Africans had benefitted from Apartheid, and things were about to change (Van Vuuren, 2015).

By 2010, President Zuma enacted a 'Secrecy Bill,' which was not unlike many Apartheid policies (Van Vuuren, 2015). This bill sought to criminalize the act of possessing or disseminating any information or press that could expose abuses of power within the country (Van Vuuren, 2015). It was not unlike Section 6 of the Terrorism Act under Apartheid (Michigan State University, n.d.; Phillips, 2001). Yet, South Africa had/has moved on from this dark past of secrecy and hopefully into the light.

Figure 19. Picture of Constitution Square in Johannesburg, South Africa (August 27, 2021)
Source: Janelle Christine Simmons, Ed.D. © 2021

Figure 20. The Old Fort in Johannesburg (August 27, 2021)
Source: Janelle Christine Simmons, Ed.D. © 2021

Solutions and Recommendations

Considering the topic and the fact that Apartheid has ended since 1994, it is hard to consider what the solutions or recommendations should be. Nonetheless, it appears to be clear that the initial issue was that of colonization and a split country (i.e., the Boers and the British fighting over the land of Africa) (A. Coleman, personal communication, August 20, 2021; Golden,

2004; Holland, 1988; South African History Online, n.d; Spielvogel, 2014; M. Wilcox, personal communication, September 21, 2022; M. Wilcox, personal communication, September 23, 2022; Willoughby-Herald, 2015). In today's world, the act of colonization is hardly ever heard of at all. Nonetheless, the concept is underwritten by a presumption of one group – that they are better than another. In a globalized society, the first solution is to seek to understand differences and other cultures. It is easy to think one is better than another without any previous experience with said people group, et al.

Second, it is important to understand the history of a country and culture. We must seek not to repeat the mistakes of the past. Thus, a full history must be presented in classrooms from elementary to high school and definitely within higher education institutions. This requires an honest reckoning with the past.

Third, in a movie titled "Inside Man" starring Denzel Washington and Clive Owens, a heist takes place. In one scene, Denzel (i.e., Detective Frazier) is speaking to his antagonist and he says; "Follow the money." Indeed, to understand the story of Apartheid in South Africa, or colonization in general – one must "Follow the money!" The story of slavery and colonization came from a story of the White man and his greed. He longed to own that which was not his and to rule those who he did not want to surpass him. This story is played out through various world powers and in the media ... even today.

Fourth, systems and laws such as Apartheid must be eradicated. While no government has the right to tell another independent government what to do, we are living in an age where it is necessary to consider how one nation influences another. At this point, a nation that continues to subjugate people, especially the original people of the land have taken part in human rights abuses. Therefore, the United Nations has played a role in establishing bans, etc. in order to encourage nations to do the right thing. However, no one organization must be involved in brokering peace. Just as the old African adage states that it takes "a village to raise a child," there needs to be a collective who come to an informed compromise without compromise their beliefs. And truth be told, for those who wish to be separate, they can willingly maintain their culture separately, without having an established government.

Fifth, protest was instrumental in ending Apartheid. It took decades. One, the protest came from within the borders of South Africa. Blacks consistently told their oppressors that apartheid was not an acceptable system and means of engagement. Two, the message was spread outside of its borders. International awareness grew and as it grew people became appalled by the human rights violations that they had heard about, read about, seen, etc.

They began to fight back. Some fought back with the pen, other fought back with civil disobedience. Still yet, others fought back by breaking unjust laws. Many were martyred. Many were and/or went missing. And finally, with the culmination of apartheid atrocities like that of the death of Steve Biko, the final outcry commenced, and an international movement ensued. Finally, in 1994, 17 years after Biko's death, South Africa was deemed a democracy. And its president was none other than one who had also been imprisoned for dissenting – Nelson Mandela.

Sixth, we are a global community. Much of the pressure that took place to end Apartheid came from international partners and sympathizers. Just as the government had supporters who sought to make money, the ANC, SASO and other organizations as well as the average South African had partners and spiritual brothers, and sisters who empathized with their struggle and their hardships, and wrote, fought, protested and some even died. Without friends overseas, South Africa may have always remained an isolated, separated and fragmented nation. Therefore, it is important for us to make injustices known worldwide.

With that being said, the author would like to make a note about her experience during her second visit in 2022. Perhaps due to load shedding and water outages, there was extra stress and pressure on the communities of South Africa. However, it appears that many have turned to their own. There is an internal apartheid that is taking place. It was quite unpleasant to watch and to endure as the author is multiracial. However, during my whole visit Black South African women made it clear that their men only like local tribal women. The author was confused as her sole goal was to complete tours and collect further data for this book. Additionally, Caucasians and Indians treated her in some time of way. By the end of her trip, she had determined not to return as there was no need to spend money to be disrespected for being a multiracial American. It appears that South Africa has much work to do on itself before it can continue to engage others honestly.

CONCLUSION

In conclusion, the history of South Africa was a bloody history that was wrought with contradictions. Colonial powers brought with them various wars and divvying up of a land. As soon as the British and Boers came, an arrogance was brought with them, which offended chiefs of various tribes such as the Xhosa. Then more policies of 'separateness' increased until finally the official policy of Apartheid was introduced, reformed, and established. The policy of Apartheid was a devastating policy that had physical, emotional, intellectual and spiritual implications. A country became divided based on race and color. It was then further divided based on location (i.e., the industrialized city versus the rural lands). It was divided further based on tribes and homelands, et al. Every part of the apartheid history led to division(s). However, hardly ever was there unity amongst the people except based on said divisions. This took place for decades. In doing so, one of the worst race experiments took place and graciously came to an end.

With the first presidential election occurring in 1994, Nelson Mandela came into power. Once, the head of the ANC, and imprisoned due to a strike he led asking for a democratic nation; he became the first Democratic president of South Africa representing the African National Congress. He was also the first modern Black African leader to be established in South Africa. History had been made. However, more than that, the country began to mend. One notable way this was done was through the Springboks. He also welcomed leaders from the old Apartheid government to be his police and security detail.

After Mandela left in 1999 or so, there were to be transitions and new presidents. However, there were still issues, such as the institution of President Zuma from 1999 to 2018 -- who was not only power-hungry and had his coiffeurs filled but who also tried to implement Apartheid-like tactics such as the 'Secrecy Bill.' With new and present dangers to democracy and to wounds that are still healing, even 18 years later – South Africa is still transforming into the nation that the ANC hoped for so many decades ago.

REFERENCES

Ager, S. (2022). *Afrikaans*. Omniglot. https://omniglot.com/writing/afrikaans.htm

Biko, S. (n.d.). White racism and Black consciousness. *SA History*. FtFeb84.1683.7118.001.001.Feb1984.7.pdf (sahistory.org.za)

Boshoff, J. J. (2018, January). *The search for the slave ship Meermin. Developing a methodology from finding intertidal shipwrecks*. University of South Africa. https://uir.unisa.ac.za/bitstream/handle/10500/24734/dissertation_boshoff_j.pdf;sequence=1

Burns, J. F. (1977, September 14). Young black leader dies in detention in South Africa, raising fears of unrest. *New York Times,* p. 3. https://www.nytimes.com/1977/09/14/archives/young-black-leader-dies-in-detention-in-south-africa-raising-fears.html

Carnegie Corporation of New York. (2022). *Our approach.* Carnegie. https://www.carnegie.org/programs/

Dubow, S. (2000). *The Africa national congress.* Jonathan Ball Publishers.

Ellis, D. (2019, Summer). Apartheid. *Israel Studies, 24*(2), 63–71. doi:10.2979/israelstudies.24.2.06

Encyclopedia Britannica. (2022). *Steve Biko.* Encyclopedia Britannica. https://www.britannica.com/biography/Steve-Biko

Fabian, A. (Director). (2008). *Skin.* [Film]. MPI Media Group.

Gibson, N. C. (2011). *Fanonian practice in South Africa: From Steve Biko to Abahali base Mjondola.* University of KwaZulu-Natal Press.

Golden, M. (2014, Winter). *Carnegie corporation in South Africa: A difficult past leads to a commitment to change.* Carnegie. https://media.carnegie.org/filer_public/f3/54/f354cbf9-f86c-4681-8573- c697418ee786/ccny_cresults_2004_southafrica.pdf

Grobbelaar, P. (1987). *Reader's digest Afrikaans-Engelse Woordeboek English-Afrikaans.* Reader's Digest Association of South Africa.

Hilton, B. T. (2011, December). Frantz Fanon & colonialism: A psychology of oppression. *Journal of Scientific Psychology*, 45–59. http://psyencelab.com/uploads/5/4/6/5/54658091/frantz_fanon_and_colonialism.pdf

Holland, H. (1989). *The struggle: A history of the African National Congress.* Toronto, CA: Grafton Paperback.

Hook, D. (2004). *Frantz Fanon, Steve Biko, 'psychopolitics' and critical psychology. LSE Research Online*. Juta Academic Publishing.

IMDb. (2002). *Inside man.* IMDb. https://www.imdb.com/title/tt0454848/?msclkid=9b40a20bce8111ecbe7d45cc09b5ed2f

Journeyman Pictures. (2000). *The incredible apartheid story with a difference.* [Video]. Youtube. https://www.youtube.com/watch?v=cYZyvxpsCjQ&list=PLFE71DB5172BB3D46

Karimi, F. (2013, December 5). *Nelson Mandela, anti-apartheid icon and father of modern South Africa, dies.* CNN. https://www.cnn.com/2013/12/05/world/africa/nelsonmandela/index.html?msclkid=15894e81ced611ecbfb54ac0c0c85ad5

Kihato, C. W. (2014). Lost dreams? Tales of the South African city twenty years after apartheid. *African Identities, 12*(3-4), 357–370. doi:10.1080/14725843.2015.1009616

Lafraniere, S. (2005, August 24). Tracing a mutiny by slaves off South Africa in 1766. *New York Times.* https://www.nytimes.com/2005/08/24/world/africa/tracing-a-mutiny-by-slaves-off-south-africa-in-1766.html

Laurence, P. (2010). *Race classification: Then and now.* Politics Web. https://www.politicsweb.co.za/news-and-analysis/race-classification-then-and-now

Lynch, H. (Ed.). (1976). *The great contemporary issues series – Black Africa. (Vol. 5)* New York, NY: The New York Times Arno Press.

Maylam, P. (1995, March). Explaining to apartheid city: 20 years of South Africa urban histography. *Journal of Southern African Studies, 21*(1), 19–38. doi:10.1080/03057079508708431

Michigan State University. (n.d.). *The death of Steve Biko.* Michigan State University. https://overcomingapartheid.msu.edu/sidebar.php?id=65-2584&msclkid=1b8fd8d7cecb11eca0ec014ea8fc762e

Miller, M. (2013, December 18). Sharpeville massacres marked turning point in South Africa's history. *CBS News.* https://www.cbsnews.com/news/sharpeville-massacre-marked-turning-point-in-south-africas-history/

Nelson Mandela Foundation. (2022). *The archive at the center of memory: Timeline.* Nelson Mandela Foundation. https://www.nelsonmandela.org/content/page/timeline?msclkid=320c32c9ced611ecb984658f100a6b7f

Nieftagodie, N. (2014). The Soweto uprising. Auckland Park, South Africa: Jacana Media (Pty.) Ltd.

Noah, T. (2019). *Born a crime: Stories from a South African childhood.* Spiegel and Grau.

Phillips, J. H. (2001, May 1). Room 6/9 – The tragedy of Steve Biko. *Journal of Forensic Sciences, 33*, 3–8.

Public Broadcasting Service. (2019). *Slave ship mutiny.* PBS. https://www.pbs.org/black-culture/shows/list/slave-ship-muti ny/

South African History Online. (n.d.). *English settlement in South Africa.* SA History. https://www.sahistory.org.za/article/english-settlement-sout h-africa?msclkid=913ee8bfcdba11eca89fcce63fef6f72

Spielvogel, J. J. (2014). *Discovering our past: A history of the world.* McGraw Hill Education.

Timetoast. (2022). Apartheid game. *Timetoast.* https://www.timetoast.com/timelines/apartheid-regime

United Nations. (2021, July 17). *"The blood we sacrificed was worth it": Sharpeville Massacre.* UN. https://southafrica.un.org/en/135812-blood-we-sacrificed-was -worth-it-sharpeville- massacre?msclkid=9b9122c8ceea11ec9d5355ec461 5bbe1.

United States Holocaust Memorial Museum. (n.d.). *Mein kampf.* USHMM. https://encyclopedia.ushmm.org/content/en/article/mein-kampf

Van der Westhuizen, C. (2008). *White power and the rise and fall of the National Party.* Struik Publishers.

Van Vuuren, H. (2015). Apartheid, guns and money: A tale of profit. Auckland Park, South Africa: Jacana Media (Pty) Ltd.

Willoughby-Herald, T. (2015). *Waste of a White skin.* University of California Press. doi:10.1525/california/9780520280861.001.0001

KEY TERMS AND DEFINITIONS

Apartheid: 'Apartness' or 'separateness.' A term used to describe a period of time in South Africa where the government purposely kept Whites and Blacks separate.

Colonialism: the act of invading a country and taking it over in part or in whole and including its capture into one's Kingdom or already accrued land mass.

Uprising: the act of rebelling or revolting.

Xhosa: A people group of Bantu ethnic origin. They are the second largest group, and they are represented in Botswana, South Africa and Zimbabwe.

ENDNOTES

1. A Bantu ethnic group, which is the second largest group and is mainly located in South Africa, Botswana and Zimbabwe.
2. This study was led by two American sociologists known as Dr. Kenyon L. Butterfield and Dr. C.W. Coulter who acted as consultants (Golden, 2004).
3. The SASO is the South African Student Organization. It was founded in 1969.

APPENDIX

Table 1. List of Prime Ministers, State Presidents, and Presidents of South African from 1910 to Present

Name	Position Held	Elected	Political Party	Location Position Was Held	Began Term/Ended Term	Born/Died
Louis Botha	MP MP	1910 1915	South African Party	Standerton, Transvaal Province (Until 1915) Losberg, Transvaal Province (Until 1915)	May 31, 1910/August 27 1919	1862/1919
Jan Christiaan Smuts	MP	1920 1921	South African Party	Wonderboom, Transvaal Province	September 3, 1919/June 30, 1924	1870/1950
James Barry Munnik Hertzog	MP	1924 (5th) 1929 (6th) 1933 (7th) 1938 (8th)	National Party (Until 1934) United Party (From 1934)	Smithfield, Orange Free State Province	June 30, 1924/September 5, 1939	1866/1942
Jan Christiaan Smuts	MP	(8th) 1943 (9th)	United Party	Standerton, Transvaal Province	September 5, 1939/June 4, 1948	1870/1950
Daniel Francois Malan	MP	1948 (10th) 1953 (11th)	National Party	Piketberg, Cape Province	June 4, 1948/November 30, 1954	1874/1959
Johannes Gerhardus Strijdom	MP	(11th) 1958 (12th)	National Party	Waterberg, Transvaal Province	November 30, 1954/August 24, 1958	1893/1958
Hendrik Frensch Verwoerd	MP	1961 (13th) 1966 (14th)	National Party	Heidelberg, Transvaal Province	September 2, 1958/ September 6, 1966	1901/1966
Balthazar Johannes Vorster	MP	1970 (15th) 1974 (16th) 1977 (17th)	National Party	Nigel, Transvaal Province	September 13, 1966/October 2, 1978	1915/1983
Pieter Willem Botha	MP	1981 (18th) 1984 (19th)	National Party	George, Cape Province	October 9, 1978/September 14, 1984	1916/2006
Pieter Willem Botha	State President	1984	National Party	ALL	September 3, 1984/September 14, 1984 September 14, 1984/ January 19, 1989 (Resigned)	1916/2006
Jan Cristiaan 'Chris' Heunis	State President	--	National Party	ALL	January 1989/March 15, 1989	1927/2006

Continued on following page

Table 1. Continued

Name	Position Held	Elected	Political Party	Location Position Was Held	Began Term/Ended Term	Born/Died
F.W. de Klerk	State President	-- 1989	National Party	ALL	March 15, 1989/ September 20, 1989 September 29, 1989/May 10, 1994	1936/2021
Nelson Mandela	President	1994	African National Congress	South Africa	May 10, 1994/June 16, 1999	1918/2013
Thabo Mbeki	President	1999	African National Congress	South Africa	June 16, 1999 – September 24, 2008 (Resigned)	1942/
Ivy Natsepe-Casaburri	President	2008	African National Congress	South Africa	September 25, 2008 for 14 hours	1937-2009
Kgalema Motlanthe	President	2008	African National Congress	South Africa	September 25, 2008 – May 9, 2009	1949/
Jacob Zuma	President	2009	African National Congress	South Africa	May 9, 2009 – February 14, 2018	1942/
Cyril Ramaphosa	President	2018	African National Congress	South Africa	February 14, 2018 – February 15, 2018 February 15, 2018 - Incumbent	1952/

Chapter 6
Say Their Names

ABSTRACT

A list of names of the most famous and recent cases of Black deaths by the police will be listed and some of those cases will be fleshed out. Overall, this chapter focuses on the myriad of cases of police brutality that have led to brutal rapes and deaths in the United States amongst the African American population. It will primarily focus on cases such as those of George Floyd, which was one of the most recent cases that was finally successfully adjudicated; Amadou Diallo, i.e., a personal case that I assisted on, et al. The resolve of this chapter is to remember the wounded and the fallen. Like war, many African Americans feel like they live within a battlefield. For many of the names that will be listed, they were merely minding their own buisness doing the everyday activities that go unnoticed.

"We've got to unify or you and I soon will die, People will text us and there will be no reply…"-Neelam, Ride on Our Enemies (2020)

"You just a black man in this world, You just a barcode, ayy

You just a black man in this world, Drivin' expensive foreigns, ayy

You just a big dawg, yeah, I kenneled him in the backyard

DOI: 10.4018/978-1-7998-9304-2.ch006

No probably ain't life to a dog, For a big dog"

- (Childish Gambino, 2018)

INTRODUCTION

James Baldwin stated the following: "The story of the Negro in America is the story of America. It is not a pretty story" (Magnolia Pictures, 2017, [0:27]. Indeed, the story of many of the ancestors of Black or African American people who came to America was not a pretty story. And yet, their stories were the tapestry that built America to be the nation that she is now. However, when we say their names, we are bringing attention to the poverty of man's soul that has led to the death of either innocent people who are citizens of the United States or those who were not able to stand their day in court because the police used excessive force, which led to their premature deaths. The African American community and institutions that stand with said community has asked the world to remember and "Say Their Names."

Figure 1. Exhibit at Stanford University libraries of 65 of the most prolific cases of police brutality
Source: Stanford University, n.d. (2022).

MAIN FOCUS OF CHAPTER

Black Deaths in Custody has continued to be an issue within the United States and worldwide. While America has not existed for over 500-600 years, slavery did (Blight, 2018; Buckland, 1908; Davis, 2021; Smith, 2021). By the time the New World was founded and began to be established, Africans were brought to its shores and forced into labor. While enslaved, to control the population, slave patrols were established in the 1700s (Davis, 2021). When the country was established as America in 1776 (Blight, 2018; Smith, 2021), slavery was still taking place. It is now 2022, and not only do Black or African Americans often face undue hardships, earn less pay for the same job, they must climb to reach a glass ceiling, find themselves with educational inequalities and less intergenerational wealth; they still have to contend for their lives. One of these contentions can and sometimes does come from regular interactions with the police force of the United States of America.

In Chapter 3, the author discussed a Black Death that shook her to the core, i.e., the death of Amadou Bailo Diallo in 1999 (CBS Interactive, Inc., 2020; Sebok, 2004; The Amadou Diallo Foundation, 2022). The 41 shots that officers took at an unarmed man were the 41 shots heard all around the world (CBS Interactive, Inc., 2020; Sebok, 2004; The Amadou Diallo Foundation, 2022). For a more specific analysis, refer to Book 1. Another case that this author chose to open this book with was that of George Floyd, which is a pivotal case within the Black community and America as a whole as well as that of Rodney King, which can also be read about in Chapter 1.

However, there were and are other cases that have shaken the core of this country. For example, just recently in January of 2023, the case of Tyre Nichols was brought to the public's attention (Finton, 2023; Lynch, 2023). Said cases have led to protests within major cities and throughout the country. They have even led to the world being appalled as they also followed the news and interviewed people. One such example was that of Michael Brown (Smith, 2021; The New Yorker, 2020).

Michael Brown

Michael Brown died at the hands of a police officer in Ferguson, Missouri (Department of Justice, n.d.; Fagen & Harcourt, 2014; Smith, 2021; The New Yorker, 2020; The Telegraph, 2014; Waheeda, 2015). Video footage from various witnesses went viral regarding the death of this 18-year-old male on

August 9, 2014 (Department of Justice, n.d.; Fagen & Harcourt, 2014; Smith, 2021; The New Yorker, 2020; The Telegraph, 2014; Waheeda, 2015). It is still unclear what occurred during the exchange between Michael Brown and Police Officer Darren Wilson, a Caucasian Officer. However, within minutes of the film footage, Michael Brown was dead.

Figure 2. High school graduation picture of Michael Brown. (date unknown)
Source: Waheeda – The Source Magazine (2015).

After his death, Ferguson, MO exploded in protest (Department of Justice, n.d.; Fagen & Harcourt, 2014; Smith, 2021; The New Yorker, 2020; The Telegraph, 2014; Waheeda, 2015). According to the U.S. Department of Justice (n.d.), within twenty-fours, their unit called the Community Relations Service (CRS) was sent out to quell the concerns of the people (U.S. Department of Justice, n.d.). Protest still ensued due to the public's belief that there was "perceived biased policing nationwide" (U.S. Department of Justice, n.d.). People were tear gassed, pushed back behind protest lines and they were frustrated, crying, tired, worn (Smith, 2021). There were a multitude of arrests (Smith, 2021).

At the same time, the CRS claimed that they were handling the situation (U.S. Department of Justice, n.d.). They had reduced student tensions, began community dialogue through town halls and the like (U.S. Department of Justice, n.d.). The CRS even worked to establish "rumor control measures" (U.S. Department of Justice, n.d., p. 1). Eventually, they worked on long-term solutions (U.S. Department of Justice, n.d.). Until this day, no one knows what really happened in Ferguson.

A grand jury was conferred (Fagan & Harcourt, 2014). According to Fagan & Harcourt (2014), the 5th Amendment gives one a right to a grand jury indictment for felony cases. This is the same Amendment that enables one to not self-incriminate (Smith, 2021). After a strange and abnormal grand jury, a "no bill of indictment" was passed regarding Officer Wilson. In other words, the officer was not indicted (The New Yorker, 2020). In reality, the death of Michael Brown was never meted with justice. This is the opposite of what was seen in the Eric Garner case.

Eric Garner

The image(s) of Eric Garner being put in a choke hold and being ignored as he cried "I can't breathe!"[1] went viral in 2014 (The Guardian, 2014). According to the witness who recorded this video, he was breaking up a fight. He died on July 17, 2014 by the hands of the police (A&E Television Networks, LLC., 2022; BBC, 2014; The Guardian, 2014; The New Yorker, 2020), but not only from a chokehold. He had had encounters with the police before over selling loose cigarettes that culminated into the incident of the chokehold (A&E Television Networks, LLC., 2022; BBC, 2014; The Guardian, 2014; The New Yorker, 2020).

Figure 3. Eric Garner and his family. (date unknown)
Source: BBC (2014), https://www.bbc.com/news/world-us-canada-30350648.

On this particular day (i.e., July 17), the Staten Islander who had been married for 25 years (BBC, 2014), had six children (A&E Network Television, LLC., 2022; BBC, 2014) and two grandchildren - had also been arrested at least 30 times before (BBC, 2014) and was as he noted – minding his own business (The Guardian, 2014). Eric was sick of being harassed by the police (BBC, 2014; The Guardian, 2014). After breaking up a fight and trying to keep the peace, Officers Daniel Pantaleo and Justin D'Amico were called to the scene as peace officers to keep the peace (A&E Network Television, LLC., 2022). After being harangued for selling loosies; he was surrounded by officers and Daniel Pantaleo put him in a chokehold and ignored his cries of having a breathing issue (A& E Network Television, LLC.; BBC, 2014; The Guardian, 2014; The New Yorker, 2020) although many knew that he had various health issues such as asthma and obesity (BBC, 2014).

According to the History Channel, "Garner die[d] after losing consciousness as a police officer lock[d] him in an illegal chokehold, and within hours, a video of the incident [...] spark[ed] outrage across the country" (A&E Network Television, LLC., 2022, p. 1). While his death was more than unfortunate, and it could hardly be called an accident, his death also reminds the Black community to be careful in their interactions with the police. More specifically, one needs to be cognizant of how they interact with the NYPD. He, like others, have been remembered in artwork such as that of Kadir Nelson's (The New Yorker, 2020), or through their own artwork such as Tyre Nichols (Finton, 2023), and at exhibits like that of Stanford University (Stanford University, n.d.) such as Sandra Bland.

Sandra Bland

Sandra Bland was stopped by a State Trooper in Prairie View, Texas (Gerber, 2016; The New Yorker, 2020; WGN News, 2019) for a traffic violation (CBS Interactive, Inc., 2016; Gerber, 2016; WGN News, 2019). As depicted from Car Cam footage or Dashboard Footage (Gerber, 2016), and her own cell phone footage, (CBS Interactive, Inc., 2016) the officer approached her vehicle, yanked her car door open and pulled a gun on her (CBS Interactive, Inc., 2016; Gerber, 2016; WGN New, 2019). She was ceremoniously arrested (CBS Interactive, Inc., 2016; Gerber, 2016; The New Yorker, 2020; WGN News, 2019).

Figure 4. Picture of Sandra Bland (date unknown)
Source: CBS Interactive, Inc., 2016.

Figure 5. Legal presentation on police brutality and the case of Sandra Bland
Source: Redden Law, PLLC. (2022).

On July 10, 2015, Sandra was stopped and arrested north of Houston (Gerber, 2016). After been jailed, she was found dead three days later (Gerber, 2016). Reminiscent of cases in Australia, Sandra was found dead hanging by a plastic bag (Gerber, 2016). State Trooper Brian T. Encinia who had made the stop and conducted the arrest of the 28-year-old, was indicted by a grand jury (Gerber, 2016). It was found that he had lied about why he forced Bland out of her vehicle (Gerber, 2016). Encinia plead "Not Guilty," but he was fired from his position as a State Trooper (Gerber, 2016). Her family finally settled for $1.9 million dollars (CBS Interactive, Inc., 2016; Gerber, 2016). However, the country refused to acknowledge that a wrongful death had taken place (Gerber, 2016). The author contends that a wrongful stop and arrest took place which led to an unnecessary death.

While these are only a few cases that have been highlighted here, the author encourages you to read their names and say their names out loud. She encourages you to pray for their families and for the Black community as a whole. She asks you to remember that the struggle is real and that the job is not yet done. It is time for America to reckon with America. There are a multitude of issues, controversies and problems that will be addressed below.

Issues, Controversies, Problems

The main issues, controversies and problems that are addressed in this chapter are that of Black Deaths, Black Deaths in custody, et al. that were caused by the hands of police officers. The list of names is long (Stanford University, n.d.) and every case cannot be discussed in this chapter and done its full justice. Nevertheless, the author has chosen cases that struck a chord with her or that were wildly publicized while listing many of the others. At the reader's leisure, they may go through each case.

Before these issues are discussed, it should be noted that Black Deaths in Custody is a term that is usually used in the case of Aborigines in Australia. However, the author has expanded its use to specifically cover the topic of the death of Black men and women during an encounter with a police officer, especially when the death was unwarranted. Moreover, in truth, Black Deaths in Custody have occurred in various countries worldwide ever since slavery began in the 15th century (Blight, 2018; Buckland, 1908; Davis, 2021; Smith, 2021). In other words, Blacks have had over 500-600 years of Black Deaths in Custody (Blight, 2018; Buckland, 1908) cases that have finally culminated to an overall protest of the depravity of humanity. Yet, there are still remedies.

First, the issue that countless Department of Justice publications and other reports have addressed is the fact that many Blacks (Baker, 2021; Cha-Jua, 2014; Davis, 2021; Smith, 2021) and Latinos are treated differently during the stop, frisk and/or arrest process for even minor alleged infringements of the law such as marijuana (The Sentencing Project, 2022). They are also disproportionately sentenced (Smith, 2021; The Sentencing Project, 2022). This issue is an issue that continues to be addressed through various means. It will be further discussed in Chapter 16: An Examination of Solutions.

Second, an issue that is a controversy is the frivolousness of some of these stops (Cha-Jua, 2014). For example, why was Eric Garner alleged crime of breaking up a fight and the accusation of him selling loosies more important than the breath of life that God had given him? Why was Sandra Bland's traffic violation in need of having her personal space and safe zone within a car violated and then why was she forced to get out of her car by gunpoint? Why was it necessary for Michael Brown to be shot down in the streets like a dirty dog for an undetermined reason? In the author's opinion, it was not necessary. It was just brutal. This moment is when one knows that excessive force has been utilized. Thus, the underlining issue is of excessive force, but why do some police officers use excessive force and why do some cases lead to the deaths of unarmed Black men and women?

Third, fear is another underlining issue (Baker, 2021; Smith, 2021). What is fear? Fear is defined as "an unpleasant often strong emotion caused by anticipation or awareness of danger" (Merriam-Webster, Inc., 2022). This emotion was embedded in Europeans from the moment that they started kidnapping Africans from Africa and bringing them to Europe, the West Indies and even the New World/America. That fear never left. The slave trader feared a revolt once their captured property was on a ship (Baker, 2021; Blight, 2018; Cha-Jua, 2014; Newtown, 1788; Smith, 2021). He was scared of Africans gaining power (Baker, 2021; Blight, 2018; Cha-Jua, 2014; Davis, 2021; Newtown, 1788; Smith, 2021). He was scared of them staying in community. He was scared of them not having his DNA. He was scared of their impending freedom. He was scared he would lose money if he could not control them after their legal emancipation. He was scared of their progress. And in some situations, some White men and women are still scared now.

According to Meeks (2011), "Fear is immobilizing and it keeps us separated" (p. 3). However, perhaps, in some circumstances -- that fear also keeps us together. The fact is, fear has driven many of the relationships that Whites and Blacks (i.e., a misnomer at best) continue to have today. While many Caucasians have adopted the correct lingo, they continue to slight Black people in certain circumstances or so it seems to the author of this book. This is especially the case when it comes to employment and titles. Unfortunately, that same fear is linked to racism.

Fourth, racism is another challenge for America (Baker, 2021; Blight, 2018; Cha-Jua, 2014; Davis, 2021; Smith, 2021). While prejudice may be classified as a cognitive shortcut, racism leads to discrimination, ostracization and violence, and racism is a whole and another beast. What is racism? According to the American Psychological Association (2022), "The causes of racism and related intolerance and the means for their perpetuation are complex, involving legal vulnerability and discrimination, economic and educational disadvantage, social and political marginalization, and psychological victimization" (p. 1). While the author will not assume that she knows all of the causes of racism, she defines racism as such; "An actualized fear due to a perceived difference regarding another people group, race, creed or religion." Discrimination is and act based on forms of prejudice and racism.

According to PsyPost (2016), when it comes to implicit bias and racism, "many people hold negative evaluations of Blacks that are outside of their conscious awareness" (p. 1). Baker (2021) refers to this reality in a term coined "Negrophobia." Davis (2021) a Black officer discusses it as the reason he created an organization titled B-Cap or Black Cops Against Police Brutality in order to work on improving relations between the community and the police. Nonetheless, the reality of "Negrophobia" leads to other issues and lack of privileges such as wanting individuals to have Voting IDs, etc. (PsyPost, 2016). Why these biases exist is another discussion for another book that I will not be writing. However, the fact is that the idea that Black people are still inferior or somehow incapable of expressing themselves intelligibly is laughable and laudable. The fact remains that in this inherent bias is not only fear but a base insecurity which in the author's opinion cannot be addressed by any Black person but has to be addressed by the White man and woman. Nonetheless, there are some solutions and recommendations that the author has listed below.

Solutions and Recommendations

First, I think it is important to flesh these events out in schools, especially amongst school-aged children, teens and adults across various higher education institutions. After the countless acts of terrorism that the Black community has faced, police brutality is one more nail that has been placed in the coffin.

The fact is, in many ways this has been happening. Toolkits (Indianapolis Public Schools, n.d.) and other forms of curriculum (e.g., Share My Lesson) (Feinberg, n.d.) have been created to open up discussions around Black deaths, police brutality, protest and why protest continues to rise from within the Black community, etc.

Second, I think it is often necessary to report crimes and seek legal remedies (Smith, 2021). For example, after the video of Eric Garner went viral, an investigation took place. There was no trial (Holcombe, Moshtaghian, & Akbarzai, 2021). However, Pantaleo was fired from the police force in August of 2019 (Holcombe, Moshtaghian, & Akbarzai, 2021). It was not until seven years later that Eric Garner's family finally garnered approval from a judge's decision that will allow them to finally question the Mayor Bill de Blasio's administration as well as the New York Police Department (NYPD) about the circumstances and events that led to this man's death (Holcombe, Moshtaghian, & Akbarzai, 2021). This was a victory for the Garner family as a whole.

Third, as previously discussed, memorial is a necessary act on occasions like these. Memorial is the act of remembering (Blight, 2018). That act can come from a written statement, an artwork, or as usually thought of a statue or structure. In the case of Amadou Bailo Diallo, this came in the form of a foundation (The Amadou Diallo Foundation, 2022). In the case of Sandra Bland, Michael Brown, Eric Garner, and others; it came in the form of artwork, murals, and the like. One example of this was the beautiful picture created by Kadir Nelson called "Say Their Names." Memorial not only helps us to remember, but it also often helps us to grieve and to be encouraged. If there is any group of people that need to remember, grieve, and be encouraged, it is that of Black people everywhere.

Fourth, is the reality of protest (Blight, 2018; Cha-Jua, 2014; Smith, 2021). This form of a solution continues to repeat itself throughout this book. The protest that occurred around the Michael Brown case led to newspaper articles, interviews, TV segments, books and the like. In Episode 3 of Amend, the episode starts off discussing Michael Brown and the protests that took place in Ferguson, Missouri (Smith, 2021). There is no stronger cry of an "unheard" people nor fight for justice other than the pen (Newtown, 1788), and a voice in protest (Blight, 2018).

Fifth, another solution and recommendation that the author is proffering is that of spiritual rest. The Garner family created a family gathering to remember Eric Garner.[2] The author also pointed to spiritual practices such as prayer and attending religious meetings (e.g., Harriet Tubman) (Smith,

2021). The interaction with God and the "spirit man," which we all possess, often allows us to process events, release negative energy, break spiritual strongholds and connect with our Creator. In many ways, our ancestors did the same and they pressed on – as should we press on as well.

Sixth, the author is also recommending neutral organizations to come in and address community unrest (Blight, 2018; Davis, 2021; Smith, 2021). While the CRS (U.S. Department of Justice, n.d.) does a wonderful job, the fact is that it is part of a government agency. If the government in some facets has already been seen as being unjust, it is highly improbable that some of the same issues do not play out in units like the CRS under the auspices of the U.S. Department of Justice (DOJ). The goal or mission of the DOJ is as follows:

To enforce the law and defend the interests of the United States according to the law; to ensure public safety against threats foreign and domestic; to provide federal leadership in preventing and controlling crime; to seek just punishment for those guilty of unlawful behavior; and to ensure fair and impartial administration of justice for all Americans (p. 1).

This mission is profound. However, when it comes to this particular case and the abnormalities of said case (e.g., the grand jury trial) (Fagan & Harcourt, 2014), and the fact that a man is dead and no one knows why – a more neutral firm of mediation organization would most likely have been preferable (U.S. Department of Justice, n.d.).

CONCLUSION

In conclusion, police brutality is not a new reality. Throughout this book, slavery, slave patrols, the end of slavery via the 13th Amendment, Black Codes, Jim Crow Laws, and the like have been discussed, and or touched upon. In fact, overseers and slave patrols were the precursor of the police force within the United States. They were created with the express job of terrorizing slaves and punishing them for minor infractions to keep the Black population "low." With that being said, there is no surprise that generational patterns continue to exist. The question in this chapter is not how to fix a broken system. Rather, the question in this chapter is as follows; "How will we remember those who have died while being apprehended by the police or actually in custody?" My response is, read about them, remember them by saying their names, and remember their families in your prayers, in your protest, in your history for that name could have easily been yours!

REFERENCES

A&E Television Networks, LLC. (2022). Eric Garner dies in NYPD chokehold. *History.com.* https://www.history.com/this-day-in-history/eric-garner-dies-nypd-chokehold

American Psychological Association. (2022). *Psychological causes and consequences of racism, racial discrimination, xenophobia and related intolerances (2008).* APA. https://www.apa.org/pi/oema/programs/racism/un-conference-plenary

Baker, E. (2021, May 20). *Police brutality: An epidemic in America.* Sandiego. https://sites.sandiego.edu/blackhistoryatusd/2021/05/20/police-brutality-an-epidemic-in-america/

BBC. (2014, December 5). *Profile; Eric Garner.* BBC. https://www.bbc.com/news/world-us-canada-30350648

Blight, D. W. (2018). *Frederick Douglass: Prophet of freedom.* Simon & Schuster.

Buckland, W. W. (1908). *The Roman law of slavery: The condition of the slave in private law from Augustus to Justinian.* Cambridge University Press.

Cha-Jua, S. K. (2014, Spring). We believe it was murder: Mobilizing black resistance to police brutality in Champaign, Illinois. *The Black Scholar, 44*(1), 58–85. doi:10.1080/00064246.2014.11641212

Fagan, J., & Harcourt, B. (2014, November 26). *Questions and answers for Columbia Law students about grand juries.* Columbia. https://www.law.columbia.edu/news/archive/fact-sheet-michael-brown-case/

Feinberg, A. (n.d.). Police brutality/Excessive force assignment. *Share My Lesson.* https://sharemylesson.com/teaching-resource/police-brutality excessive-force-assignment-267266

Finton, L. (2023, April 7). *Activists to host Tyre Nichols photo exhibits, lantern ceremony before city hall.* Retrieved on April 10, 2023 from https://www.yahoo.com/entertainment/activists-host-tyre-nichols-photo-152701684.html

Gerber, M. (2016, September 20). $1.9-million settlement in Sandra Bland death is the latest big payout in police misconduct lawsuits. *LA Times.* https://www.latimes.com/nation/la-na-police-death-settlements-20160920-snap-htmlstory.html

Holcombe, M., Moshtaghian, A., & Akbarzai, S. (2021, July 19). Eric Garner's family commemorates his death as judge allows litigation against police and city officials. *CNN.* https://www.cnn.com/2021/07/19/us/eric-garner-family-commemoration-judge-litigation/index.html

Indianapolis Public Schools. (n.d.). *"Say their names" toolkit.* Indianapolis Public Schools. https://myips.org/get-involved/racial-equity/say-their-names-toolkit/

C.B.S.Inc.(2016,September15).Lawyer:$1.9settlementreachedinSandraBland case. *CBS.* https://www.cbsnews.com/video/lawyer-1-9m-settlement-reached-in-sandra-bland-case/#x

C. B. S. Inc. (2020, June 9). Police fired 41 shots when they killed Amadou Diallo. His mom hope's today's protests will bring change. *CBS News.* https://www.cbsnews.com/news/amadou-diallo-kadiatou-protests-george-floyd-police/

Lynch, J. (2023, January 17). Memphis police relieve officers pending investigations into the arrest of man who later died, chief says. *CNN.* https://www.cnn.com/2023/01/16/us/memphis-tennessee-arrested-man-dies-hospital/index.html/

Malcolm, X. (2012). *The House negro and the field negro.* Bing. https://www.bing.com/videos/search?q=I+Am+Not+Your+Negro&&view=detail&mid=4CC268E118D2B546E9A24CC268E118D2B546E9A2&rvsmid=EE7CB61FA93C401B7FB1EE7CB61FA93C401B7FB1&FORM=VDMCNR

Meeks, C. (2011, October 5). Racism is fueled by fear. *Huffington Post.* https://www.huffpost.com/entry/post_2501_b_992066

Merriam-Webster, Inc. (2022). Fear. *Meriam Webster*. https://www.merriam-webster.com/dictionary/fear

News, W. G. N. (2019, May 7). *Sandra Bland's own cellphone video surfaces.* Bing. https://www.bing.com/videos/search?q=sandra+bland&docid=6080 09482127036521&mid=BE7E3AB9998E BE414DD6BE7E3AB9998EBE414DD6& view=detail&FORM=VIRE

Newtown, J. (1788). *Thoughts upon the African slave trade.* London: Printed for J. Buckland, in Pater-Noster Row, & J. Johnson, in St. Paul's Church-yard.

PsyPost. (2016, October 16). Fear causes Whites high in implicit racism to be more supportive of voter ID laws. *PsyPost.* https://www.psypost.org/2016/10/fear-causes-whites-high-impl icit-racism-supportive-voter-id-laws-45408

Redden Law, P. L. L. C. (2022). *The case of Sandra Bland as an example of police brutality in Texas.* Redden Law. https://www.reddenlawtexas.com/the-case-of-sandra-bland-as-a n-example-of-police-brutality-in-texas/

Sebok, A. J. (2004, January 12). *The Amadou Diallo case was New York City's $3 million settlement too low, too high, or a just amount?* Find Law. https://supreme.findlaw.com/legal-commentary/the-amadou-dial lo-case.html

Smith, W. (2021, February 17). *Amend: The fight for America.* [Net Series]. Netflix.

Stanford University. (n.d.). *Say their names: Green Library supporting the Black lives matter movement.* Stanford University. https://exhibits.stanford.edu/saytheirnames

The Amadou Diallo Foundation. (2022). *Amadou Diallo.* ADF. https://www.amadoudiallo.com/about-amadou/

The Guardian. (2014, December 4). 'I can't breathe': Eric Garner put in chokehold by NYPD officer – video. *The Guardian.* https://www.bing.com/videos/search?q=eric+garner&view=detail &mid=C6A4C096C0122EFC50D8C6A4C096C0122EFC50D8&FORM= VIRE

The New Yorker. (2020, June 14). Kadir Nelson's "Say their names." *The New Yorker.* https://www.newyorker.com/culture/cover-story/cover-story-2020-06-22

The Sentencing Project. (2022). *Race & justice news: Blacks disproportionately arrested for marijuana in Alabama: October 30, 2018.* The Sentencing Project. https://www.sentencingproject.org/news/race-justice-news-blacks-disproportionately-arrested-marijuana-alabama/

The Telegraph. (2014, August 20). *Eyewitness describe Michael Brown killing as new footage released.* Bing. https://www.bing.com/videos/search?q=Michael+Brown+Video+Footage&&view=detail&mid=46AFF2A1F65D860B5E0046AFF2A1F65D860B5E00&&FORM=VRDGAR&ru=%2Fvideos%2Fsearch%3Fq%3DMichael%2BBrown%2BVideo%2BFootage%26FORM%3DVARSQP

United States Department of Justice. (n.d.). *About us.* USDJ. https://www.justice.gov/about

United States Department of Justice. (n.d.). *Shooting death of Michael Brown – Ferguson. Missouri: 2014.* USDJ. https://www.justice.gov/crs/timeline-event/shooting-death-michael-brown-ferguson-mo/

Waheeda. (2015, January 22). Civil rights charges highly unlikely for Michael Brown case. *The Source.* https://thesource.com/2015/01/22/fbi-has-completed-investigation-into-the-shooting-of-michael-brown-civil-rights-charges-not-expected/

KEY TERMS AND DEFINITIONS

Black Deaths in Custody: A term coined or usually related to Australia. Black Deaths in Custody as a term is often linked to police abuses and the disproportionate number of Aborigines who allegedly suicide while in custody or who are killed by the police. The author has used this term universally to depict this phenomenon worldwide.

Memorial: A statement of facts, a structure or statute to commemorate a person(s) or an event(s), et al. It often people to "remember."

Negrophobia: An inherent fear of Black people coupled with a great dislike for said people.

ENDNOTES

1 The same words that Eric Garner cried were cried out by George Floyd. These words were "I can't breathe!"

2 The family had a family gathering to commemorate the death of Eric Garner in 2021 (Holcombe, Moshtaghian, & Akbarzai, 2021).

Chapter 7
Social Justice Issues Examined

ABSTRACT

This chapter focuses on social justice issues. What does that mean? In short, it has many meanings. However, in this chapter, it will revolve around discussions of oppression. Throughout this book, a foundation was laid to examine three cases. Those case studies were of three countries, which are as follows: America, Australia, and South Africa. In each country, there was a form of colonization via European powers. From the moment colonization was a goal, oppression became a reality. Examining social justice issues revolves around educating people about oppressions and in this setting exposing those issues calls us to a clearer examination of what issues we are not left with at present. These are the issues that will be examined, i.e., discrimination, privilege, racism, modern segregation, and more.

"Lately we've been feeling it the hardest

Dead in the street with a knee on his jaw and

Never been a felon but I'm treated like it often

I don't want to be a hashtag out jogging"

--KB, Dark Skin (2021)

DOI: 10.4018/978-1-7998-9304-2.ch007

Not everything faced can be changed...but nothing can be changed until it is faced." -James Baldwin

INTRODUCTION

The moment that colonization occurred, one group of individuals was given preference over another (Blight, 2018; Cha-Jua, 2014; Fanon, 2008; Hilton, 2011; Hughes & Meltzer, 1956; Newtown, 1788; Smith, 2021). This became the situation when slavery entered the equation in Europe, the United States, etc. (Hughes & Meltzer, Jones, 2017; Newtown, 1788). Laws were created to keep this social division (Smith, 2021). For example, the "one drop rule" was established in the United States of America to classify people past their appearance or racial identification (African American Registry, 2022; Bradt, 2010; Browning, n.d.; IMDb, 2022; Johnson, 2006; Smith, 2021). The determination was that "[…] those having any African ancestry as black, a standard known as the "one-drop rule," which defined "white" as a state of "absolute purity" in relation to "black" (Johnson, 2006; p.20) were Black. In other words, white was celebrated as being pure and black was celebrated and associated with that which was impure.

In the same way, in Australia, outside of the process of assimilation, most Aboriginal people were kept segregated from Whites until they were deemed Australian (Chang, 2019). In the same vein, in South Africa, apartheid was instituted as a policy to keep the races separate with the thought that Whites were purer, better, or more significant (Ellis, 2019; Holland, 1989; TimeToast, 2022), and this was repeated in Champaign-Urbana, Illinois (Cha-Jua, 2014). Yet, in many cases, oppressed people around the world such as the Algerians (Fanon, 2008; Hilton, 2011), the Aboriginals (Chang, 2019) and even the Black people were maintaining various standards of conservatism and purity (Chang, 2019; Hughes & Meltzer, 1956).

The ugly reality is that the classifications were unnecessary. It is the author's position that many of the Whites who continued to focus on the differences were merely insecure and found their only confidence in subjugating another group who had differences in build, looks, culture and origin, etc. (Baker, 2021). By emphasizing and exaggerating these differences, they hoped to continue to cause the "other" to swell with insecurities, which they may or could manipulate them by (Fanon, 2008; Hilton, 2011). This would maintain the power structure with Whites on top and Black people on the bottom (Baker, 2021) According to Bradt (2010), the racial hierarchy that was still in existence as of 2010 was that the Whites were the best group, then Asians, then Latinos and finally Blacks. This predetermined hierarchy is a sham and a disgrace to a nation like the United States that claims in the words of Thomas Jefferson in the Preamble of the Declaration of Independence the following: "We hold these truths to be self-evident, that all men are created equal, that they are endowed, by their Creator, with certain unalienable Rights, that among these are Life, Liberty, and the pursuit of Happiness." Even though these words were written when some of "our" forefathers owned slaves in America, it is hard to believe that in 2010 or 2020 or even 2022, that such pervasive patterns of racism would still exist. And yet, even in 2023, they still do.

Specific to the phenomenon of hypodescent, Bradt (2010) stated the following: "The persistence of hypodescent serves to reinforce racial boundaries" (p. 3). These racial boundaries lead to segregation in one's personal life (Johnson, 2006), segregation in housing (Johnson, 2006; Vrieland, 2022), segregation in work and work positions, etc. (Johnson, 2006). The reality is that Whites continue to "control" (Baker, 2021; Cha-Jua, 2014; Johnson, 2006). They control various job positions, and they [...] control [...] schools, government, the police, and most other resources and sources of power" (Johnson, 2006, p. 22). This leads to other forms of discrimination and glass ceilings (Baker, 2021; Cha-Jua, 2014; Johnson, 2006). For example, Blacks and Latinos often have higher rates of unemployment, lower salaries and earn less wages overall, and are not represented in management or leadership positions even when they have earned a degree (Johnson, 2006), or more than one degree. In general, Blacks are known to take lower wages to hold a position and therefore are at the mercy of some White people and are used as pawns to get other Whites to do their jobs (Johnson, 2006) or even highly ticketed to accrue city revenue (Cha-Jua, 2014).

The fact of the matter is that there are so many issues to unwrap, consider and discuss at any time. There have been grievous acts against African Americans and acts on the family of Blacks since slavery began in this country and in others (Baker, 2021; Blight, 2018; Cha-Jua, 2014; Ellis, 2019; Fanon, 2008; Hilton, 2011; Hughes & Meltzer, 1956; Irons, 2002; Johnson, 2006; United Nations, 2022; Woodward, 1966). In addition to the issue(s) of police brutality, an example of the government funding an unethical and dishonest experiment to save their own is that of the Tuskegee Experiment (Alsan, Wanamaker & Hardeman, 2019; Anekwe, 2014). The Tuskegee Experiment took place within the United States from 1932-1972 (Alsan, Wanamaker & Hardeman,

2019; Anekwe, 2014). It was officially titled 'The US Public Health Syphilis Study on the Negro (Alsan, Wanamaker & Hardeman, 2019; Anekwe, 2014).

This experiment was carried out on Black males in order to study the effects of syphilis as well as compare those with syphilis without treatment to those without syphilis (Alsan, Wanamaker & Hardeman, 2019; Anekwe, 2014). For those with syphilis, they were often subjected to painful spinal taps, which virtually left them unable to walk (Alsan, Wanamaker & Hardeman, 2019; Anekwe, 2014). Of 600 poor Black men who were mostly illiterate, 400 of them had syphilis and 200 did not (Alsan, Wanamaker & Hardeman, 2019; Anekwe, 2014). Regardless, those with syphilis were promised free medical care and were used as guinea pigs instead (Alsan, Wanamaker & Hardeman, 2019; Anekwe, 2014). After 40 years, the experiment was exposed and in 1974 a settlement of $9 million was reached (Alsan, Wanamaker & Hardeman, 2019). This experiment caused peripheral trauma to the Black community, which has also been seen due to systematic racism and police brutality (Alsan, Wanamaker & Hardeman, 2019).

Questions of trust continue to be an issue when it comes to people's trust in the democratic government of the United States. Questions of trust continue to be an issue when one considers the relationship between the police and the community. This is especially the case with Black and brown populations.

Figure 1. Picture of Sophia Tupuola (32) and Dante Steve (30) of Hunters Point. Standing at a protest against police brutality at Candlestick Park in San Francisco, California. June 6, 2020.
Source: Library of Congress Prints & Photographs, Division of Washington, D.C. © 2020 https://www.loc.gov/pictures/resource/ppbd.01267/.

In this chapter, social justice issues will be examined further.

MAIN FOCUS OF CHAPTER

As previously noted, "the history of law enforcement being politicized to act as an intimidating force against African Americans citizens began with the deputizing of fugitive slave catches in the 19th century" (Normore & Scott, 2021, p. 79), which were possibly based on the Fugitive Slave Laws (i.e., in America) of 1793 (Hughes & Meltzer, 1956). Slavery, especially in the United States created an unbalanced and hostile relationship between Black slaves and slave patrols as well as Blacks and police officers (Baker, 2021;

Davis, 2021; Jones, 2017). According to Jones (2017), "In the United States, violence directed at people of color is as old as the country itself" (p. 872). One cannot forget the phenomenon of lynching like in the case of Emmet Till or the sung truth such as with Billie Holiday's "Strange Fruit" (Jones, 2017).

This phenomenon turned into further injustices (Jones, 2017). In 2020, names like Ahmaud Arbery, George Floyd and Breonna Taylor splashed across the pages of newspapers in the United States and worldwide (Normore & Scott, 2021). Other names like Amadou Diallo, Eric Garner, Freddie Gray; Rodney King, Abner Louima, Laquan McDonald, Walter Scott and are synonymous with police brutality (Maule, 2017). Shall we forget Sandra Bland, Michael Brown, or Oscar Grant Lyle & Esmail, 2016)? And now, we must even remember the name of Tyre Nichols as of January 2023 (Baker, 2021; Finton, 2023; Lynch, 2023). The fact is that a citizen's race in this nation (i.e., the United States of America) affects their experience (Alsan, Wanamaker & Baker, 2021; Hardeman, 2019; Jones, 2017; Normore & Scott, 2021; Jones, 2017), especially with the law.

Policies and systems of systemic racism appear in a myriad of places and ways within this country (Baker, 2021; Hughes & Meltzer, 1956; Jones, 2017; Kuumba, 2021; Lyle & Esmail, 2016; Normore & Scott, 2021; Worland, 2014). Normore & Scott (2021) point to the fact that the school-to-prison-pipeline system has led to unjust policies where incarceration is increased for young Black men and criminalization becomes a way of life. Youth are incarcerated at alarming rates (Baker, 2021; Normore & Scott, 2021). Racial profiling still takes place (Baker, 2021; Normore & Scott, 2021). This country has a culture of adopting policies that encourage force and create tensions (i.e., stop and frisk) as well as failing to reprimand officers (Baker, 2021; Normore & Scott, 2021). Moreover, the police continue to be silent perpetuating the theme of a "Blue Wall of Silence" (Normore & Scott, 2021). Communities continue to see due process issues, etc. (Normore & Scott, 2021). It appears to be so many issues that they cannot be addressed. A thorough discussion of some of the aforementioned issues as well as additional ones, controversies and problems will now be discussed. After all, "This is America!"[1]

Issues, Controversies, Problems

Issues that have been briefly touched upon above are manifold. The author will focus on some of the most prominent issues, controversies and problems that arise when one looks at the roots of and the precipitators of police brutality.

Some of the issues that will be discussed are as follows; the Blue Wall of Silence, Due Process, Police Brutality, Poor Police and/or Governmental processes, Racial profiling, Racism, School-to-Prison-Pipeline System and the Criminalization of Blacks, especially Black males to name several. This is by no means an extensive list, but it is a list that has been identified as some of the repetitive issues that have been seen throughout the literature.

First, the Blue Wall of Silence (Ariel, Farrar & Sutherland, 2015; Levine, 2016; Normore & Scott, 2021) or silence (Ariel, Farrar & Sutherland, 2015) in general is a repetitive theme in the literature. Police departments across the country and perhaps the world have an insular culture where police officers protect other police officers (Normore & Scott, 2021). Moreover, there are various subcultures within the main police culture (Ariel, Farrar & Sutherland, 2015). In general, police do not report on other police (Ariel, Farrar & Sutherland, 2015; Levine, 2016; Normore & Scott, 2021). According to Ariel, Farrar & Sutherland (2015), most police officers view cases of police brutality or other forms of misconduct as being tiered such that some acts are seen as "dead wrong," some acts are seen as being "wrong but not bad," and some acts are deemed as being "wrong and everybody knows" about it. Yet, that does not mean that everybody or even anybody will report about the wrongdoing (Ariel, Farrar & Sutherland, 2015) everybody knows.

In fact, police often refuse to testify against a fellow officer and prosecutors have a challenging time making a case (such as was the case with Eric Garner Even worse, sometimes officers collude to present a fraudulent representation of the facts or the events of the alleged indiscretion (Baker, 2021; Levine, 2016). This occurred when it came to the Abner Louima case (Maule, 2017, p. 28). Officer Charles Schwartz wound up being convicted for ten years on a perjury charge trying to protect his partner regarding the Abner Louima case (Maule, 2017). They try to present stories in the "least criminal light" (Levine, 2016, p. 749) to protect a fellow officer (Maule, 2017) as in the movie "Training Day" with Denzel Washington. Overall, this leads to a "lack of criminal accountability for police" (Levine, 2016, p. 745). This causes a lot of problems for those citizens who are trying to address crimes that have been committed against them from police officers.

Second, due process issues have been a repetitive problem. The fact of the matter that it is not unheard-of during police interrogations or even perp apprehension that due process violations occur. These violations often deal with the fifth (5th) and fourteenth (14th) amendments (Normore & Scott, 2021). Not giving Miranda rights before an interrogation would lead to a violation of one's 5th amendment rights. Exercising cruel and unusual punishment would be a violation of one's 14th amendment rights (Normore & Scott, 2021) such as in the case of Abner Louima (Maule, 2017). It would also and has led to allegations of misconduct throughout precincts throughout the country (Maule, 2017). Regardless, these actions also lead to another issue, which is that of civil liability (Maule, 2017). This issue will not be touched upon in this book.

Other due process issues may be related to the length of time it takes for a trial to take place (Levine, 2016). Often enough prosecutors refuse to charge police officers who have murdered people during the course of their duties (Levine, 2016: Maule, 2017) even when they know there may be a constitutional issue. This is even the case when the suspects are or were unarmed. Moreover, this holds true even when it is a White officer who has shot and killed and unarmed Black male (Levine, 2016).

Third, police brutality is the glaring issue of this book. In the United States, "police brutality is at the center of a growing national conversation on state power, race and our problematic law enforcement culture" (Levine, 2016, p. 745). Police officers are allowed to utilize a "...legitimate use of force" (Maule, 2017, p.3) as the authority was given to them to do so (Lyle & Esmail, 2016). In other words, they can utilize reasonable force (Lyle & Esmail, 2016; Maule, 2017). Whenever a police officer utilizes more force than is necessary to apprehend or even to subdue a perp, he has committed this heinous crime (Ariel, Farrar & Sutherland, 2015; Jones, 2017; Lyle & Esmail, 2016; Kuumba, 2021; Normore & Scott, 2021; Worland, 2014). According to Lyle & Esmail (2016), "police abuse is the purposeful practice of unwarranted coercion, frequently physical, but potentially in the form of verbal assaults and psychological intimidation by police which, constitutes abuse and official misconduct" (p. 155).

Unfortunately, that force is often used with POCs or people of color (Baker, 2021; Jones, 2017; Lyle & Esmail, 2016; Normore & Scott, 2021). Organizations like the 5points Law Group (2020) focused on data to flesh out racial disparities when it comes to police brutality, shootings, and black deaths in custody (Normore & Scott, 2021). Of all contacts with police officers, five (5%) percent to ten (10%) percent of those interactions wind up involving force (Ariel, Farrar & Sutherland, 2015). Moreover, 5Points Law Group found that approximately 30% of African Americans are unarmed when they are shot and killed by the police (Normore & Scott, 2021).

According to Lyle & Esmail (2016), that is 31% while Blacks only make up 13% of the population. In addition, since January 2015 (to 2016) or at the point of their publication, 175 Black males had been killed by police while being unarmed while only making up 6% of the overall population (Lyle &

Esmail, 2016). One of 1,000 Black men are stopped and killed by the police versus one of 2,500 White men (Baker, 2021). More ironically, it should be noted that off-duty Black officers are 52x more likely to be fatally shot as opposed to off-duty White officers (Jones, 2017). In fact, police brutality in the United States costs $1.8 billion annually (2010) as reported by the Centers for Disease Control (Baker, 2021).

The United States is not the only country with some of these issues (Jones, 2017; Tupper, 2021). While American police are more likely to use force overall, places like the United Kingdom had 3,000 active investigations of police brutality and other forms of misconduct by 2017, i.e., the printing of this printed journal article (Jones, 2017). And the United Kingdom is investigating officers still (Jones, 2017) as is Australia. Moreover, the Netherlands also had issues with police misconduct and racial profiling (Jones, 2017). Countries like Australia also have issues with the police and police brutality overall.

The police in Australia operate in a paramilitary-style, which may contribute to increasing conflicts (Gooding, 2017). Due to deinstitutionalization in 1986, mental health legislation may have inadvertently "authorized coercive treatment in certain circumstances, may have also led to increasing encounters with police" (Gooding, 2017, p. 438). From 1993-1994, cases had increased immensely (Gooding, 2017). This was the case in the case of a woman by the name of Colleen Richman who bore a hatchet (Gooding, 2017). Standing at 5'1", she had an altercation with the police and wielding a hatchet she asked them to leave (Gooding, 2017). They left after shooting her in the province of Victoria and leaving her for dead in 1994 (Gooding, 2017). This Indigenous woman was probably just defending her way of life (Gooding, 2017). Over two decades later, a study was carried out in Australia that used narrative therapy to address previous victims of police brutality (Tupper, 2021). There were various issues such as the concern with publicizing said stories, feeling disconnected from social norms, and the like (Tupper, 2021). Participants also had concerns with being ostracized within their communities and legal liabilities (Tupper, 2022). And yet, they shared their stories and these stories pointed to a growing problem. Not unlike that in the entire continent of Africa.

In the continent of Africa, there is a history of police brutality and police corruption (Hatungimana, 2022). In Tunisia, Mohamed Bouazizi was abused by the police and as a form of protest, he self-immolated (i.e., set himself on fire) on December 17, 2010 (Hatungimana, 2022). Thus, sparking protest known as the Arab Springs. In Nigeria, there has been a history of colonization as well of which the police force was a rooted in and from (Hatungimana, 2022). Due to this, the police had duties that supported the economic ends of the leaders, and they met this end by "pacifying" the natives (Hatungimana, 2022). Acts such as bribes to keep them at bay is not unheard of (Hatungimana, 2022). Protests broke out when a young man was shot to death in the Delta state by SARS or the Special Anti-Robbery Squad (Hatungimana, 2022). Like its African counterparts, South Africa also has a number of issues with police brutality and misconduct as well that are entrenched in and from the system of Apartheid.

As far as South Africa, which was one of the countries that was used as a case for this book, there have been ongoing issues with the militarization of the police force that has led to further abuses (McMichael, 2016). From 2012 to 2013, the rates of crimes like assault, murder and rape by police officers was up by 213% (McMichael, 2016). A radio advert was played that asked for citizens to report police brutality against the SAPS (South African Police Services) (McMichael, 2016). This led to other reports that were given and/or reported to the IPID or the Independent Police Investigation Directorate (McMichael, 2016). Other issues arose such as the murder of thirty-four striking miners by the police, which became known as the Marikana massacre in Durban (McMichael, 2016). At each turn, police brutality may have shown a different side of its head, but the result was the same – more dead bodies and many of them were Black.

Fourth, poor police and/or governmental policies is another controversy which is an underlining issue. Several of the policies regarding policing are just "bad" (McMichael, 2016). Unjust policies exist that are described by the school-to-prison-pipeline system (See below!) (Normore & Scott, 2021). Policies such as this drive schoolchildren to prison or to prison sooner (Normore & Scott, 2021). Another policy that is an issue is that of stop and frisk (Jones, 2017; Normore & Scott, 2021). Other policies such as zero tolerance/mandatory minimum sentences and the three-strike rule have imprisoned people, especially people of color at astronomical rates, which disrupts their learning, their families, etc. (Jones, 2017; Normore & Scott, 2021). Often the transgressions are seemingly minor compared to the actual sentences. What is even more troubling is that of stand-your ground laws, which basically support the use of lethal force (Jones, 2017). Stand-your ground laws exist in thirty-three of the 50 contiguous United States as of 2014 (Jones, 2017).

Unjust policies also exist when it comes to dealing with police misconduct as well as police brutality cases (Hatungimana, 2022; Normore & Scott, 2021). Often when police are accused of misconduct, there is an aggressive plan of attack that comes to their aid (Normore & Scott, 2021) or a sweeping under the rug (Americans Who Tell the Truth (n.d.). Even worse, is when police officers are not reprimanded at all (Normore & Scott, 2021). Rather, these accusations should be investigated with all honesty and transparency. The call for transparent accountability from the government is a cry that is heard worldwide (Hatungimana, 2022).

Fifth, racial profiling continues to lead to more stops and arrests and chances for black deaths in custody. Racial profiling "… assumes guilt based on race or ethnicity, a problem that mostly affects those individuals who have a higher lifetime risk of dying because of police brutality" (Normore & Scott, 2021, p. 83). Racial profiling increased after World War II (Normore & Scott, 2021). For example, RBP or racially biased policing addresses the fact that some police officers believe racial minorities inherently commit more crimes, and they do not (Jones, 2017). However, this may contribute to the reality of more minorities being arrested at a higher rate and imprisoned at a higher rate. Even in the Netherlands, racial profiling has become a grave issue (Jones, 2017). Nor are Black people, especially Black men more dangerous because they wear hoodies (i.e., the Hoodie Effect) as in the case of teen Trayvon Martin (Jones, 2017). The answer to racial profiling in New York, specific to Manhattan in 2013 was the wearing of body cams (Ariel, Farrar & Sutherland, 2015).

Sixth, racism, which is linked to discrimination has been a problem since slavery began during the transatlantic slavery trade until present-day (Baker, 2021; Blight, 2018; Cha-Jua, 2014; Hughes & Meltzer, 1956; United Nations, 2022). It is also the basis for racial profiling. It has been a problem throughout different forms of colonization. Racism is defined as "a belief that race is a fundamental determinant of human traits and capacities and that racial differences produce an inherent superiority of a particular race" (Merriam-Webster, Incorporated, 2022, p. 1). As previously noted, race and ethnicity usually play a role in how police treat suspects or citizens during routine stops (Jones, 2017). According to Jones (2017), "Yes, race matters in the killing of racial and ethnic minorities, whether they are by police or civilians and especially when they are unarmed" (p. 873). In other words, race plays a role in police shootings (Jones, 2017). But they would not play a role if police officers did not have certain biases regarding individuals of certain races or ethnicities. This is especially the case since police officers target people of color on a regular basis (Baker, 2021).

Seventh, the school-to-prison-pipeline system is a continuous issue. It also leads to the criminalization of Black people in general. Specific to the United States, the United States is the world leader when it comes to incarceration in general (Normore & Scott, 2021). However, incarceration at such high rates was never supposed to come to the children. The fact is that many of America's and other countries' students are brought into the mass incarceration system at an alarming rate (Normore & Scott, 2021). When youth are incarcerated, it leads to a disruption in their education and to further educational deficits (Normore & Scott, 2021).

Eighth, another controversy surrounds that of "qualified immunity" (Normore & Scott, 2021). Qualified immunity is a legal doctrine (Normore & Scott, 2021). It is specific to the United States, and it is how the federal law shields or protects government officials, which includes police officers who are performing their duties within an official governmental capacity (Normore & Scott, 2021). In other words, when a police officer has utilized "reasonable force," he is covered by qualified immunity (Maule, 2017). This derives from Anderson v. Creighton, 483, US 1987). The exception of said defense is if they violate any and all specifically delineated federal and/or constitutional rights, etc. (Normore & Scott, 2021). To understand what rules police must follow, one may look below at a discussion of the patrol guide/manual.

Patrol Guide

Patrol guides are manuals police officers must follow, such as the "NYPD's patrol guide [which] contains the rules that NYC police officers must follow in carrying out their official duties (City of New York, 2022, p. 1). (See https://guides.lib.jjay.cuny.edu/nypd/procedure). For example, pertinent to the discussion of collusion, giving a false statement is punishable by disciplinary action and can be found in the NYPD Patrol Guide (2016/2017) under P.G.203-08: Making false statements (City of New York, 2022). Officers are not supposed to advocate hate or show disrespect for citizens such as is referenced in P.G.203-10 nor participate in biased incidents such as referenced in P.G.207-10 (City of New York, 2022). Moreover, the NYPD is at no time to participate in racial profiling P.G.203-25 (City of New York, 2022). It states the following in Section 1:

Members of the service are reminded that the New York City Police Department is committed both to the impartial enforcement of law and to the protection of constitutional rights. To reinforce these commitments and to ensure that all members of the service engage only in constitutionally sound policing practices, the Department prohibits the use of racial and bias-based profiling in law enforcement actions. Conducting enforcement activities in an unbiased manner fosters and strengthens relationships between police officers and members of the community, and inspires confidence in, and support for, policing efforts (City of New York, 2022, p. 1).

Thus, while the NYPD has a higher number of incidents, it is clear that the manual has already made clear what behaviors are becoming of an officer (City of New York, 2022). Therefore, if it is written, the question always becomes why it is not followed? Nonetheless, regardless of the "why?," there are some solutions and recommendations that the author has regarding the issues, controversies and problems that have contributed to police brutality. In addition, of course she also has comments regarding police brutality directly.

Solutions and Recommendations

The next chapter will discuss solutions and recommendations to the issues previously provided and discussed here. The fact of the matter is that there are no clear-cut answers. How does one cure racism? How can you force someone to be less racist when they live in a democracy and have a 1st Amendment right to believe and profess whatever they want to believe and/or profess? The author herself is a born-again Christian with a Jewish heritage and she would not want anyone trampling on her 1st Amendment right.

First, with that being said, for the average American citizen – the aforementioned argument of having a 1st Amendment right is a valid argument. However, for a police officer, the standard is higher because they are called to "protect and serve." How does one "protect and serve" their neighbor if they see their neighbor as an animal? Perhaps, this points to what Maule (2017) discussed in what characteristics one looks for when choosing a police officer such as high moral standards and integrity. Regardless of one's beliefs, they must complete their job duty to the best of their ability and that includes understanding how their biases may interfere with the commission of their job duties (Davis, 2021). That takes a mature man or woman. These are the thoughts, beliefs and characteristics traits that must be examined before one is even hired to the NYPD (i.e., my local police force) or any other police force.

Second, the hiring process must be re-examined with an honesty that may not have occurred in the past. Who do you want to work side by side with every day? Who is best equipped to "protect and serve" the members of the community they are assigned to at present? If an officer is assigned to a lily-White district, this may not be an issue as long as no people of color (POC) walk or drive through that area. However, for a racist officer in Los Angeles which has a large Black and Latino population, the chance of a Black death or Latino death in custody will most likely substantially increase, especially if the verbal exchange becomes hostile. Thus, the interview process, the psychiatrist's exam, etc. must be completed with the utmost honesty and thoroughness.

If racism is addressed properly, racial profiling may decrease. This requires White officers to be called to interact with people who are not like them. Perhaps, part of the pre-training of a police officer can be them attending religious meetings, school meetings, community events and being asked to put in their 40 hours for a month or two or three as they learn about other cultures. It would be considered an on-boarding internship and they would be paid at a predetermined internship rate and benefits would apply once approved for the NYPD's job onboarding process. Key community leaders would also be able to speak with the brass and give their opinions and key assessments of the potential officers without the community knowing who they were initially. This would also do wonders for police-community relations. Before one gets married, do they not usually date or court the individual to get to know them. This process would be considered the "courtship stage."

Third, due process of the law. Due process is promised via the 4th Amendment. Once a police officer is brought up on charges, a thorough process of the law should take place. Prosecutors should not take the matter lightly. In the case of Tamir Rice, the trial did not come about until a year or so later and multiple reports had already been published indicating the innocence of the officers. This tainted fruit ruins grand jury and jury pools. If proper due process was followed and if police officers were held accountable for an accusation of police misconduct, at the worst-case scenario, the officer would be found guilty and would be charged appropriately. At the best-case scenario, the officer would be deemed innocent, but the public would have more trust in the promise of due process as well as legal remedies.

Fourth, poor police policies and procedures lead to mistrust within the community (Baker, 2021; Davis, 2021). One of the main policies that have angered Black citizens is that of stop-n-frisk. The idea that someone can be stopped and frisked without necessarily doing something is an issue. Even if thought to be guilty of a crime, the increased number of stop and frisk incidents within the Black community is too high, which is indicative of racial profiling playing a role. There are other ways to deal with the public such as having conversations, attending community meetings, and listening, etc.

When attending, let it be known that you are an officer as not to perpetuate old hostilities.

Fifth, community policing in schools is a program that needs to be revisited. Watching police dance on YouTube with students does not mean that students are treated well while attending school nor does it mean that they are not adjudicated at a higher rate. The issue of the school-to-prison pipeline system and the criminalization of Black males specifically is not just an unfortunate accusation (Baker, 2021). It has become a way of life. Instead of slavery, Black Codes, and Jim Crow (Hughes & Meltzer, 1956), we have youth and young males sitting in prison being robbed of their youth and sometimes the ability to have a family. This reality does not just affect that individual, it affects his family, his community, and the Black community at-large. It also leads to the legacy of Black families having less generational wealth. Moreover, if linked to poverty, one being poor has often been correlated with higher incidences of crimes such as theft and drug dealing. Thus, leading to issues such as the three-strike policy, which after three strikes would leave a Black male and possibly a Black female in prison for life.

Finally, something that is harder to address is the "Blue Wall of Silence" (Davis, 2021). In fact, the author is not sure what the recommendation would be. The fact is that police officers do need to band together. No one can understand the stress, the trauma or perhaps the isolation – especially in the case of an undercover cop as does another police officer. Regardless, when police officers commit crimes (Baker, 2021), and other officers knowingly stay silent, they are choosing to criminalize their own profession (Davis, 2021). An officer takes an oath to "protect and serve" people in the community. And while some of the people in the community may be fellow police officers, their standard is higher.

It is the same with religious leaders, especially Christian leaders, the Bible says in James 3:1 the following: "My brethren, be not many masters, knowing that we shall receive the greater condemnation" (KJV). In applying this to police officers as visible leaders in the community, it is clear that police officers who do not maintain their integrity and follow and obey a moral compass, regardless of what other officers or even superior officers do within the force, they shall be held accountable by God. And in 2023 and beyond, they will also most likely be held more accountable by the public.

In other words, officers like Serpico were the ultimate officers. They risked their life/lives to report corruption from within the department. In I Peter 4:17, we are told that "For the time *is come* that judgment must begin at the house of God: and if *it* first *begin* at us, what shall the end *be* of them that obey not the gospel of God?" If one applied this principle of the church and its standards to the precincts and the department as a whole, they would come to realize, the first judgment for crimes must begin with the distributors of justice. If the judgment begins in the precinct, at the courts, at the house(s) of legislation then when the judgment came/comes to everyday citizen, each individual would be more confident in the process.

If that happened, once the force went to address criminals of the greater population or their local communities, less people would question their actions. Moreover, more citizens would probably assist with reporting crimes and testifying if they knew they could trust the police, trust the prosecutors, trust the judges, etc., and if they knew they were really about the business of "protecting and serving," etc. Additionally, there would be less need for undercover cops. Therefore, there would be more transparency, and this would also foster more trust with the community. Overall, the entire system would work like a finely oiled machine, a machine that is fed with truth and that distributes true justice in all its forms of purity.

CONCLUSION

In conclusion, America as a case study is an interesting case indeed. America, previously known as the New World, has had a checkered past and a colored history. Nonetheless, it is important to consider how Black Deaths in custody occurred and continue to occur as well as other acts of Police Brutality. The history of America sheds light on this reality. With that being said, America has come a long way from the slaughter of many Native American tribes to slavery, the Civil War and its end, the forming of the Ku Klux Klan and Blacks Codes as well as Jim Crow Laws, etc. Today, many of these laws have been eradicated. They have been replaced with the 13th, 14th, 15th, etc. Amendments, and changes to local, state, and federal laws.

The average citizen has stood up to protest through various means such as writing, sit-ins, refusing to move from the front of the bus like Rosa Parks, etc. With each injustice has come an equal or greater reaction. To address false imprisonment, excessive punishments, etc. organizations like the Equal Justice Initiative have sprouted up and even had impacts through subsidiary organizations and institutions on public spaces and remembrance via museums, etc. One of the greatest tools in the fight for justice has not been the invention of a story, but the telling and re-telling and the documentation of the actual and factual occurrences. From 1865 until the present-day, the journey of the

African American in America has crossed space and time to continue the public outcry for freedoms in a country that claims to be the "land of the free and the home of the brave." Through their own boldness and acts of bravery they have garnered more freedom. And people of other cultures and religions have traveled with them to make America great again!

Like America, Australia is an interesting case of a country that has moved from being a colonized Commonwealth to a Commonwealth Democracy. Considering that Australia's form of government is a blend of England, America with some references to Canada with England and Ireland listed within the preamble of its constitution as motherlands; some similarities in issues as well as solutions will be in common. Like Australia, South Africa was a Commonwealth, but it meandered to being a repressive regime known as an Apartheid State. In 1994, it became a Commonwealth Democracy along with its predecessor Australia and like the United Kingdom, which includes England, Ireland, Scotland, Wales, and Gibraltar (which is located in Spain). Thus, its form of government is heavily influenced by America and the UK as well. Nonetheless, each of these countries had been colonies/colonized. Moreover, each of these countries has had a colored past. The issue of police brutality or a militarized force is not a new one. Thus, solutions and recommendations will be addressed in the next chapter with the hopes that as a global community "we" can reduce the amounts of deaths in custody, especially Black deaths in custody, when Blacks (i.e., with an emphasis on Black males) make up an astronomical numerical representation of said deaths.

REFERENCES

Alsan, M., Wanamaker, M., & Harderman, R. R. (2019). The Tuskegee study of untreated syphilis: A case study in peripheral trauma with implications for health professionals. *Journal of General Internal Medicine*, *35*(1), 322–325. https://www.ncbi.nlm.nih.gov/pmc/articles/PMC6957600/pdf/11606_2019_Article_5309.pdf. doi:10.100711606-019-05309-8 PMID:31646456

Anekwe, O.N. (2014, May). The Tuskegee experiment. *International Journal of Clinical and Medical Imagining*, *1*(5), 1. doi:. file:///C:/Users/janel/OneDrive/Desktop/Publications/the-tuskegee-experiment. May.2014.05.14.2022.pdf. doi:10.4172/ijcmi.1000211

Ariel, B., Farrar, W. A., & Sutherland, A. (2015). The effect of police body-worn cameras on use of force and citizens' complaints against the police: A randomized controlled trial. *Journal of Quantitative Criminology*, *31*(3), 509–535. doi:10.100710940-014-9236-3

Baker, E. (2021, May 20). *Police brutality: An epidemic in America.* San Diego University. https://sites.sandiego.edu/blackhistoryatusd/2021/05/20/police-brutality-an-epidemic-in-america/

Blight, D. W. (2018). *Frederick Douglass: Prophet of freedom.* Simon & Schuster.

Bradt, S. (2010). *'One-drop rule' persists racial hierarchy.* Harvard. https://news.harvard.edu/gazette/story/2010/12/one-drop-rule-persists/

Cha-Jua, S. K. (2014, Spring). We believe it was murder: Mobilizing black resistance to police brutality in Champaign, Illinois. *The Black Scholar*, *44*(1), 58–85. doi:10.1080/00064246.2014.11641212

Chang, C. (2019, January 21). How early Australians treated Aboriginal people. *News.com.* https://www.news.com.au/national/politics/how-early-australians-treated-aboriginal-people/news-story/e984d3a453382c59a1d5d81f99a9ad8c

City of New York. (2022). *New York patrol guide.* NYC Gov. https://www1.nyc.gov/site/ccrb/investigations/nypd-patrol-guide.page#:~:text=The%20NYPD%27s%20Patrol%20Guide%20contains%20the%20rules%20that,must%20follow%20in%20carrying%20out%20their%20official%20duties

Davis, D. L. (2021). From the field: Why I founded black cops against police brutality. *Journal of Ethnicity in Criminal Justice*, *19*(3-4), 201–222. doi:10.1080/15377938.2021.1979159

Ellis, D. (2019, Summer). Apartheid. *Israel Studies*, *24*(2), 63–71. doi:10.2979/israelstudies.24.2.06

Ewing, E. L. (2020, August 25). *Blue bloods: America's brotherhood of police officers.* Retrieved on April 30, 2022 from https://www.vanityfair.com/culture/2020/08/americas-brotherhood-of-police-officers

Fanon, F. (2008). *Black skin, White masks.* Grove Press.

Finton, L. (2023, April 7). *Activists to host Tyre Nichols photo exhibits, lantern ceremony before city hall.* Yahoo. https://www.yahoo.com/entertainment/activists-host-tyre-nichols-photo-152701684.html

Fulbright, L. (2000, March 6). "*Wanted: Female cops.*" file:///C:/Users/janel/OneDrive/Desktop/Publications/Examining%20Black%20Deaths%20in%20Custody%20-%202022/Women_may_be_solution_to_polic.pdf.

Hatungimana, W. (2020). How people approve their governments: Corruption perceptions of police legitimacy in Africa. *Journal of Modern Studies, 60*(1), 1-22. . doi:10.1017/S0022278X21000392

Hilton, B. T. (2011). Frantz Fanon and Colonialism: A Psychology of Oppression. *Journal of Scientific Psychology*, 45–59.

Holland, H. (1989). *The struggle: A history of the African National Congress.* Grafton Paperback.

Hughes, L., & Meltzer, M. (1956). *A pictorial history of the negro in America.* Crown Publishers.

Johnson, A. G. (2006). *Privilege, power, and difference*. McGraw Hill Companies.

Jones, J. M. (2017). Killing fields: Explaining police violence against persons of color. *The Journal of Social Issues*, *73*(4), 872–883. doi:10.1111/josi.12252

Kaba, M. (n.d.). *Yes, we mean literally abolish the police.* https://drive.google.com/file/d/1KR-D1GBoOQzT_IljgqOoEaPOareRQ0xD/view

Levine, K. (2016). How we prosecute the police. *The Georgetown Law Journal*, *104*(4), 745–776.

Lyle, P., & Esmail, A. M. (2016). Sworn to protect: Police brutality – A dilemma for America's police. *Race, Gender. Class, New Orleans*, *23*(3/4), 155–185.

Lynch, J. (2023, January 17). Memphis police relieve officers pending investigations into the arrest of man who later died, chief says. *CNN.* https://www.cnn.com/2023/01/16/us/memphis-tennessee-arrested-man-dies-hospital/index.html/

Maule, B. A. (2017). *Police misconduct in Brooklyn: Documenting, understanding and preventing*. Springer Publications. doi:10.1007/978-3-319-66814-7

McMichael, C. (2016). Police wars and state repression in South Africa. *Journal of Asian and African Studies*, *51*(1), 3–16. doi:10.1177/0021909614541086

Merriam-Webster, Incorporated. (2022). *Racism.* Meriam-Webster. https://www.merriam-webster.com/dictionary/racism

New York City Police Department. (2019, April 3). *Patrol guide.* NYCPD. https://www1.nyc.gov/assets/nypd/downloads/pdf/public_information/public-pguide1.pdf

Newtown, J. (1788). *Thoughts upon the African slave trade*. J. Buckland, in Pater-Noster Row, and J. Johnson in St. Paul's Church-yard.

Normore, A. H., & Scott, W. R. (2021). Police brutality and the militarization of Black and Brown communities: Transforming the culture of policing through education and training. *New Directions for Adult and Continuing Education*, *2021*(170), 79–88. doi:10.1002/ace.20427

Project, N. I. A. (2020, October 13). *Defund police.* [Video]. Youtube. https://www.youtube.com/watch?v=bT0YpOmk8NA

Smith, W. (2021, February 17). *Amend: The fight for America.* [Net Series]. Netflix.

Tupper, N. M. (2021). Working with victims of police brutality: Conducting and documenting multistoried interviews. *The International Journal of Narrative Therapy and Community Work*, *2*, 48–57.

United Nations. (2022, March 25). *Resistance to slavery and unity against racism: Rhythms of resistance.* UN. https://www.youtube.com/watch?v=VUhHhW1__sg

U.S. Commission on Civil Rights in New York City. (2000, August). *Police practices and civil rights in New York City.* GPO. https://permanent.access.gpo.gov/lps13167/main.htm

U.S. Department of Health and Human Services. (2021). *Tuskegee experiment.* CDC. https://www.cdc.gov/tuskegee/timeline.htm?msclkid=9d69f9a7cd4711ecba7d3de204e661d5

Vrieland, D. (2022). *Dr. King comes to Grosse Pointe.* Academia Letters. *Article, 4541*. doi:10.20935/AL4541

Wells, D., Umansky, E., & Syed, M. (2020, July 26). *The NYPD files: Search thousands of civilian complaints against New York City police officers.* Prop Publica. https://projects.propublica.org/nypd-ccrb/

KEY TERMS AND DEFINITIONS

Discrimination: Discernible treatment where one is treated differently based on their race, creed, religion, sex, culture, etc.

Hypodescent: When it comes to mixed children, the act of classifying them by the "lesser" considered or subordinate race.

One-drop Rule: The idea that if someone has one drop of blood that is non-White, they cannot be considered a White person.

Privilege: Usually refers to a right or preferential treatment for belonging to a particular group. Usually, when one refers to being privileged, they refer to someone being rich. However, in the use of this term, the author is referring to White privilege, which means that Caucasians receive extraordinary circumstances that are not associated with their education or work but the color of their skin.

Racism: Believing and classifying various groups along certain characteristics in a deterministic way that sets one group above another socially, economically, et al.

Segregation: The act of separating groups due to race with the intent of keeping the races separate.

Social Justice Issues: Identifying controversies or problems with the intent of understanding issues and educating others on those topics that have led to another's oppression.

ENDNOTE

1 Allusion to Childish Gambino song titled "This is America."

Chapter 8
An Examination of Solutions

ABSTRACT

This chapter focuses on the solutions that both the author, politicians, activists, educators, religious leaders, etc. have proffered throughout the literature review and the analysis of the issues that have been discussed throughout this book. These solutions act as a salve to the wounds of injustice throughout the world. Many of these solutions are not panaceas or end all be all solutions. Some of the solutions are short-term remedies while other solutions are long-term remedies. To be frank, it is impossible to return land masses – in complete, return the dead to life or to heal all the wounds from the emotional abuse, physical abuse, sexual abuse, and spiritual abuses that have occurred worldwide. It is also impossible to salvage some of the cultural losses via identity as well as artifacts. None the less, an examination and discussion of said solutions may bring about a better understanding and a better solution.

"Support them, but my hope is not in law enforcement" -KB, Dark Skin (2021)

"I wish it need not have happened in my time."- Frodo, The Fellowship of the Rings

"So do I, and so do all who live to see such times. But that is not for them to decide. All we have to decide is what to do with the time that is given to us."- Gandalf, The Fellowship of the Rings

DOI: 10.4018/978-1-7998-9304-2.ch008

Figure 1. Centerpiece regarding Miranda Rights, National Law Enforcement Museum, Washington, D.C. 2022
Source: Janelle Christine Simmons, Ed.D. © 2022

INTRODUCTION

For many Black people who were slaves, they, like Frodo in Lord of the Rings, wished that it had not happened in their time or to them. Yet, some form of slavery has occurred and been experienced by almost every people group on earth. Slavery appears to be the precursor of police brutality (Baker, 2021). This is one of the key issues that is discussed in this book as it relates to Black deaths in custody. In examining solutions, it must be noted that conversations must take place. However, how those conversations take place will dictate how much truth is discussed.

At the end of a clip where Malcolm X discusses the difference between the House Negro and the Field Negro (i.e., the parable of the House Negro) at a talk he gave in Detroit, Michigan at King Solomon Baptist Church on November 10, 1963, he described James Baldwin, a famous Black author (Columbia University, Center for Teaching and Learning, n.d). Malcolm X discussed the conversation and how White people often try to control the conversation for their own benefit (Malcolm X, 2012). He stated the following: "No, it was a sellout. It was a takeover. When James Baldwin came from Paris, they would not let him talk. 'Cause they couldn't make him go by the script" (Malcolm X, 2012, [21:47]). In order to bring systematic change, it is necessary for freedom of speech (1) to be able to prevail within the borders of the United States of America.

In business, they often say – there must be an ask. What is it that you are asking for support, funding, etc.? In James Baldwin's Artist on Fire by W.J. Weatherby (1989), James Baldwin stated the following: "I suspect, though I certainly cannot prove it," he wrote ten years before he died, "that every life moves full circle …toward revelation" (p. 1). Well, James Baldwin made a hidden ask many years ago while speaking on a TV Program known as the Dick Cavett Show in 1969 (NPR, 2017; Peck, 2017) that may have moved us all towards revelation. He stated the following: "If any White man in the world says, "Give me liberty or give me death (2), the entire White word applauds. When a Black man says exactly the same thing, he is judged a criminal and treated like one, and everything possible is done to make an example of this bad nigger so there won't be any like him" [Magnolia Pictures, 2017, [0:05]. For a country that speaks of liberty and allegedly celebrates uniqueness – an apropos example is its system of capitalism; for many Black people defiance is the only way to bring about social change.

It is what James Baldwin referred to when he referenced the Defiant Ones, a movie screened in 1958, written by S. Kramer and starring Tony Curtis and Sidney Poitier (Peck, 2017), which expressed "[…] a social idea – the idea of men of different races brought together to face misfortune in a band of brotherhood" (Thompson, 1958, p. 1). James Baldwin states the following; "The root of the black man's hatred is rage, and he does not so much care about White men as simply wants them out of his way, and more than that, out of his children's way" (Peck, 2017).[1] Ironically, this statement sounds like James Baldwin may be supporting the principle of separate but equal, however, what he is really discussing is the fact that Black Americans want the freedom to be themselves in a land they either were forced to come to or freely came to at some point. Moreover, they want freedom for their children and their future generations. While physical enslavement has been left behind, there is still the issue of mental enslavement.

By all technicalities, unless imprisoned the Black man and the Black woman is free. They have human rights, civil rights – they have access to equal rights. Nonetheless, how those rights are expressed is a question for the sages and for the ages. Yet, within that question lies another question. What solutions are viable for the Black community to engage in through social reform? In addition, when it comes to the general public and the police, what solutions are viable in order to bring understanding, reform, and to build community across color lines, culture, racial identity, religious beliefs, et al.?

This chapter will focus on examining solutions to the issue of black deaths in custody. Some of these solutions will address acts that citizens can execute. Some of these solutions will address reform within the police department. Other solutions will address reform in the courts or even throughout the legislators. This is especially the case when it comes to due process and the lack thereof for some cases. Regardless of the solutions discussed, the author comes to the same conclusion that she alluded to or stated in previous chapters – it is really a matter of the heart. Police officers who are hired must be men and women of compassion, wit, discernment, and integrity. They must remember that they are not above the law but are here to enforce the law. That law is predetermined by our forefathers/founders, judges, legislators, and the like.

MAIN FOCUS OF CHAPTER

Within the United States alone, there are 14,800 police agencies (Lyle & Esmail, 2016). Fifty percent of these agencies or 7,400 do not report homicides to the FBI-UCR that involve the police (Lyle & Esmail, 2016). LEOs or law enforcement agents (Lyle & Esmail, 2016) need to be held accountable for real crimes that they commit against "innocent" or unarmed individuals. What makes the reality even more trying is the fact that the gorilla effect appears to take place, which is where and when Blacks of African descent are dehumanized (Jones, 2017). The process also does not even allow for one being considered as the outsider or part of the "out group," but leads to someone being considered as not even being part of the human group (Jones, 2017), which is known as the human race. The process of this dehumanization leads way for various forms of abuse and discrimination, which includes police brutality (Baker, 2021; Cha-Jua, 2014; Davis, 2021; Jones, 2017). Moreover, even the media has been "complicit in creating a context in which lethal actions against people of color can be justified and go unpunished" (Jones, 2017, p. 876). Yet, there have been various forms of legislation that have still been passed to address these injustices.

Various acts and laws have been established within various countries to address said issues. Specific to the United States, acts like the 1871 Civil

Rights Act, the 13th Amendment, the 14th Amendment and Title 42 US Code Section 1983 have all been written to address these issues (Lyle & Esmail, 2016). These various forms of legislation had to be put in effect to push change ahead but at each period of time of enactment, part of the populace resisted. However, even with a myriad of acts, amendments, bills, laws, etc.; there are still issues, controversies, problems, and outright crimes that have been committed.

Figure 2. Picture of a newspaper clip titled "Enforcement of the Fourteenth Amendment."
Source: Statutes and Stories (2022). https://www.statutesandstories.com/blog_html/the-ku-klux-klan-act-of-1871/.

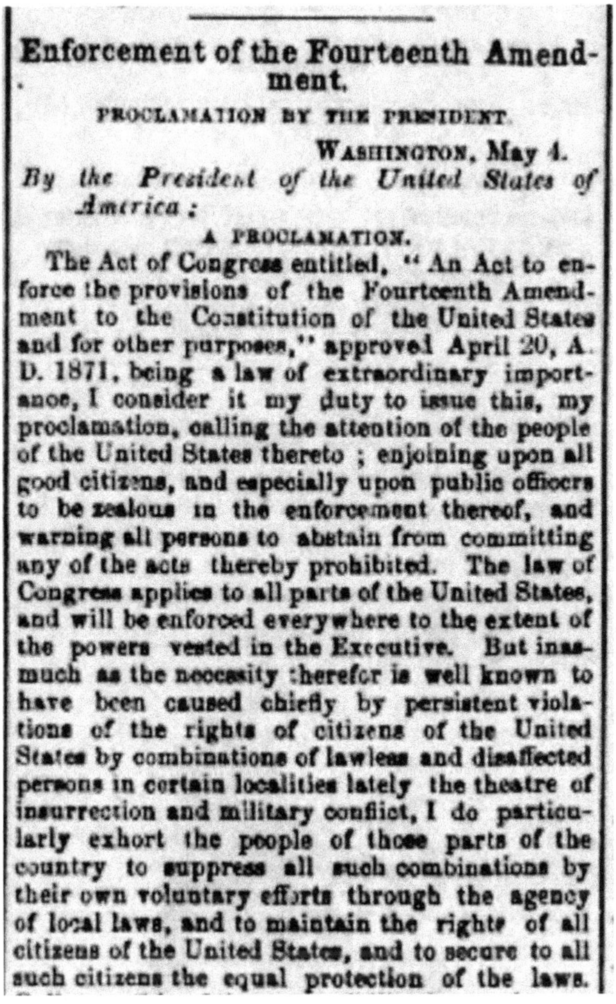

Enforcement of the Fourteenth Amendment.

PROCLAMATION BY THE PRESIDENT.

WASHINGTON, May 4.

By the President of the United States of America:

A PROCLAMATION.

The Act of Congress entitled, "An Act to enforce the provisions of the Fourteenth Amendment to the Constitution of the United States and for other purposes," approved April 20, A. D. 1871, being a law of extraordinary importance, I consider it my duty to issue this, my proclamation, calling the attention of the people of the United States thereto; enjoining upon all good citizens, and especially upon public officers to be zealous in the enforcement thereof, and warning all persons to abstain from committing any of the acts thereby prohibited. The law of Congress applies to all parts of the United States, and will be enforced everywhere to the extent of the powers vested in the Executive. But inasmuch as the necessity therefor is well known to have been caused chiefly by persistent violations of the rights of citizens of the United States by combinations of lawless and disaffected persons in certain localities lately the theatre of insurrection and military conflict, I do particularly exhort the people of those parts of the country to suppress all such combinations by their own voluntary efforts through the agency of local laws, and to maintain the rights of all citizens of the United States, and to secure to all such citizens the equal protection of the laws.

Issues, Controversies, Problems

Figure 3. Picture of "Frank" Serpico or Francesco Vincent Serpico, a former, retired NYPD officer who was the 1st to report widespread police corruption
Source: Americans Who Tell the Truth (n.d.) https://www.americanswhotellthetruth.org/portraits/frank-serpico.

Above is a picture of "Frank" Serpico (Americans Who Tell the Truth, n.d.). Many years ago, when I was a small child, I sat with my "father," Leon Ray Simmons, Jr. and I watched a movie called "Serpico." It was a 70s flick (Americans Who Tell the Truth, n.d.). The premise of the movie was that Serpico who was a Brooklynite (Shaer, 2013) a former military man had joined the police force at the age of 23 and after years of being an NYPD officer; he began to report police corruption, but no one took him seriously (Americans Who Tell the Truth, n.d.; Shaer, 2013). And then a crisis came (Americans Who Tell the Truth, n.d.).

His journey of reporting police corruption began in 1967 and it was not until the New York Times ran a story that blew up in the news in 1970, that Mayor Lindsay appointed the Knapp Commission to investigate (Americans Who Tell the Truth, n.d.; Shaer, 2013), which was made up of a five-man commission (Shaer, 2013). Serpico testified and then he was ostracized by his fellow NYPD officers (Americans Who Tell the Truth, n.d.). Thereafter, it appeared that his "fellow officers" set him up and allowed him to get shot in the face during a drug raid (Americans Who Tell the Truth, n.d.). After almost dying, he retired (Americans Who Tell the Truth, n.d.). His fellow officers did not call for help nor assist him (Americans Who Tell the Truth, n.d.), and basically had left him to die (Shaer, 2013). He survived and in 1973, a movie with Al Pacino named Serpico was made (Americans Who Tell the Truth, n.d.).

Serpico is an example of how a police officer can see corruption and break the "Blue Wall of Silence" (Ariel, Farrar & Sutherland, 2015; Normore & Scott, 2021; Shaer, 2013) even though he risked his life to do so (Americans Who Tell the Truth, n.d.). In fact, whistleblowers should be celebrated as they have sounded a mighty alarm. In Ezekiel 33:6, the Lord tells us: "But is the watchman see the sword come, and blow not the trumpet, and the people be not warned; if the sword come, and take any person from among them, he is taken away in his iniquity; but his blood will require at the watchman's hand." In other words, when applying this scripture to Serpico's story, if Serpico had failed to whistle blow on his fellow officers, they would have died for their sin, but he would have been held accountable. Why? Because Serpico was a leader. Are not police officers like watchmen on a wall? Do they not look to see where dangers come from and protect their communities? Are not these various communities representative of God's creation? When a person becomes a police officer, they are called to a high standard with difficult duties to execute whether they sit behind a desk, are monitoring traffic, or are in a high-speed chase. The truth is that more officers need to do just as "Frank" Serpico did if the force will be a police force of integrity.

Police misconduct occurs at various arenas and to various people (Ariel, Farrar & Sutherland, 2015; Cha-Jua, 2014; Jones, 2017; Kuumba, 2021; Levine, 2016; Lyle & Esmail, 2016; Maule, 2017; Normore & Scott, 2021; Worland, 2014). It can include minor infringements like sleeping on the job, taking a free meal, all the way to a case of police brutality (Baker, 2021; City of New York, 2022; Maule, 2017). The issue lies in the fact that defining police misconduct tends to get dicey. Nonetheless, this book focuses on black deaths in custody (Baker, 2021), which is a form of police brutality that falls under the broader auspices of police misconduct.

While the public, i.e., everyday citizens define police misconduct broadly, police officers and other officials define police misconduct narrowly (Maule, 2017), which may contribute to the misunderstanding. Nonetheless, the U.S. Supreme Court defines police conduct as follows: "[m]isuse of power, possessed by virtue of state law and made possible only because the wrongdoer is clothed with the authority of the state" (Lugar v. Edmondson Oil Co., Inc., 1982)" (Maule, 2017, p. 10). Thus, police misconduct is considered to be "an affirmative 'misuse of power,' which can include non-action, corruption, ignoring one's legal obligation (Maule, 2017), and looking the other way. There continue to be actions taken to attempt to curb police misconduct (Cha-Jua, 2014; Maule, 2017). However, sometimes this seems to be of no avail as cases though minute compared to other crimes continue to appear and increase. Yet, nothing can curb the acts of police misconduct and police brutality that led to the loss of life of citizens, especially when said citizens are at home minding their business, out for a walk or run; and unarmed. This is especially the case, when the cases affect Black lives (Baker, 2021).

Solutions to Police Brutality and Misconduct: From the Wall of Blue

There are a number of solutions that have been discussed when it comes to addressing issues of blue brutality and misconduct from within the Blue Wall of Silence. Policing is a complex and an extremely unique profession (Maule, 2017). An officer is called to have high moral character (Ariel, Farrar & Sutherland, 2015; Maule, 2017). It requires one or more than one person having a high amount of emotional intelligence (Maule, 2017). They must be able to manage interactions with wisdom and delicacy (Maule, 2017).

This is one of the reasons why adding women to the force was of interest in the beginning of the 21st century (Fulbright, 2000). Outside of women, there still needs to be other forms of diversity welcomed and hired into the police department (Davis, 2021). Police officers must be responsible individuals (Baker, 2021; Davis, 2021; Maule, 2017). In other words, there are specific characteristics that one looks for in a police officer. It has been said overall that there are 12 desirable traits that police departments and Field Officer Trainers look for in police officers before the process of recruitment (Maule, 2017).

First, one topic that has been proffered is that of the hiring and training process. Regarding hiring, it has been suggested that the force continue to diversify their employee pool. From 2000, it was suggested that more women be hired (Fulbright, 2000) as an example. Fulbright (2000) stated the following regarding the hiring of female police officers: "female police officers use force less often in the line of duty and are more adept at defusing violent situations through negotiation" (p. 1). It is thought the reason there were fewer female police officers was the PDs have hostile work environments (Fulbright, 2000).

Maule (2017) states the following regarding recruitment: "There should be little if any doubt that perhaps the single most significant function of a police department if the recruitment, selection, and hiring of individuals to become members of its organization" (p. 41). This is the case since police officers are a product of their environment, their societies, and their communities (Maule, 2017), it is necessary to carefully choose candidates. Police officers need to or should maintain positive community relations (Baker, 2021; Davis, 2021; Maule, 2017). When officers execute police brutality, especially if multiple complaints have been filed against them; they have not only violated this relationship, but they have violated their execution of justice (Baker, 2021; Davis, 2021; Maule, 2017).

Perhaps, this and other issues can be addressed via training.

Figure 4. Picture discussing the need for police training at National Law Enforcement Museum, March 12, 2022
Source: Janelle Christine Simmons, Ed.D. © 2022.

Previously, the initial police forces were untrained (National Law Enforcement Museum, personal communication, March 12, 2022). However, in the 21st century, there are various trainings that have been suggested (Baker, 2021, Davis, 2021; National Law Enforcement Museum, personal communication, March 12, 2022; Normore & Scott, 2021). There is cultural and competence and diversity training (Baker, 2021; Normore & Scott, 2021). There is evidence-based training, which focuses on police and diversity

(Normore & Scott, 2021). These trainings address police officers' competency in being sensitive to various cultures, etc. (Baker, 2021; Normore & Scott, 2021). There is also implicit bias training (Normore & Scott, 2021). This type of training focuses on "improving the relationship between police and minority civilians" (Normore & Scott, 2021, p. 86). It requires the officer to be aware and cognizant of their own biases (Normore & Scott, 2021). Finally, there is reality-based training, which puts police cadets and officers in scenarios in 360-degree environments so that their thought-process, physical reaction time, choices in combat, and other issues can be analyzed (Murray & Haberfield, 2021).

The fact is when it comes to police misconduct, it is unclear whether training of any kind truly helps (Baker, 2021; Maule, 2017). However, an issue that has repeatedly come up regarding police officers in various countries (e.g., Australia, Nigeria, South Africa, United States, etc.), is a militarized force (Gooding, 2017; Hatungimana, 2022; Normore & Scott, 2021). In other words, another issue that should be addressed in training is the militarization of the police force that has taken place (Baker, 2021; Gooding, 2017; Hatungimana, 2022; Normore & Scott, 2021). Many police forces have become militarized in a way that causes them to shoot first and ask questions later (Baker, 2021; Gooding, 2017; Hatungimana, 2022; Normore & Scott, 2021). This is highly problematic. Police are to "protect and serve" – not shoot first and ask questions later. Thus, police officers need to decrease their use of force (Murray & Haberfield, 2021; Normore & Scott, 2021).

First, other forms of education are necessary (Baker, 2021; Murray & Haberfield, 2021; Normore & Scott, 2021). Higher levels of education are linked with police officers who work better on duty and who do a better job overall (Normore & Scott, 2021). It has been duly noted and stated that "college-educated police officers generate fewer citizen complaints and termination is less frequent for misconduct" (Normore & Scott, p. 86). That may be the reason why Field Training Officers are college-educated (Normore & Scott). They tend to train new cadets in order to ensure that they are ready for the challenges and the stresses of being a police officer (Murray & Haberfield, 2021; Normore & Scott, 2021). In a sense they are "police leaders," and as such while training, they should lead by example (Normore & Scott, 2021).

Second, police officers should engage with the public (M. Wilcox, personal communication, September 23, 2022). It is unfortunate, but "the exercise of power by the police can potentially tarnish their relationship with the community" (Ariel, Farrar & Sutherland, 2015, p. 509). Since the 1980s, "demands escalated as sharp increases in violent crime led the public to support spending more money on local policing efforts. Police chiefs responded by experimenting with varying approaches, settling (for now) on "Community-Oriented Policing" as the "modern" approach to effective policing (Haberfeld 2002; Kimbrough 2016; Leventakis and Haberfeld 2018a, b, 2019)" (Murray & Haberfield, 2021, p. 1). Some of it was highly ineffective (Murray & Haberfield, 2021). Still, much of the public, especially the Black community, has wounds that have been unhealed due to the injustices that they have seen and endured (Normore & Scott, 2021). During some of the BLM marches, several police officers attended in an off-duty capacity (Basu, 2020; Normore & Scott, 2021). They knelt in support of the message – that they too acknowledged that too many Black people, especially men had been killed/murdered while unarmed (Normore & Scott, 2021). This type of true engagement with the public may build a sense of trust. It also goes a long way in bringing on moments where wounds that have festered can start to feel a smudge of salve and does not require training(s), but empathy and compassion (Refer to the Fourth Point for a side discussion of community policing).

Third, the second point is related to this point. Many citizens have a general mistrust for the police (Ariel, Farrar & Sutherland, 2015; Baker, 2021; Murray & Haberfield, 2021; National Law Enforcement Museum, personal communication, March 12, 2022). They do not have confidence that the everyday police officer is for them or really seeks to "protect and serve" them (Ariel, Farrar & Sutherland, 2015; Jones, 2017; Maule, 2017). This is especially the case since the basic social contract between police and citizens is that the police are to "protect and serve" them (Ariel, Farrar & Sutherland, 2015). Police are supposed to be not only legally responsible but also morally responsible (Ariel, Farrar & Sutherland, 2015; Murray & Haberfield, 2021; M. Wilcox, personal communication, September 21, 2022).

When police continue to appear to be or are abusive to the public, the citizens of the arenas they are to protect, public tensions increase (Ariel, Farrar & Sutherland, 2015; Baker, 2021; Gooding, 2017; Hatungimana, 2022; Jones, 2017; Maule, 2017; Normore & Scott, 2021; M. Wilcox, personal communication, September 21, 2022; M. Wilcox, personal communication, September 23, 2022). This usually leads to more hostility in encounters as well as more incidents (M. Wilcox, personal communication, September 21, 2022; M. Wilcox, personal communication, September 23, 2022). The solution to this issue is for police officers to be cognizant of their emotions, their beliefs and their biases and take account each day before they even attempt to put that uniform on (Murray & Haberfield, 2021). For example, Na'im Akbar and Booby Wright who are psychologists note the effects that Eurocentric values and mentalities have on Black people or POCs in general (Hilton, 2011). With that being said, these mentalities are projected onto Black people and other people of color from White/Caucasian people (Hilton, 2011). The natural extension of that, especially seeing that many police officers are White males is that they may also project these denigrating attitudes and/or possess and unconsciously exude these hegemonic effects, which also increases tension. This is especially the case since police officers are a product of their environment (Maule, 2017). Therefore, attending community events in support is positive and a step towards change, but the first change must come from within.

Figure 5. Picture of the five communities placard describing the artwork at the National Law Enforcement Museum in Washington, D.C. on March 12, 2022
Source: Janelle Christine Simmons, Ed.D. © 2022.

Figure 6. Picture depicting community policing in one of the five communities at the National Law Enforcement Museum in Washington, D.C. on March 12, 2022
Source: Janelle Christine Simmons, Ed.D. © 2022.

Fourth, community policing is a topic that continues to be discussed and questioned (Xu, Fiedler & Flaming, 2005). Unlike the traditional style of policing, community policing introduced a new form of policing (Murray & Haberfield, 2021; Potter, n.d.). Traditionally, policing involved recognizing that police officers were law enforcement agents (Xu, Fiedler & Flaming, 2005). This type of policing was "incident-oriented" (Xu, Fiedler & Flaming, 2005, p. 153). Their role is to intercept crimes (Xu, Fiedler & Flaming, 2005). Due to this, it was difficult to stay that the average police officer in that context is able to establish "healthy" relationships (Glaser & Denhardt, 2009). This is especially the case when officers were known to be overly aggressive at events like protests with the aim of breaking them up instead of listening (Baker, 2021). This is also especially the case when it came to the Black community (Baker, 2021; National Law Enforcement Museum, personal communication, March 12, 2022).

Ironically, events like these led to the police force trying to change and to address the community in a unique way, which led to community policing change(s) (Murray & Haberfield, 2021; National Law Enforcement Museum, personal communication, March 12, 2022). What is community policing? "[C] ommunity policing takes a more comprehensive approach and embraces the more inclusive concept, the quality of life, as the ultimate goal of policing" (Xu, Fiedler & Flaming, 2005, p. 150). It is considered to be a more proactive form of policing where crimes are prevented rather than intercepted (Xu, Fiedler & Flaming, 2005). It looks at regular citizens as being co-producers who are coproducing safe and healthy communities with low crime (Glaser & Denhardt, 2005). It is based on the premise the "public safety is best achieved when police and community members work together to solve problems" (Glaser & Denhardt, 2005, pgs. 309-310). Through trust and the belief that citizens bound by sociographic neighborhoods have a personal stake in their neighborhoods, it is thought that crimes can be prevented and not just solved (Glaser & Denhardt, 2005; Murray & Haberfield, 2021).

How community policing is to be measured is questionable (Murray & Haberfield, 2021). There are still various debates on its efficiency or efficacy (Xu, Fiedler & Flaming, 2005). After all, Crimestats or Compstats are not a particularly accurate measure of how police are performing their duties (Xu, Fiedler & Flaming, 2005). Moreover, it has not been determined that community policing gone past its initial stage in meeting its goal (Murray & Haberfield, 2021; Xu, Fiedler & Flaming, 2005). Xu, Fiedler & Flaming (2005) put it like this: "Although many believe that community policing has advanced beyond the defining stage, its ability to meet its goal remains largely untested (Sadd & Grinc, 1996) [...]" (p. 148). Nonetheless, it is clear that Glaser & Denhardt (2005) have established the author's basic belief, which is as follows: "effective implementation of community policing not only requires policy and organizational change, at its core, it is a 'battle for the hearts and minds of officers" (p. 310). Clearly, if the community policing model has been cited as being ineffective (Murray & Haberfield, 2021), it would appear that is because the "hearts and the minds of officers" (Glaser & Denhardt, 2005, p. 310) have not been won over in over 40 years.

Fifth, much of the policy that has been established for the police force is flawed (Ariel, Farrar & Sutherland, 2015). Policies differ from precinct to precinct, from locale to locale and from state to state. Some of the policy is addressed in manuals such as police manuals (City of New York, 2022). And some policies have been adjusted such as the implementation of programs like community policing (Glaser & Denhardt, 2005; Murray & Haberfield,

2021; National Law Enforcement Museum, personal communication, March 12, 2022). Nonetheless, what is written is not always followed, and some policies leaves for loopholes. This must be addressed from the brass as well as from legislative bodies.

Sixth, while there has been debate about the benefits of police using body cams, it appears that there have been positive outcomes from said use (Ariel, Farrar & Sutherland, 2021) and that they are a positive solution to the conversation of police brutality and misconduct (Baker, 2021; Lyle & Esmail, 2016; Murray & Haberfield, 2021; Normore & Scott, 2021). When police officers utilize body cams, they tend to use less force and there are less complaints about police regarding police misconduct (Ariel, Farrar & Sutherland, 2015; Lyle & Esmail, 2016; Normore & Scott, 2021). It also tends to reduce or prevent the act of racial profiling as was seen in Manhattan – NYPD since 2013 (Ariel, Farrar & Sutherland, 2015).

The use of body cams leads to more transparency for police officers in the field overall (Ariel, Farrar & Sutherland, 2015; Lyle & Esmail, 2016). In other words, police legitimacy is enhanced (Ariel, Farrar & Sutherland, 2015) while said officers are being held accountable for their actions or lack thereof (Lyle & Esmail, 2016). They have been used to keep police officers accountable for their interactions with the public, especially during stops and arrests (Lyle & Esmail, 2016). Moreover, it appears to be a win-win situation for the police because it also allows them to improve their process of evidence collection (Ariel, Farrar & Sutherland, 2015). Therefore, this increases their rates of prosecution (Ariel, Farrar & Sutherland, 2015). It may also lead to higher reporting rates of incidents. In 2015, 20% of lethal police killings were not even disclosed (Lyle & Esmail, 2016). They only cost approximately $1,000 per body cam (Lyle & Esmail, 2016) and with this small investment, there may be less headaches for police officers, police departments, citizens as well as the actors of the criminal justice system.

Solutions to Police Brutality and Misconduct: From the Courthouse and the Legislative

Houses

As was aforementioned, throughout this book, there have been many times that Blacks have sought remedies (Baker, 2021), and legal remedies from the court (Chestnut, 2008). With that being said there is no reason to stop seeking such remedies when the court of public opinion fails. There are established laws, bills, and amendments, which allow for jurisprudence to take place (Ariel, Farrar & Sutherland, 2015; Brown, 2020; Levine, 2016; Maule, 2017; Smith, 2021). From cases like Dred Scott to Brown v. Board of Education, Black Americans/African Americans sought legal remedies. Sometimes they lost but other times they won (Smith, 2021).

Nonetheless, when it comes to police brutality and misconduct cases, due process is often a flawed process (Baker, 2021; Levine, 2016; Normore & Scott, 2021). There are issues with everything from grand juries to police testimony (Levine, 2016). In fact, Levine (2016) suggests that "grand juries should be treated as evidence-weighing bodies, rather than prosecutorial rubber stamps (p. 750). Issues with the length of trials are another issue (Levine, 2016). Nonetheless, regardless of the issues, there needs to be a rehauling of the system. The criminal justice system has always been a flawed one (Baker, 2021; M. Jacobs, personal communication, August 27, 2021).

Figure 7. Quote about the purpose of the law, George Mason University School of Law
Source: Janelle Christine Simmons, Ed.D. © 2019.

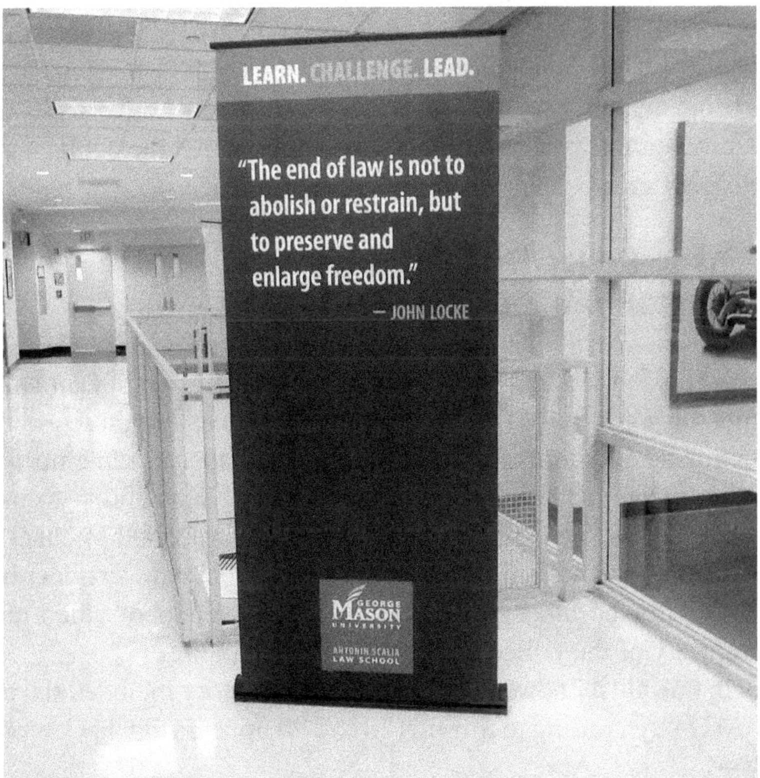

The fact that there are multiple amendments that refer to due process should indicate how important it was to the Founding Fathers. The 14th Amendment of 1868 noted that due process was to be equally protected under the law (Smith, 2021; University of Minnesota Human Rights Library, n.d.). The 4th Amendment discusses that the act of excessive force violates one's rights under the auspices of the Constitution of the United States as well (Brown, 2020; Maule, 2017). It is also necessary to know that police are not to engage in cruel and unusual punishment (Brown, 2020; Levine, 2016; Maule, 2017).

Due process for citizens who complain about police misconduct or cases of police brutality is often disrupted by the lack of cooperation from the "men in blue" (Baker, 2021; Davis, 2021; Levine, 2016). As aforementioned, police tend to refuse to testify (i.e., pleading the 5th Amendment, which is their right) (Levine, 2016). It is also the right of citizens not to be forced to self-incriminate and to have their Miranda rights read (Brown, 2020; Levine, 2016). Not only do these issues exist, but the issue of collusion exists within the police force (Levine, 2016; Maule, 2017).

Police officers sometimes have been found to collude and concoct a fraudulent statement, which is a crime (Levine, 2016); Maule, 2017). Often, even though the victims/suspects were killed without any evidence of any type of weapon, prosecutors refuse to charge officers (Levine, 2016). This is most likely because of their working relationship and the need to have police officers bring evidence for them to be able to prosecute other cases (Levine, 2016). However, this probably adds to the mistrust that the public has for not only police officers but for the entire criminal justice system.

Solutions to Police Brutality and Misconduct: From the Citizens

The average citizen can address police brutality and misconduct in a myriad of ways. First, in NYC, the MTA has a motto that states: "If you see something, say something." Well, the author is asking the reader to remember that "If they see something or hear something, record it." This ability to use one's phone to record has shed light on cases like Eric Garner and Michael Brown. Moreover, other countries like Nigeria note that police misconduct has been able to be addressed more readily because of such acts of video recording the impropriety of the police force (Hatungimana, 2022).

Second, one must know the history and this history includes slave patrols (Baker, 2021). According to Spruill (2016), "It appears that law enforcement reformers have little interest or at a minimum, limited understanding of how slave patrolling influences present-day police operations in Black neighborhoods and how this knowledge may play a constructive role in conversation about resolving conflict between police officers and black citizens" (p. 43). However, for those who do know, it may assist them with their duties as modern-day police officers. Specific to African Americans throughout the United States, and for Africans and Blacks worldwide (Baker, 2021); there is something called the gorilla effect, which leads to the dehumanization of Africans and Black people (Jones, 2017). What many officers may not be aware of is that for those who know their history; "knowing Black history [helped to mediate] racial differences in perceptions of racial discrimination" (Jones, 2017, p. 878). Seeing that racial discrimination is related to racial profiling, this would also help in reducing the act of racial profiling.

Third, by protesting and using various forms of resistance with the goal of it being peaceful, people have altered societies. There are many ways to protest and there are many ways to honor protest. In the photo below, the Accidental Talmudist (n.d.) brought reference to the historical necessity of walking next to one's brother regardless of color, race, or religion. Jim Letherer walked ~54 miles from Selma to Montgomery in 1965 in support of the civil rights of his fellow man (National Museum of African American History and Culture – Smithsonian, n.d.).

Figure 8. Picture of Jim Letherer walking 50 miles during the Civil Rights Movement to fight for the rights of the African American and other underdogs, 1965
Source: Facebook of the Accidental Talmudist, Date Unknown.

Others protested such as entertainers (Belafonte & Shnayerson, 2011). Attorneys like Gandhi protested through hunger strikes (M. Jacobs, personal communication, August 27, 2021; M. Wilcox, personal communication, September 21, 2022). We have also seen modern-day protests such as the various protests that were organized by BLM (Basu, 2020; Lyle & Esmail, 2016; Normore & Scott, 2021). Through protest, the whole citizenry learns about an issue(s), and they are able to find ways to address it if they so choose.

Fourth, is the roots of protest, which is activism. In 1967, the communities on the border of Grosse Pointe did not want African American living in their communities due to fear of riots and the like (Vrieland, 2022). The Grosse Pointe Human Relations Council was formed, and King was invited to speak (Grosse Point Historical Society, n.d.; Vrieland, 2022). Despite various protests and obstacles, King made it to Grosse Pointe and spoke on March

14, 1968 - only three weeks before he was to be assassinated (Grosse Point Historical Society, n.d.; Vrieland, 2022). Just as King went to Gross Pointe to fight for fair practices in housing (Vrieland, 2022), African Americans and all others who believe that police brutality is a stain on our democracy need to and should do the same.

This book does not address fair housing issues. This book is addressing an ill that if it continues to exist could be much greater, police brutality. The question the author poses is this: What can be done? What role should activists play in our modern society? What is the best way to advocate for fair treatment, and human rights as a citizen of the country that has promised to protect your rights and not to infringe upon your livelihood? There are a number of ways that this issue can be addressed. One way is through artistic displays. Another way is through educational programs such as conferences. In the Spring of 2014, John Jay College held their its yearly conference called Left Forum. During that conference I heard several people speak such as Harry Belafonte and Angela Davis. I like the others were able to absorb wisdom from our elders who had been activists the better part of their lives.

Figure 9. Alice Walker quote about activism. Michigan State University, East Lansing, MI
Source: Janelle Christine Simmons, Ed.D. © 2019

Harry Belafonte has been referred to already (Belafonte & Shnayerson, 2011). Angela Davis, however, had not been. Angela Yvonne Davis was/ is known for her affiliation with the Communist Party as well as the Black Panther Party (The U.S. National Archives and Records Administration, n.d.). She had been held in prison for crimes that had been committed with her weapons with the trial beginning in 1970 (The U.S. National Archives and Records Administration, n.d.). After one year she was freed. She continued to be an activist and became a professor at the University of California (The U.S. National Archives and Records Administration, n.d.). She has long advocated for the abolishment of prison systems/prisons (The U.S. National Archives and Records Administration, n.d.), which would solve the issue of mass incarceration at exceedingly high rates for people of color within the United States (Normore & Scott, 2021).

During the Left Forum conference, I walked up to her to thank her for her part in the struggle. Please note: I am not a Communist party member by any stretch of the imagination. She spoke to a friend and then turned back to speak to me. (See https://rosalux.nyc/events/left-forum-2014/).

Figure 10. Picture of Angela Davis, activist at John Jay College's Left Forum Conference from May 30, 2014 to June 1, 2014
Source: Janelle Christine Simmons. © 2014

Figure 11. Picture of Angela Davis and I at the Left Forum Conference at John Jay College of Criminal Justice in New York City. (2014)
Source: Unknown. Stranger. © 2014

Fifth, another solution/recommendation is that of monument and memorial/honor and remembrance. Creating monuments (e.g., statues), museums, and other institutions of remembrance build a legacy for the person's family and for the whole community (M. Jacobs, personal communication, August 27. 2021; M. Wilcox, personal communication, September 21, 2022; M. Wilcox, personal communication, September 23, 2022).

Figure 12. Picture of the entrance of the Eugenie Blake Memorial Jazz Institute and Cultural Center, Baltimore, Maryland (2019)
Source: Janelle Christine Simmons, Ed.D. © 2019.

African Americans have decided to move forward by honoring their ancestors, honoring their history, and working towards acts, just like organizations like the Equal Justice Initiative (2022), which is led by Bryan Stevenson who founded the initiative in 1989. He is not only an attorney but also wrote *Just Mercy*, which became a famous movie (Equal Justice Initiative, 2022). EJI works to advocate for public interests in four primary areas or arenas, which are as follows: criminal justice reform, museum and memorial, public education, and racial justice. Within the realm of memorial(s), there have been a number of initiatives.

The EJI worked on establishing the Legacy Museum: from Enslavement to Mass Incarceration (Museum (eji.org) and the National Memorial for Peace and Justice (Memorial (eji.org) (Equal Justice Initiative, 2022). While the museum focuses on depicting and historicizing slavery being converted to a system of mass incarceration (Equal Justice Initiative, 2022); the National Memorial charts the violence and historical markers and the story of lynchings throughout the United States of America (Equal Justice Initiative, 2022). In utilizing memorial, this organization hopes to change the association and the correlational relationship that was expressed by slavery and jail and prison sentences as well as lynchings, and monuments throughout the United States. According to Dr. Andrea Douglas (2022), the EJI found a relationship had existed between the areas of the United States that had the highest lynchings and monuments in those towns and cities that depicted the South's heroes such as Robert E. Lee (AARP Virginia, 2022). This fact was established in 2015 (AARP Virginia, 2022).

For example, one man by the name of John Henry James was lynched near Charlottesville, VA or allegedly raping a White woman on July 12, 1898. Stories like these were/are revisited and the legality of the story as well as the unjust punishment are discussed and shed in the light of justice (AARP Virginia, 2022). Outside of lynchings, some African Americans, usually males were just falsely imprisoned. Bryan Stephenson, a Harvard University trained defense attorney defended poor or indigent clients in the south and came across the case of Walter McMillian, who was sitting on death row and wound up being innocent and the story was depicted in a major motion picture film (AARP Virginia, 2022; Bing Images, 2022; IMDb, 2022).

Figure 13. Picture of the book cover of Just Mercy, which was written by Bryan Stevenson
Source: Bing Images (2022).

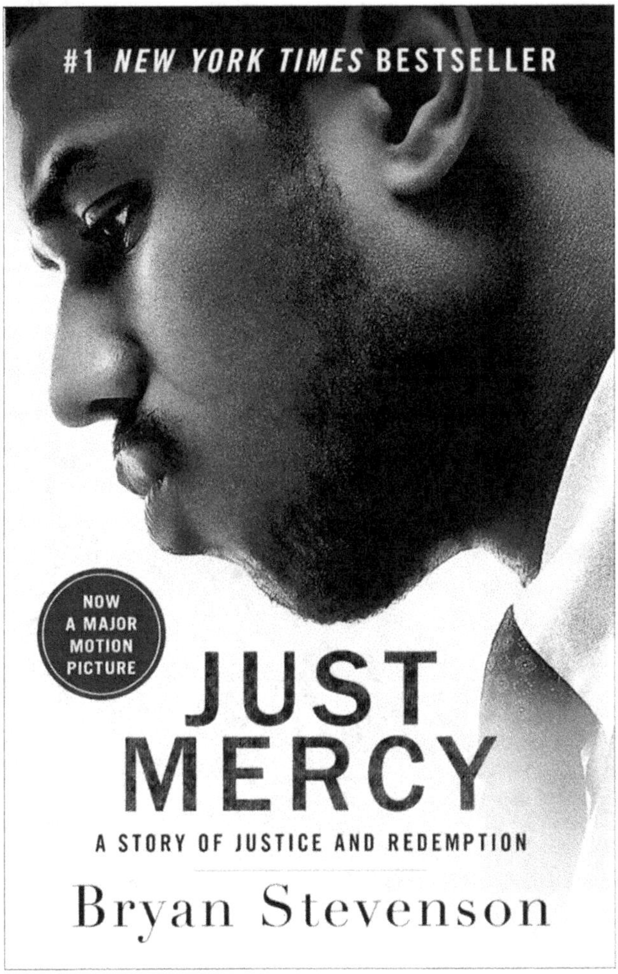

Figure 14. Cover of the movie named Just Mercy
Source: Bing Images. (2022).

Figure 15. Picture of a placard where Café Society use to stand, New York, NY (2019)
Source: Janelle Christine Simmons, Ed.D. © 2019

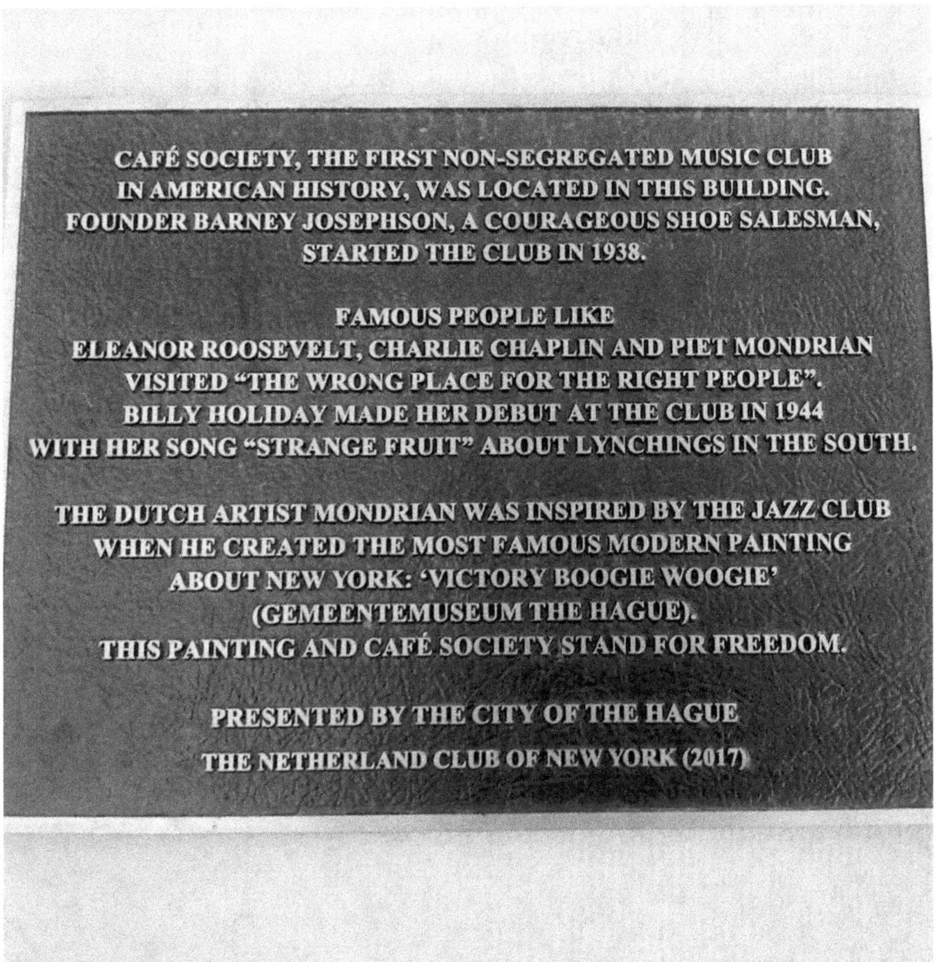

Sixth, a secondary form of education, memory and protest is that of artistic expression. The arts and music have led to various forms of resistance. There are many forms of artistic expression that have galvanized the masses to take a stand such as art, music, and poetry. One form of protest that seems to resonate with people at a greater pace appears to be music (Simmons, 2014). A prime example of an artist who continues to push the envelope is Locksmith. He recently released a song titled "Lemme Breathe," which was the cry of George Floyd and many others. For the full lyrics, refer to Appendix A.

Figure 16. Sticker/Artwork about shaming racists, Brooklyn, NY (2019)
Source: Janelle Christine Simmons, Ed.D. © 2019.

Figure 17. Mural on Callowhill Avenue and 3rd Street of Philadelphia, PA
Photographer: Janelle Christine Simmons, Ed.D. © 2022
Source: "The History of Immigration" – Mural by the Philadelphia Anti-Graffiti Network © 1993

Solutions to Police Brutality and Misconduct: From the Organizations/Movements

The United Nations

The United Nations, a human rights organization has stood up against police brutality (Kuumba, 2021; Worland, 2014). In fact, the United Nations has criticized the police force within the United States for repeated acts of police brutality (Kuumba, 2021; Worland, 2014). Part of the reasoning for said behavior was the existence of institutionalized discrimination that exists within America (Worland, 2014) as well as systemic racism in the United States and worldwide (Kuumba, 2021). This organization began investigating more reports of police brutality around November 2015 and decided to return to the issue on a semi-yearly basis (Kuumba, 2021). Much of the police brutality that was researched, reported (i.e., via testimony) was regarding police abuse, brutality and violence that affects Black people around the world (Kuumba, 2021). They also noted that this leads to mistrust for the justice system (Worland, 2014). This mistrust continues to be an issue for the Black community within the United States (Baker, 2021), and throughout the Europeanized world.

Figure 18. Picture of the Route to Human Rights: An International Solidarity for Human Rights Project as seen in Miami, Florida. (May 2, 2022)
Source: Janelle Christine Simmons, Ed.D. © 2022

Figure 19. Picture of the Route to Human Rights: An International Solidarity for Human Rights Project as seen in Miami, Florida. (May 2, 2022)
Source: Janelle Christine Simmons, Ed.D. © 2022

BLM

One movement that has taken the world by storm is the Black Lives Matter Movement better known as BLM (Baker, 2021; Basu, 2020; Lyle & Esmail, 2016; Normore & Scott, 2021). The Black Lives Movement, despite of the controversy surrounding it – is a "[...] decentralized political and social movement protesting incident of police brutality and all racially motivated violence against Black people" (Normore & Scott, 2021, p. 2). This movement has brought more recognition and has placed a spotlight on black deaths in custody (Lyle & Esmail, 2016; Normore & Scott, 2021). Nonetheless, the issue racist policing and of Black Deaths in custody continues within America (Baker, 2021; Cha-Jua, 2014; Davis, 2021).

Figure 20. Picture of a BLM protest
Source: Basu (2020).

Universities

Colleges and universities are institutions of higher education. Within those institutions, some of the brightest and best are being trained to fill positions that require "knowing." Not only are there various majors, minors, and other educational events but such institutions can use their position to remember, celebrate and teach all at the same time. At the author's alma mater, John Jay College of Criminal Justice holds an event known as the John Jay Medal for Justice. It celebrates those who use their position to be activists for change and to fight for civil rights around the world.

Earlier in this book, Harry Belafonte and his friendship with Martin Luther King, Jr. is discussed as they both fought against civil rights infringements when it came to the Black man (Belafonte & Shnayerson, 2011). People like Harry Belafonte used their status as entertainers in order to not only protest, but to fly to and fund various acts of trainings and protest (Belafonte & Shnayerson, 2011). It is for the work that he did during the Civil Rights Movement through the 21st century that he was honored by my alma mater, John Jay College of Criminal Justice.

Figure 21. Harry Belafonte poses with the Board of John Jay College of Criminal Justice in New York City
Source: Janelle Christine Simmons, Ed.D. (Then known as Janelle Christine Simmons). **© 2012**

Figure 22. Harry Belafonte and I on the stage of John Jay College of Criminal Justice
Source: Janelle Christine Simmons, Ed.D. (Then known as Janelle Christine Simmons). © 2012

CONCLUSION

Though it is innately human to resist total domination and barbaric treatment by others, slaves' aspirations to change their status and condition made them a threat to whites from every socio-economic class. Slave resistance was expressed in theft of crops and livestock, arson, poisoning, plotting uprisings and running away. They were an ominous peril to white livelihoods and security and considered most dangerous in areas where they approached numerical majorities. That resistance came from watching the superiority of African civilization being dismantled by the Europeans while Europeans dehumanized and de-culturated[2] the Black man and woman as Dr. Henrik Clarke would have attested to if here. That Manichean color line still exists today through microaggression and acts of discrimination that are linked to racism that tends to be systemic and institutionalized.

That color line leads to a perpetual conflict. The foes fight to prove they are better, healthier, richer than the other. It is subtle but it is there. However, that would have been fine enough until African Americans and people of color worldwide watched their neighbors, their friends and their family members being gunned down like dogs in their home and in the streets. Thus, the author and the reader have to come to a number of conclusions about what has been presented juxtaposed to what they have read and then determine what will be done about it at present.

In conclusion, this chapter was quite meaty. There were a number of issues to unpack and to discuss. Mainly the solutions and recommendations proffered were not only for the police departments throughout the United States and around the world, but for the Legal System, towards Legislators, towards institutions and organizations as well as every other citizens of the United States. This chapter was focused on introducing and examining solutions to social justice issues. In Chapter 7, social justice issues were examined. While there was not a perfect match in response to the issues discussed in Chapter 7, many of those issues were addressed. The truth is that there were too many to mention.

Nonetheless, this chapter was set up with an introduction and then a further discussion of the previous issues through the solutions that were proffered. The chapter was sub-divided between how the community can bring light to said issues of injustice as various forms of solutions as well as how the police and other legal actors (e.g., judges, prosecutors, legislators, etc.) could address injustices from within their organizations and through mediations, the courts, etc. Also, injustices that could be addressed by organizations/institutions as well as universities as institutions of higher learning were addressed.

The bulk of this chapter looked at re-examining the issues that have been discussed throughout this book. In re-examining said issues, the author hoped to build a solid case for the proffered solutions. Solutions such as training to prevent a militarized police force, body cams, reforming legislation and addressing due process flaws, protest, police reform, community building, a reduction in undercover cops, especially in places of worship; etc. were either touched upon in a brief introduction or introduced and discussed thoroughly. It is the author's hope that local police forces will be able to have a heart change that leads to a change in procedure, in policy and in "protecting and serving" the public. Most citizens are not the enemies of the police forces, however, after years of injustice; they often question whether they can trust the police. This is unfortunate, because while police officers are sworn officers of the law; they are in a partnership with their neighbors, their communities, and the communities they serve. Without the everyday citizen, it is almost impossible for any police officer to get the job done. Let it be that we are able to sharpen each other and create a safe, healthy and happy community and duplicate that in every community within the United States and beyond.

"Iron sharpeneth iron; so a man sharpeneth the countenance of his friend."
– Proverbs 27:17

REFERENCES

Ariel, B., Farrar, W. A., & Sutherland, A. (2015). The effect of police body-worn cameras on use of force and citizens' complaints against the police: A randomized controlled trial. *Journal of Quantitative Criminology*, *31*(3), 509–535. doi:10.100710940-014-9236-3

Baker, E. (2021, May 20). *Police brutality: An epidemic in America.* SDU. https://sites.sandiego.edu/blackhistoryatusd/2021/05/20/police-brutality-an-epidemic-in-america/

Basu, A. (2020, July 21). Black lives matter: US workers stage nationwide strike against racial injustice. *News 24 Online.* https://news24online.com/news/world/black-lives-matter-us-workers-stage-nationwide-strike-against-racial-injustice-697f313e/

Brown, C., Esq. (2020, November 30). *What amendment does police brutality violate?* Brown Firm. https://www.brownfirmpllc.com/what-amendment-does-police-brutality-violate/

Cha-Jua, S. K. (2014, Spring). We believe it was murder: Mobilizing black resistance to police brutality in Champaign, Illinois. *The Black Scholar, 44*(1), 58–85. doi:10.1080/00064246.2014.11641212

City of New York. (2022). *New York patrol guide.* NYC Gov. https://www1.nyc.gov/site/ccrb/investigations/nypd-patrol-guide.page#:~:text=The%20NYPD%27s%20Patrol%20Guide%20contains%20the%20rules%20that,must%20follow%20in%20carrying%20out%20their%20official%20duties

Columbia University Center for Teaching and Learning. (n.d.). *The autobiography of Malcolm X: Speeches and interviews.* CUCTL. https://ccnmtl.columbia.edu/projects/mmt/mxp/speeches/mxt29.html

Community Oriented Policing Services. (2014). *Community policing defined.* USDOJ. https://cops.usdoj.gov/RIC/Publications/cops-p157-pub.pdf#:~:text=Community%20policingis%20a%20philosophy%20that%20promotes%20organizational%20strategies,of%20crime.%20Community%20policing%20comprises%20three%20key%20components%3A

Davis, D. L. (2021). From the field: Why I founded black cops against police brutality. *Journal of Ethnicity in Criminal Justice, 19*(3-4), 201–222. doi:10.1080/15377938.2021.1979159

Equal Justice Initiative. (2022). *About EJI.* EJI. https://eji.org/about/

Fulbright, L. (2000, March 6). *"Wanted: Female cops."* file:///C:/Users/janel/OneDrive/Desktop/Publications/Examining%20Black%20Deaths%20in%20Custody%20-%202022/Women_may_be_solution_to_polic.pdf.

Glaser, M. A., & Denhardt, J. (2009, August 5). Community policing and community building: A case study of officer perception. *American Review of Public Administration*, *40*(3), 309–325. doi:10.1177/0275074009340050

Gooding, P. (2017). The government is the cause of the disease, and we are stuck with the symptoms: Deinstitutionalization, mental health advocacy and police shootings in 1900s Victoria. *Continuum (Perth)*, *31*(3), 436–446. doi:10.1080/10304312.2016.1275146

Grosse Point Historical Society. (n.d.). *Dr. Martin Luther King's 1968 speech at Grosse Pointe High School.* GP Historical Society. http://gphistorical.org/mlk/index.htm

IMDb. (2022). *Just mercy.* IMDb. https://www.imdb.com/title/tt4916630/

John Jay College of Criminal Justice. (2012). *Harry Belafonte, Dr. Hawa Abdi, Vivian Nixon and the late justice William O. Douglas to receive 2012 John Jay medal for justice.* John Jay College. http://johnjay.jjay.cuny.edu/newsroom/5715.php

Kuumba, C. (2021, February 14). *The United Nations follow-up on police brutality and abuse.* Bing. https://www.bing.com/search?q=united+nations+and+police+brutality&cvid=03773022b10848cf991013caa37b8d2b&aqs=edge.69i57j69i64.40944j0j1&pglt=2211&FORM=ANNTA1&PC=HCTS

Magnolia Pictures. (2017, January 5). *I am not your negro: Official trailer.* Bing. https://www.bing.com/videos/search?q=I+Am+Not+Your+Negro&docid=608001557737573582&mid=EE7CB61FA93C401B7FB1EE7CB61FA93C401B7FB1&view=detail&FORM=VIREHT

Murray, K. R., & Haberfield, M. R. (2021). *Use of force training in law enforcement: A reality based approach.* Springer. doi:10.1007/978-3-030-59880-8

National Museum of African-American History and Culture - Smithsonian. (n.d.). *Jim Letherer, Selma to Montgomery march.* NMAAHC. https://nmaahc.si.edu/object/nmaahc_2015.129.58

Peck, R. (Director/Producer). 2017. *I am not your negro.* [Film]. Magnolia Pictures and Amazon Studios.

Potter, G. (n.d.). *The history of policing in the United States*. file:///C:/Users/janel/Desktop/Publications/Examining%20Black%20Deaths%20in%20Custody%20-%202022/The%20History%20of%20Policing%20in%20the%20United%20States.GaryPotter.8.22.2021.pdf.

Shaer, M. (2013, September 30). 134 minutes with Frank Serpico – NY Magazine: A Hudson troll with the NYPD's most famous whistle-blower and aging Casanova. *NY Magazine*. https://nymag.com/news/intelligencer/encounter/frank-serpico-2013-10

Simmons, J. C. (2014, May 30-June 1). *Seeing evil, hearing evil, speaking good: Social media as a tool for transformative justice*. [Conference presentation]. Left Forum, New York, NY.

Smith, W. (2021, February 17). *Amend: The fight for America*. [Net Series]. Netflix.

Spruill, L. H. (2016). Slave patrols, "Pack of Negro dogs," and policing Black communities. *Phylon*, *53*(1), 42–66.

Statutes and Stories. (2022). Enforcement of the fourteenth amendment. *Statues and Stories*. https://www.statutesandstories.com/blog_html/the-ku-klux-klan-act-of-1871/

The U.S. National Archives and Records Administration. (n.d.). *Angela Davis (January 26, 1944)*. US National Archives. https://www.archives.gov/research/african-americans/individuals/angela-davis

Thompson, B. C. (1958, September 25). Screen: A forceful social drama; 'The Defiant Ones' has debut at Victoria. *New York Times*. https://www.nytimes.com/1958/09/25/archives/screen-a-forceful-social-drama-the-defiant-ones-has-debut-at.html

Virginia, A. A. R. P. (2022). *Sunday sit-ins with AARP Virginia and Richmond ASALH*. [Video]. Youtube. https://www.youtube.com/watch?v=JQATlH1lRWE

Vrieland, D. (2022). *Dr. King comes to Grosse Pointe*. Academia Letters. *Article*, *4541*. doi:10.20935/AL4541

Weatherby, W. J. (1989). *James Baldwin: Artist on fire*. Dell Publishing.

Worland, J. (2014, November 28). U.S. panel sharply criticizes police brutality in US. *Time.* https://time.com/3609811/police-brutality-united-states-un-ferguson-torture

Xu, V., Fiedler, M.L. & Flaming, K.H. (2005, May 1). Discovering the impact of community policing: The broke windows thesis. Collective efficacy, & citizens' judgment. *Journal of Research in Crime and Delinquency, 42*(2), 147-186. . doi:10.1177/0022427804266544

KEY TERMS AND DEFINITIONS

Equal Justice Initiative: An organization that fights to put an end to excessive forms of punishment and mass incarceration. Founded by Bryan Stevenson in 1989. See https://eji.org/about-eji/.

Institutionalized Discrimination: Unfair and unequal treatment that is usually hidden that operates or group membership and affects institutions on a daily basis.

Lynching: The killing of a person usually by a mob and usually the person(s) dies by hanging. An act that was commonplace down South and the punishment for perceived slights that Black people, usually did by White people.

Monument(s): any structure, usually a building or a statue used to commemorate a person, etc.

Parable: a moral or spiritual insight usually hidden and told within a story.

Public Spaces: any area such as an alleyway, a street, a park, etc. that is in the public and accessible to the public.

ENDNOTES

1. Also referenced at/through Goodreads.com. Goodreads, Inc. (2023). *James Baldwin: Quotes.* Retrieved on April 15, 2023 from https://www.goodreads.com/quotes/9023663-the-root-of-the-black-man-s-hatred-is-rage-and.
2. De-culturated – Term coined by the author. The act of the colonizer or an oppressor stripping the colonized or oppressed of their culture. It is almost like they are depleted of self.

APPENDIX A: COMPARATIVE TABLES OF SOLUTIONS (INTRODUCTION TO CONCLUSION)

Table 1(a). Part I of Comparative Solutions

Table 1: Part I of Comparative Solutions	Activism	Add Protective Laws	Art/Create Art as Memorial and Protest	Build Health and Strong Families (Black and Indigenous)	Body Cams
Introduction	--	--	--	--	--
Chapter 1: Transitioning Governments and Laws					
Chapter 2: A Comparative Analysis of Laws Amongst Western Powers through the 20th Century		X		X	
Chapter 3: Case Study: America					
Chapter 4: Case Study: Australia					
Chapter 5: Case Study: South Africa					
Chapter 6: Say Their Names					
Chapter 7: Social Justice Issues Examined	X				X
Chapter 8: An Examination of Solutions	X				X
Conclusion	X	X	X	X	X

Table 1(b). Part I of Comparative Solutions

Create Curri-culums and Toolkits	Create a Legacy	Create Memorials/ Monuments/ Museums	Create Orgs to Fight Injustice	Engage with Public (Police)	Eradicate Unjust Laws	Escape or Run
--	--	--	--	--		--
						X
	X		X			
X		X				
		X		X		
				X	X	
X	X	X	X	X	X	X

Table 2(a). Part II of Comparative Solutions

Table 2: Part II of Comparative Solutions	First Amendment (Utilize It as a Citizen)	Follow the Money (Find the Truth)	Global Community (Seek International Assistance)	Hiring and Training Process (Change/ Adapt)	Hold Gov't Account-able
Introduction	--	--	--	--	--
Chapter 1: Transition-ing Governments and Laws					
Chapter 2: A Comparative Analysis of Laws Amongst Western Powers through the 20th Century					
Chapter 3: Case Study: America					
Chapter 4: Case Study: Australia					
Chapter 5: Case Study: South Africa		X	X		
Chapter 6: Say Their Names					
Chapter 7: Social Justice Issues Examined	X				X
Chapter 8: An Examination of Solutions	X			X	
Conclusion	X	X	X	X	X

Table 2(b). Part II of Comparative Solutions

ID Problem and Form Solution	Know the History/ About Slave Patrols	Look at and to Movements, Universities, etc.	Maintain Tribal Law	Need Formal Education (Police)	Neutral Orgs
--	--	--	--	--	--
			X		
X					
					X
				X	
	X	X		X	
X	X	X	X	X	X

Table 3(a). Part III of Comparative Solutions

Table 3: Part III of Comparative Solutions	Open Dialogue (Maintain)	Protest/ Revolt	Publicize Civil Rights Injustices	Question and Address	Question The Rate/#/ of Black Deaths in Custody	Re-Address Police Dept.'s Hiring Process
Introduction	--	--	--	--		--
Chapter 1: Transition-ing Governments and Laws		X				
Chapter 2: A Comparative Analysis of Laws Amongst Western Powers through the 20th Century		X				
Chapter 3: Case Study: America			X			
Chapter 4: Case Study: Australia	X				X	
Chapter 5: Case Study: South Africa		X				
Chapter 6: Say Their Names		X				
Chapter 7: Social Justice Issues Examined		X		X		X
Chapter 8: An Examination of Solutions		X		X		X
Conclusion	--	--	--	--	--	--

Table 3(b). Part III of Comparative Solutions

Remodify Behavior	Report Crimes/ Police Brutality	Seek to Under-stand	Spiritual Rest	Train New Black/ Indigenous Attorneys	Under-stand History and Culture	World Leaders (No False Apologies)
--	--	--	--	--		
				X		
						X
		X			X	
	X					
X			X			
X	X					
--	--	--	--	--	--	--

Conclusion

"Throughout life people will make you mad

Disrespect you and treat you bad

Let God deal with the things they do

Cause hate in your heart will consume you too." – Will Smith, Just the Two of Us (1997)

This chapter focuses on reviewing what has been introduced, discussed, analyzed, fleshed out and established as narrative and fact throughout the length of this book. The author has introduced the reality of the transatlantic slave trade in the Introduction with six points. Then transitioning governments with countries such as America, Australia and South Africa are discussed briefly. Finally, a comparative analysis of laws amongst western points through the 20th century tasks place. Then case studies are introduced of each country for a further analysis of the issues. Finally, an examination of the names of many victims of Black Deaths in Custody are introduced with the purpose of further examining social justice issues and deriving solutions.

INTRODUCTION

The precursor to freedom for the colonized, was colonization and other forms of slavery (Baker, 2021; Fanon, 2008; Hilton, 2011; Smith, 2021). As noted in the first book of this two-book series as well as in the Introduction of this book, the transatlantic slave trade led to the transportation of millions of

Africans (Newtown, 1788; United Nations, 2022; Smith, 2021) – illegally – throughout Europe, parts of Africa like South Africa, Brazil, Portugal, the West Indies and finally America. The wounds from this reality continue to be felt throughout generations of families and people groups. Like a birth pang, the bell tolls for the dead.

In Chapter 1, transitioning governments and laws were discussed. How countries created new governments or adapted them as slaves were freed and land(s) was/were reapportioned are discussed. Additionally, how Blacks accrued their freedom and wealth by appeasing the White man is explored (Fanon, 2008; Hilton, 2011). Then a comparative analysis of laws takes place in Chapter 2 across Western powers during the 20th century, which explains specific laws that addressed grievances of aboriginal and Black people or BIPOC people in countries or kingdoms like America, Australia, Britain, Canada (i.e., briefly), South Africa, et al. A comparison of laws took place. The reader was able to see the development of said laws as well as laws that developed throughout the 20th century. As current citizens of the 21st century, "we" will surely see many more laws written and established will what effect – "we are unsure. Nonetheless, this comparison of laws showed us a pattern of distress as well as a pattern of progress.

From Chapters 3-5, we saw case studies of countries. America, the author's home country, Australia and South Africa were discussed. In each chapter, one could see the damage that was done to a native people and to a kidnapped people. Often these abuses of powers came from outsiders known as colonizers. These colonizers were always of European descent (Blight, 2018; Hilton, 2011; Smith, 2021). For the countries chosen as cases for this book, these countries were originally part of the British empire. As one knows, America became independent of Great Britain but still shares a "special" relationship with her. Australia still has many British and Irish descendants living within its borders and South Africa as Afrikaners and their descendants still within its borders. The richness of the narrative of each country is indispensable and informative of abuses that should NEVER be repeated! More specifically, the author will now delineate a blurb for each country, i.e., America, Australia, and South Africa.

By Chapter 3, the first Case Study begins, which is that of America. This Case Study discusses the original inhabitants, the colonization of America, the first slaves brought to the continent, and then the transition from being the New World to the United States of America. Thereafter, the end of slavery, which took place in 1865 due to the ratified 13th Amendment is (Blight, 2018; Hughes & Meltzer, 1956) introduced as well as restrictive codes known as

Black Codes, and laws known as Jim Crow laws (Alchin, 2017; Hughes & Meltzer, 1956; Irons, 2002) that were meant to control Blacks in America even after the Civil War had been won (Blight, 2018; Hughes & Meltzer, 1956; Smith, 2021). In Chapter 4, the second Case Study is introduced, and the reader learns about the colonization of Australia and its prison colonies. The reader also learned about the atrocities that the Aboriginal people endured as well as the Torres Strait Islanders (Australian Law Reform Commission, 2010; Healing Foundation, 2022). Finally, a discussion of a new government being installed, i.e., a Commonwealth Democracy and the delayed rights of a people is explained. In addition, the tool of protest is discussed regarding citizen rights and land and water rights.

In Chapter 5, the last Case Study is presented, which is that of South Africa. The Apartheid government and the continued fight for the freedom to be recognized and not oppressed was explored (M. Jacobs, personal communication, August 27, 2021; M. Wilcox, personal communication, September 21, 2022; M. Wilcox, personal communication, September 23, 2022). Police corruption and governmental corruption were also explored regarding the African continent (Hatungimana, 2022; Holland, 2011), and more specifically South Africa. The fact is that international outcries came as more and more South Africans were killed culminating with the death of Steve Biko (Biko, n.d.; M. Jacobs, personal communication, August 27, 2021; M. Wilcox, personal communication, September 21, 2022; M. Wilcox, personal communication, September 23, 2022).

Finally, specific to America, the reader is asked to say their names (Chapter 6). These names are the names of the dead. Not unlike the Jews in Warsaw (IMDb, 2022). As the Nazis had killed the Jews, so the Europeans continue to kill us (i.e., the Black man and woman and child). Thus, the author asked you to say their names, remember their stories, and fight for justice whenever you see it deprived. Remember people like Rosa Parks who said, I refuse to be separated, I am tired and worn and I need a seat just like everybody else (Hughes & Meltzer, 1956; McGovern Library and Dakota Wesleyan University, 2022). Remember the Montgomery Boycott that ensued for 381 days as Blacks throughout Alabama and that throughout America rose up. That one act of defiance by Rosa Parks to sit[3] down led people to rise up and stand and march as Rosa Parks led millions to struggle against the powers that be. Not unlike a slave called Harriet Tubman who not only said one day that enough was enough but then after garnering her freedom went back and led hundreds to freedom as well as they crossed the border into Canada (McCall Bronxwood Funeral Home, 2022).

In Chapter 7, an examination of solutions took place. Policies were introduced, discussed and in some cases critiqued. Is stop and frisk appropriate? Does community policing work? Should a woman be arrested for a routine traffic stop and wind up dead? What policy aor training can address some happenstance like this? Cases and policies were looked at and while some further solutions and recommendations were made, the author informed the reader/her audience that policies and laws cannot ensure a change of a man's heart. According to Leviticus 19:17, God informed us through Moses of the following: "Thou shalt not hate thy brother in thine heart: thou shalt in any wise rebuke they neighbor, and not suffer sin upon him." And in I John 4:20, the reader is informed of the following: Thou shalt not hate they brother in thine heart: thou shalt in any wise rebuked they neighbour, and not suffer sin upon him." For the police force to change, more than a policy change is required. They must truly look at every citizen and visitor as their brother or sister and not hide any hate in their heart. This though brought the reader and the author of this book to the conclusion of the whole matter (Chapter 8).

FINAL SOLUTIONS AND RECOMMENDATIONS: THE CULMINATION

In Chapter 1, two solutions were proffered. Due to tribalism, a self-explanatory solution was that tribes have their own governing bodies. Thus, whether one was in America (Legends of America, 2022; Petersen, 2022), Australia was tribal and had been inhabited by its native people called Aborigines (Bringing Them Home, n.d.; Chang, 2019), or South Africa (Golden, 2004; Holland, 1989; M. Jacobs, personal communication, August 27, 2021; Lynch, 1976; Noah, 2019; M. Wilcox, personal communication, September 21, 2022), M. Wilcox, personal communication, September 23, 2022; Van Vuuren, 2015). tribes had their own practices, responsibilities, and their own laws to regulate their actions, and the use of land (Chang, 2019; Legends of America, 2022; Petersen, 2022; The Arizona Board of Regents, 2022).

Second, once these tribes and tribal lands were colonized by Europeans, the tribesmen fought, and many died to re-establish their position (Petersen, 2022). Then new governments were established that promised freedom (Australian Law Reform Commission, 2022; Hughes & Meltzer, 1956; M. Jacobs, personal communication, August 27, 2021; M. Wilcox, personal communication, September 21, 2022; M. Wilcox, personal communication, September 23, 2022; Smith, 2021). Through those governments, protest came and continued (Belafonte & Shnayerson, 2022; Blight, 2018; Bringing Them Home, n.d.; M. Jacobs, personal communication, August 27, 2021; Noah, 2019; Petersen, 2022; M. Wilcox, personal communication, September 21, 2022). Protest brought about changes to the law that were more just (Belafonte & Shnayerson, 2022; Blight, 2018; Hughes & Meltzer, 1956; M. Jacobs, personal communication, August 27, 2021; Noah, 2019; M. Wilcox, personal communication, September 21, 2022; Van Vuuren, 2015).

In Chapter 2, a handful of solutions were discussed. First, there needs to be a form or rebellion against unjust laws and protest (Blight, 2018; Davis, 2021; Equal Justice Initiative, 2023; Healing Foundation, 2022; Hughes & Meltzer, 1956; Petersen, 2022; Smith, 2021). Second, specific to being enslaved, one needs to find a way to run to freedom (Blight, 2018). And more so even theoretically, one needs to find the courage to be bold, go and speak. Third, just laws need to be established (Blight, 2018; Smith, 2021) as well as practices (Baker, 2021; Blight, 2018; Hughes & Meltzer, 1956; Smith, 2021). Fourth, one needs to continue to record history (Equal Justice Initiative, 2023a; Hughes & Meltzer, 1956; Smith, 2021). Fifth, Aboriginals and Blacks and other minorities who have fought oppression and police brutality must seek to build healthy and strong families and relationships (Baker, 2021; Biko, n.d.; Fanon, 2008; Hilton, 2011; Healing Foundation, 2022).

In Chapter 3, a handful of solutions were proffered. First, one must continue to identify problems and form strategies to address the racial and systemic issues of America as a nation in totality and within other countries as well (Biko, n.d.; Blight, 2018; McGovern Library and Dakota Wesleyan University 2022). Second, one must document and publicize incidents (Biko, n.d.; Blight, 2018; Hughes & Meltzer, 1956; Smith, 2021) such as the video utilized in the George Floyd case or Tyre Nichols (See the Introduction of this book!). Third, one must create organizations to fight injustices[2] (Biko, n.d.; Equal Justice Initiative, 2023; Healing Foundation, 2022; M. Jacobs, personal communication, August 27, 2021; Smith, 2021). Organizations like the Equal Justice Initiative (Equal Justice Initiative, 2023), or even B-CAP (Davis, 2021) address legal injustices as well as issues that Black cops face to maintain justice, to serve and protect. Fourth, one must create legacies (M. Wilcox, personal communication, September 23, 2022) such as the New Legacy Museum created by EJI (Equal Justice Initiative, 2023a). This museum was created to explore slavery through mass incarceration (Equal Justice Initiative, 2023a). Fifth, the author suggests that Black attorneys be trained in specialties that address atrocities such as the Holocaust, Slave Reparations, Indigenous/Tribal laws, etc.

In Chapter 4, there are a few solutions that the author has delineated to address the Case Study of Australia. First, there needs to be an open dialogue (Healing Foundation, 2022). This is especially the case when it comes to Britain and the pre-established government of Australia during the colonization period (Australian Law Reform Commission, 2010). Third, need to hold the government accountable for past atrocities (Australian Law Reform Commission, 2010; Harrison, 2020; Healing Foundation, 2022; Trigger, 1985).

In Chapter 5, there are a myriad of solutions and recommendations that were made. First, a point about colonization is made (A. Coleman, personal communication, August 20, 2021; Golden, 2004; Holland, 1988; South African History Online, n.d; M. Wilcox, personal communication, September 21, 2022; M. Wilcox, personal communication, September 23, 2022; Spielvogel, 2014; Willoughby-Herald, 2015). Colonization must always be addressed (A. Coleman, personal communication, August 20, 2021; Spielvogel, 2014; Golden, 2004; Holland, 1988; South African History Online, n.d; M. Wilcox, personal communication, September 21, 2022; M. Wilcox, personal communication, September 23, 2022; Willoughby-Herald, 2015). Second, it is important to understand the country's history and culture and to be honest in its critique (Biko, n.d.; South African History Online, n.d.; Spielvogel, 2014; Van Vuuren, 2015; M. Wilcox, personal communication, September 21, 2022; M. Wilcox, personal communication, September 23, 2022). Third, to understand Apartheid, one must follow the money (Van Vuuren, 2015). Fourth, Apartheid systems and laws had to and must be eradicated (i.e., if there are new laws that claimed the same injustice – they must be eradicated) (Biko, n.d.; Van Vuuren, 2015). Fifth, there must always be protest (Biko, n.d.; Blight, 2018; Hughes & Meltzer, 1956; McGovern Library and Dakota Wesleyan University 2022; M. Jacobs, personal communication, August 27, 2021; Spielvogel, 2014; M. Wilcox, personal communication, September 21, 2022; M. Wilcox, personal communication, September 23, 2022). Sixth, one must reach out and mobilize the global community (Al-Jazeera Media Network, 2019; Australian Together, 2022; Biko, n.d.; Spielvogel, 2014; Van Vuuren, 2015; M. Wilcox, personal communication, September 21, 2022; M. Wilcox, personal communication, September 23, 2022).

In Chapter 6, there were approximately a handful of solutions and recommendations that the author came up with to address the issues of Black Deaths in custody. First, each community needs to flesh out the events that surrounded each Black Death in Custody (Indianapolis Public Schools, n.d.). Second, civilians need to report crimes and seek legal remedies (Holcombe,

Moshtaghian & Akbarzai, 2021; Smith, 2021). Third, memorial (i.e., a solution and recommendation that was aforementioned throughout this book) is necessary. It is imperative for one to remember (Blight, 2018). In Deuteronomy 8:11, the Israelites are told the following:

Beware that you do not forget the LORD your God by not keeping His commandments, His Judgments, and His Statues which I command you today.

While this context is religious, memorial can be religious in nature or irreligious. Nonetheless, one is called to remember an event, a chapter of history and even certain families, etc. in order to learn from those histories in some way. Fourth, protest is a continuous solution that has been proffered. Protest is necessary, especially when established laws are unjust in their own nature (Biko, n.d.; Blight, 2018; Cha-Jua, 2014; Newtown, 1788; Smith, 2021; U.S. Department of Justice, n.d.). Fifth, the author has suggested that outside of protest, spiritual rest is needed (Smith, 2021). Sixth, it is imperative to utilize neutral organizations to address civil unrest (Blight, 2018; Davis, 2021; Smith, 2021; U.S. Department of Justice, n.d.) such as was the case with Eric Garner (U.S. Department of Justice, n.d.).

In Chapter 7, there are six solutions and recommendations that the author gives to the reader. First, as a community, we must be cognizant of the 1st Amendment (Maule, 2017). Everyone has a right to say what they feel. However, there are certain characteristics that must be considered when choosing an officer for the police force (Maule, 2017) to complete certain job duties (Davis, 2021). This is especially the case when issues of racial profiling come up (Baker, 2021; Davis, 2021; Jones, 2017; Maule, 2017). Second, the author believes that the hiring process must be re-examined and there should be a "courtship." Perhaps, a community internship can be instituted. Third, the 4th Amendment must be re-examined when it comes to due process (Normore & Scott, 20121), especially when African Americans are dying due to police brutality (Baker, 2021; Normore & Scott, 2021). Fourth, some of the police policies and procedures continue to contribute to mistrust within the community (Davis, 2021). Fifth, it should be noted that community policing in schools needs to be revisited especially since Black males are still adjudicated at higher rates (Baker, 2021). These rates affect families, communities, and generational wealth. Sixth, there must be a way to address the "Blue Wall of Silence." The police force needs to address police impropriety legally (Ariel, Farrar & Sutherland, 2015; Davis, 2021; Jones, 2017; Lyle & Esmail, 2016; Kuumba, 2021; Normore & Scott, 2021;

Worland, 2014). Testimony against officers who participate in police brutality and Black Deaths in Custody needs to become a reality. Also, there needs to be remedies for those who interact with corrupt police officers or even abusive police officers such as the research completed regarding therapy in Australia (Tupper, 2021).

In Chapter 8, education for the police force is necessary (Baker, 2021; Murray & Haberfield, 2021; Normore & Scott, 2021). Hiring police officers who are well-qualified is important to the health of the police department (Harmon, 2017). Especially when it comes to addressing stress (Murray & Haberfield, 2021; Normore & Scott, 2021). Higher education needs to be an explored option (Murray & Haberfield, 2021; Normore & Scott, 2021). Part of that education after passing the Police Academy needs to be proper police training (Baker, 2021; National Law Enforcement Museum, personal communication, March 12, 2022; Normore & Scott, 2021).

Second, the police should engage with the public (M. Wilcox, personal communication, September 23, 2022) in a positive manner (Baker, 2021). While community-oriented policing was utilized (Normore & Scott, 2021); it has many flaws. "Police play a critical, but complicated, role in any free society (Harmon, 2017, p. 27). This is especially the case when it comes to the Black community (Baker, 2021; Davis, 2021; Normore & Scott, 2021).

Third, the community and more specifically the Black community has a general mistrust for the police already (Baker, 2021; Davis, 2021; Murray & Haberfield, 2021). Thus, officers need to know themselves and their own biases to address them properly (Murray & Haberfield, 2021). Not to mention that the police project their prejudices on the public and vice versa (Hilton, 2011). Officers also need to be cognizant of the public, especially minorities (Baker, 2021).

Fourth, community policing is a form of policing that was created with the public in mind (Harmon, 2017; Murray & Haberfield, 2021). However, it has been an ultimate "fail" in some arenas and its effectiveness has been questioned (Baker, 2021; Davis, 2021; Harmon 2017; Xu, Fiedler & Flamingo, 2005). Not only is this type of policing hard to determine but establishing "healthy" relationships can be difficult (Glaser & Denhardt, 2009). However, police officers can be aggressive and antagonistic (Baker, 2021) towards the public, especially at protests (Baker, 2021). Black people are often maltreated by the police also (Baker, 2021; National Law Enforcement Museum, personal communication, March 12, 2022), and even by some Black officers (Davis, 2021).

Fifth, much of the policy that has been established for the police force is flawed (Ariel, Farrar & Sutherland, 2015; Harmon, 2017). Since policies differ, it is often hard to address each precinct (City of New York, 2022). Additionally, when the police finally react and act on their own prejudices and behaviors, criminal prosecution of a police officer is often difficult – if not impossible (Harmon, 2017). However, they can be prosecuted for constitutional violations (Harmon, 2017).

And some policies have been adjusted such as the implementation of programs like community policing (Glaser & Denhardt, 2005; Murray & Haberfield, 2021; National Law Enforcement Museum, personal communication, March 12, 2022). Nonetheless, what is written is not always followed, and some policies leave for loopholes. This must be addressed from the brass as well as from legislative bodies.

Sixth, while there has been debate about the benefits of police using body cams, it appears that there have been positive outcomes from said use (Ariel, Farrar & Sutherland, 2021) and that they are a positive solution to the conversation of police brutality and misconduct (Baker, 2021; Lyle & Esmail, 2016; Murray & Haberfield, 2021; Normore & Scott, 2021). When police officers utilize body cams, they tend to use less force and there are less complaints about police regarding police misconduct (Ariel, Farrar & Sutherland, 2015; Lyle & Esmail, 2016; Normore & Scott, 2021). It also tends to reduce or prevent the act of racial profiling as was seen in Manhattan – NYPD since 2013 (Ariel, Farrar & Sutherland, 2015).

The use of body cams leads to more transparency for police officers in the field overall (Ariel, Farrar & Sutherland, 2015; Lyle & Esmail, 2016). In other words, police legitimacy is enhanced (Ariel, Farrar & Sutherland, 2015) while said officers are being held accountable for their actions or lack thereof (Lyle & Esmail, 2016). They have been used to keep police officers accountable for their interactions with the public, especially during stops and arrests (Lyle & Esmail, 2016). Moreover, it appears to be a win-win situation for the police because it also allows them to improve their process of evidence collection (Ariel, Farrar & Sutherland, 2015). Therefore, this increases their rates of prosecution (Ariel, Farrar & Sutherland, 2015). It may also lead to higher reporting rates of incidents. In 2015, 20% of lethal police killings were not even disclosed (Lyle & Esmail, 2016). They only cost approximately $1,000 per body cam (Lyle & Esmail, 2016) and with this small investment, there may be less headaches for police officers, police departments, citizens as well as the actors of the criminal justice system.

CONCLUSION

In conclusion, there is no real conclusion. There is an epiphany and moments of accountability. "Keith Ellison, the Minnesota attorney general who led the prosecution of Mr. Chauvin, said the sentence did not reflect justice but was a "moment of real accountability on the road to justice" (Arango, 2021, p. 4). The "road to justice" has been a long road with a myriad of twists and turns.

Previous musical quotes in this book pointed to incongruities in justice, a lack of justice, abuses of power, etc. The image of the police overall has been a schizophrenic or bipolar personality as a blue force collective. From the roots of slavery to the overhauling of the police department, community policing initiatives and more black deaths in custody; our communities are hurt and angry. However, that is not the only image of the police. While 2 Pac told the police to go F&*k themselves, there are also reputable police officers in the force.

"Okay, here's a story I'd like to tell about two young fellas in the ATL

We don't never cause trouble when we out in the streets

But then, "Woop, woop," that's the sound of the police

I was shook (He was shook)" – Andy Mineo featuring Lecrae, Been About It (2021)

The song continues. Basically, they were scared they would be casualties as the song implies. However, when they were finally pulled over, the lyrics continued, and noted that they remained calm. When the officers left their vehicles to interact with Andy and Lecrae they told them how they liked the lyrics to their rap songs. In other words, we as citizens of any country must be on guard due to certain circumstances and realities. Nonetheless, this does not mean that every officer that pulls us over will ticket us, beat us, or kill us.

There are officers of all creeds, colors, religions, heights, etc. They are doing their best to be a Wall of Honor to the Blue Wall of Shame. Nevertheless, there are still issues of social justice that need to be dealt with in the present and probably in the future. At this point, this country has a reckoning. It may not be an issue of police training at this point, but an issue of the hearts of men. If at the core, a police officer, or a prison officer (e.g., Corrections Officer) – as in the case of Australia is racist, can we expect equal treatment of all people regardless of color? Wouldn't we expect escalation of emotions, exchanges of words and then violence?

In a country like America, it would be wrong to erode our rights deemed to us from the Constitution and the Declaration of Independence. Therefore, we must remember that people can say whatever they want (i.e., 1st Amendment) and people can choose to bear arms (2nd Amendment), and some of those same people can choose not to incriminate themselves (5th Amendment). Regardless, whether a Black person or even a White person says whatever they want, bears arms or even chooses not to incriminate themselves in a crime that they may have been associated with – does not mean that they can kill or be killed indiscriminately. This is especially the case when it comes to the police force. The police force cannot become a vigilante system or a militarized system. And while other countries, especially other European countries around the world suggest eradicating some of our protections, these protections are in place in a country with a colored past for a reason.

Black deaths in custody will happen from time to time, due to a person's illnesses or preexisting conditions. That would have probably occurred across any race or culture represented within any country. However, when a pattern forms and when there is no reason for the death (i.e., as in the case of Michael Brown), or there are too many shots (i.e., as in the case of Amadou Bailo Diallo) and even if the person(s) has a criminal record (i.e., as in the case of George Floyd and Eric Garner); there is no reason that a suspected perp without a weapon should be shot down like a dog in the streets of any town or city in the United States of America. With each death, each of us regardless of our color are a little less free. But today, even with possible restricted freedom due to circumstances like this or even COVID-19; many of us are becoming a little more brave! Perhaps, one day we can all truly say together, hand in hand: "Free at last, Free at last, Thank God Almighty we are free at last!,"[1] and not have a bullet in our head within five years (i.e., April 4, 1968).

"Let [Us] breathe!"

REFERENCES

Alchin, L. (2017). *Black codes.* American Historama. https://www.american-historama.org/1866-1881-reconstruction-era/blackcodes.htm#:~:text=Definition%20and%20Summary%3A%20The%20Black%20Codes%20were%20a,War%20at%20the%20beginning%20of%20the%20Reconstruction%20Era.

Ariel, B., Farrar, W. A., & Sutherland, A. (2015). The effect of police body-worn cameras on use of force and citizens' complaints against the police: A randomized controlled trial. *Journal of Quantitative Criminology, 31*(3), 509–535. doi:10.100710940-014-9236-3

Australian Law Reform Commission. (2010). *Australian law as applied to Aborigines: August 28, 2010.* ALRC. https://www.alrc.gov.au/publication/recognition-of-aboriginal-customary-laws-alrc-report-31/4-aboriginal-customary-laws-and-anglo-australian-law-after-1788/australian-law-as-applied-to-aborigines/

Baker, E. (2021, May 20). *Police brutality: An epidemic in America.* SDU. https://sites.sandiego.edu/blackhistoryatusd/2021/05/20/police-brutality-an-epidemic-in-america/

Biko, S. (n.d.). *White racism and Black consciousness.* DISA. https://disa.ukzn.ac.za/sites/default/files/pdf_files/FtFeb84.1683.7118.001.001.Feb1984.7.pdf

Blight, D. W. (2018). *Frederick Douglass: Prophet of freedom.* Simon & Schuster.

Bringing Them Home. (n.d.). *Historical context: The stolen generations.* BTH. https://bth.humanrights.gov.au/significance/historical-context-the-stolen-generations?msclkid=e1774539cf4711ec8c533f37dc49e321

Cha-Jua, S. K. (2014, Spring). We believe it was murder: Mobilizing black resistance to police brutality in Champaign, Illinois. *The Black Scholar, 44*(1), 58–85. doi:10.1080/00064246.2014.11641212

Chang, C. (2019, January 21). How early Australians treated Aboriginal people. *News.com.* https://www.news.com.au/national/politics/how-early-australians-treated-aboriginal-people/news-story/e984d3a453382c59a1d5d81f99a9ad8c

City of New York. (2022). *New York patrol guide.* NYC Gov. https://www1.nyc.gov/site/ccrb/investigations/nypd-patrol-guide.page#:~:text=The%20NYPD%27s%20Patrol%20Guide%20contains%20the%20rules%20that,must%20follow%20in%20carrying%20out%20their%20official%20duties

Davis, D. L. (2021). From the field: Why I founded black cops against police brutality. *Journal of Ethnicity in Criminal Justice*, *19*(3-4), 201–222. doi:10.1080/15377938.2021.1979159

Ellis, D. (2019, Summer). Apartheid. *Israel Studies*, *24*(2), 63–71. doi:10.2979/israelstudies.24.2.06

Equal Justice Initiative. (2023). *Equal justice initiative.* EJI. https://eji.org/

Equal Justice Initiative. (2023a). *Plan your visit.* EJI. https://museumandmemorial.eji.org/visit/

Fanon, F. (2008). *Black skin, White masks.* Grove Press.

Fulbright, L. (2000, March 6). *Wanted: Female cops.* file:///C:/Users/janel/OneDrive/Desktop/Publications/Examining%20Black%20Deaths%20in%20Custody%20-%202022/Women_may_be_solution_to_polic.pdf.

Glaser, M. A., & Denhardt, J. (2009, August 5). Community policing and community building: A case study of officer perception. *American Review of Public Administration*, *40*(3), 309–325. doi:10.1177/0275074009340050

Golden, M. (2014, Winter). *Carnegie corporation in South Africa: A difficult past leads to a commitment to change.* Carnegie Media. https://media.carnegie.org/filer_public/f3/54/f354cbf9-f86c-4681-8573-c697418ee786/ccny_cresults_2004_southafrica.pdf

Harmon, R. A. (2017). *Legal remedies for police misconduct. In Academy for Justice, a Report in Scholarship and Criminal Justice reform.* Virginia Public Law & Legal Theory Research Paper No. 40. https://law.asu.edu/sites/default/files/pdf/academy_for_justice/2_Reforming-Criminal-Justice_Vol_2_Legal-Remedies-for-Police Misconduct.pdf

Harrison, K. (2020, June 10). I can't breathe: The suffocating truth of Australia's race relations. *Newsroom.* https://newsroom.unsw.edu.au/news/social-affairs/i-cant-breathe-suffocating-truth-australia%E2%80%99s-race-relations

Hatungimana, W. (2022). How people appraise their governments: Corruption perceptions of police legitimacy in Africa. *Journal of Modern Studies, 60*(1), 1-22. . doi:10.1017/S0022278X21000392

Healing Foundation. (2022). *Who are the stolen generations?* Healing Foundation. https://healingfoundation.org.au/who-are-the-stolen-generations/#:~:text=The%20Stolen%20Generations%20refers%20to%20a%20period%20in,Aboriginal%20children%20to%20be%20removed%20from%20their%20parents

Hilton, B. T. (2011). Frantz Fanon and Colonialism: A Psychology of Oppression. *Journal of Scientific Psychology*, 45–59.

Holcombe, M., Moshtaghian, A., & Akbarzai, S. (2021, July 19). *Eric Garner's family commemorates his death as judge allows litigation against police and city officials.* https://www.cnn.com/2021/07/19/us/eric-garner-family-commemoration-judge-litigation/index.html

Holland, H. (1989). *The struggle: A history of the African National Congress.* Grafton Paperback.

Hughes, L., & Meltzer, M. (1956). *A pictorial history of the negro in America.* Crown Publishers.

Indianapolis Public Schools. (n.d.). *"Say their names" toolkit.* IPS. https://myips.org/get-involved/racial-equity/say-their-names-toolkit/

Irons, P. (2002). *Jim Crow's children: The broken promise of the Brown decision.* Penguin Books.

Jones, J. M. (2017). Killing fields: Explaining police violence against persons of color. *The Journal of Social Issues, 73*(4), 872–883. doi:10.1111/josi.12252

Kaba, M. (n.d.). *Yes, we mean literally abolish the police.* https://drive.google.com/file/d/1KR-D1GBoOQzT_IljgqOoEaPOareRQ0xD/view

Legends of America. (2022). *Native American tribes list.* Legends of America. https://www.legendsofamerica.com/na-tribelist/?msclkid=e81c0039d03c11ecaf9b4525ddec4ae0

Levine, K. (2016). How we prosecute the police. *The Georgetown Law Journal, 104*(4), 745–776.

Lynch, H. (Ed.). (1976). *The great contemporary issues series: Black Africa* (vol. 5). The New York Times Arno Press.

Maule, B. A. (2017). *Police misconduct in Brooklyn: Documenting, understanding and preventing*. Springer Publications. doi:10.1007/978-3-319-66814-7

McGovern Library and Dakota Wesleyan University. (2022). *Martin Luther King, Jr.: The civil rights movement.* DWU. https://library.dwu.edu/martin_luther_king/civil_right

Murray, K. R., & Haberfield, M. R. (2021). *Use of force training in law enforcement: A reality based approach.* Springer. doi:10.1007/978-3-030-59880-8

Newtown, J. (1788). *Thoughts upon the African slave trade*. J. Buckland, in Pater-Noster Row, and J. Johnson in St. Paul's Church-yard.

Noah, T. (2019). *Born a crime: Stories from a South African childhood.* Spiegel and Grau.

Normore, A. H., & Scott, W. R. (2021). Police brutality and the militarization of Black and Brown communities: Transforming the culture of policing through education and training. *New Directions for Adult and Continuing Education, 2021*(170), 79–88. doi:10.1002/ace.20427

Petersen, T.T. (2022, August 12). *Military conquest of the prairie: Native American resistance, evasion & survival, 1865-1890.* Liverpool University Press.

Smith, W. (2021, February 17). *Amend: The fight for America* [Net Series]. Netflix.

Spielvogel, J. J. (2014). *Discovering our past: A history of the world.* McGraw Hill Education.

The Amadou Diallo Foundation. (2022). *Amadou Diallo.* ADF. https://www.amadoudiallo.com/about-amadou/

The Arizona Board of Regents. (2022). *Tribe.* AZ Regents.https://azregents.edu/

Trigger, D.S. (1985, June). *Doomadgee: A study of power relations and social action in North Australian Aboriginal settlement* [Doctoral dissertation]. University of Queensland.

Tupper, N. M. (2021). Working with victims of police brutality: Conducting and documenting multistoried interviews. *The International Journal of Narrative Therapy and Community Work, 2*, 48–57.

United Nations. (2022, March 25). *Resistance to slavery and unity against racism: Rhythms of resistance.* UN. https://www.youtube.com/watch?v=VUhHhW1__sg

United States Department of Justice. (n.d.). *Shooting death of Michael Brown – Ferguson. Missouri: 2014.* USDJ. https://www.justice.gov/crs/timeline-event/shooting-death-michael-brown-ferguson-mo/

Van Vuuren, H. (2015). Apartheid, guns and money: A tale of profit. Jacana Media (Pty) Ltd.

Xu, V., Fiedler, M.L., & Flaming, K.H. (2005, May 1). Discovering the impact of community policing: The broke windows thesis. Collective efficacy, & citizens' judgment. *Journal of Research in Crime and Delinquency, 42*(2), 147-186. . doi:10.1177/0022427804266544

ENDNOTES

1. Quote from King's speech on August 28, 1963 from his "I Have a Dream Speech." Given at the Mall on Washington, D.C.
2. In the case of Biko, it was not an organization that was built first, but organizations were built from his ideology of Black Consciousness, which led to a movement that swept through South Africa.
3. Allusion to Stand Up by Cynthia Erivo. Reference to John 14:2, which states the following: "In my Father's house are many mansions: if *it were* not *so*, I would have told you. I go to prepare a place for you. https://www.youtube.com/watch?v=sn19xvfoXv.

Appendix: Conclusion

Locksmith's Lemme Breathe Lyrics

[Intro]

Decap

[Chorus]

[…]

Lemme breathe

The blacker the berry, the tighter the noose

That's not a chip on my shoulder, that's your boot

Lemme breathe

Source: (Genius Media Group, 2022)

REFERENCES

Genius Media Group. (2022). *Lemme breathe – Locksmith.* Genius. https://genius.com/Locksmith-lemme-breathe-lyrics

Compilation of References

A&E Network Television, LLC. (2022). Jim Crow laws. *History.com.* https://www.history.com/topics/early-20th-century-us/jim-crow-laws

A&E Network Television, LLC. (2022a). Ku Klux Klan. *History.com.* https://www.history.com/topics/reconstruction/ku-klux-klan

A&E Television Networks, LLC. (2022). Eric Garner dies in NYPD chokehold. *History.com.* https://www.history.com/this-day-in-history/eric-garner-dies-nypd-chokehold

A&E Television Networks. (2022). Civil rights movement. *History.com.* https://www.history.com/topics/black-history/civil-rights-movement

A&E Television Networks. (2022a). Jim Crow laws. *History.com.* https://www.history.com/topics/early-20th-century-us/jim-crow-laws

African American Registry. (2022). *The 'one drop rule' in America, a story.* AAR. https://aaregistry.org/story/the-one-drop-rule-abriefstory/?msclkid=b7bcbe86cfa811ecb1 72602642076870.

Ager, S. (2022). *Afrikaans.* Omniglot. https://omniglot.com/writing/afrikaans.htm

Alchin, L. (2017). *Black codes.* American Historama. https://www.american-historama.org/1866-1881-reconstruction-era/blackcodes.htm#:~:text=Definition %20and%20Summary%3A%20The%20Black%20Codes%20were%20a,War%20at%20the%20beginning%20of%20the%20Reconstruction%20Era.

Alchin, L. (2017). *Black codes.* American Historama. https://www.american-historama.org/1866-1881-reconstruction-era/blackcodes.htm#:~:text=Definition%20and%20Summary%3A%20The%20Black%20Codes%20were%20a,War%20at%20the%20beginning%20of%20the%20Reconstruction%20Era

Ali, K. (2016, July 1). Muhammad Ali: Boxing, legend, human rights activist. *Crescent.* https://crescent.icit-digital.org/articles/muhammad-ali-boxing-legend-human-rights-activist#:~:text=Muhammad%20Ali%20was%20not%20only%20a%20world-class%20boxer%2C,him%20because%20he%20had%20become%20an%20international%20icon

Alsan, M., Wanamaker, M., & Harderman, R. R. (2019). The Tuskegee study of untreated syphilis: A case study in peripheral trauma with implications for health professionals. *Journal of General Internal Medicine, 35*(1), 322–325. https://www.ncbi.nlm.nih.gov/pmc/articles/PMC6957600/pdf/11606_2019_Article_5309.pdf. doi:10.100711606-019-05309-8 PMID:31646456

American Federation of Teachers. (2021, April 21). George Floyd's family vows to 'keep fighting' for just policing after Chauvin verdict. *Share My Lesson.* https://sharemylesson.com/todays-news-tomorrows-lesson/derek-chauvin-verdict

American Psychological Association. (2022). *Psychological causes and consequences of racism, racial discrimination, xenophobia and related intolerances (2008).* APA. https://www.apa.org/pi/oema/programs/racism/un-conference-plenary

Anekwe, O.N. (2014, May). The Tuskegee experiment. *International Journal of Clinical and Medical Imagining, 1*(5), 1. doi:. file:///C:/Users/janel/OneDrive/Desktop/Publications/the-tuskegee-experiment. May.2014.05.14.2022.pdf. doi:10.4172/ijcmi.1000211

Anti-Defamation League. (2021, April 21). The verdict is in: How to talk with young people about the Derek Chauvin murder trial verdict. *Share My Lesson.* https://sharemylesson.com/blog/derek-chauvin-murder-trial-verdict

Anti-Defamation League. (2022). *Civil rights movement.* ADL. https://www.adl.org/education/resources/backgrounders/civil-rights-movement

Arango, T. (2021, June 25). Derek Chauvin is sentenced to 22 and a half years for the murder of George Floyd. *New York Times.* https://www.nytimes.com/2021/06/25/us/derek-chauvin-22-and-a-half-years-george-floyd.html

Ariel, B., Farrar, W. A., & Sutherland, A. (2015). The effect of police body-worn cameras on use of force and citizens' complaints against the police: A randomized controlled trial. *Journal of Quantitative Criminology, 31*(3), 509–535. doi:10.100710940-014-9236-3

Australian Law Reform Commission. (2010). *Australian law as applied to Aborigines: August 28, 2010.* ALRC. https://www.alrc.gov.au/publication/recognition-of-aboriginal-customary-laws-alrc-report-31/4-aboriginal-customary-laws-and-anglo-australian-law-after-1788/australian-law-as-applied-to-aborigines/

Australian Law Reform Commission. (2022). *Australian law as applied to Aborigines*. ALRC. https://www.alrc.gov.au/publication/recognition-of-aboriginal-customary-laws-alrc-report-31/4-aboriginal-customary-laws-and-anglo-australian-law-after-1788/australian-law-as-applied-to-aborigines/

Australian Law Reform Commission. (2022). *Australian law as applied to Aborigines: August 28, 2010*. ALRC. https://www.alrc.gov.au/publication/recognition-of-aboriginal-customary-laws-alrc-report-31/4-aboriginal-customary-laws-and-anglo-australian-law-after-1788/australian-law-as-applied-to-aborigines/

Australians Together. (2022). *The stolen generations*. Australians Together. https://australianstogether.org.au/discover/australian-history/stolen- generations#:~:text=First%20Nations%20people%20who%20were%20removed%20were%20left,children%2C%20their%20parents%20and%20families%2C%20and%20their%20descendants

Baker, E. (2021, May 20). *Police brutality: An epidemic in America*. San Diego University. https://sites.sandiego.edu/blackhistoryatusd/2021/05/20/police-brutality-an-epidemic-in-america/

Baker, E. (2021, May 20). *Police brutality: An epidemic in America*. Sandiego. https://sites.sandiego.edu/blackhistoryatusd/2021/05/20/police-brutality-an-epidemic-in-america/

Baker, E. (2021, May 20). *Police brutality: An epidemic in America*. SDU. https://sites.sandiego.edu/blackhistoryatusd/2021/05/20/police-brutality-an-epidemic-in-america/

Basu, A. (2020, July 21). Black lives matter: US workers stage nationwide strike against racial injustice. *News 24 Online*. https://news24online.com/news/world/black-lives-matter-us-workers-stage-nationwide-strike-against-racial-injustice-697f313e/

BBC. (2014, December 5). *Profile; Eric Garner*. BBC. https://www.bbc.com/news/world-us-canada-30350648

BBC. (2019). *Rwanda genocide: 100 days of slaughter*. BBC. https://www.bbc.com/news/world-africa26875506?msclkid=9bdb2255cfb111ecb557434b79b3261d

Belafonte, H., & Shnayerson, M. (2011). *My song: A memoir*. Knopf Publishers.

Biko, S. (n.d.). *White racism and Black consciousness*. DISA. https://disa.ukzn.ac.za/sites/default/files/pdf_files/FtFeb84.1683.7118.001.001.Fcb1984.7.pdf

Biko, S. (n.d.). White racism and Black consciousness. *SA History*. FtFeb84.1683.7118.001.001.Feb1984.7.pdf (sahistory.org.za)

Biography. (2022). *The tragic story behind Billie Holiday's strange fruit*. Biography.com. https://www.biography.com/news/billie-holiday-strange- fruit#:~:text=The%20Tragic%20Story%20Behind%20Billie%20Holiday%27s%20%22Strange%20Fruit%22,the%20world%20of%20jazz%20and%20pop%20music.%20

Blight, D. W. (2018). *Frederick Douglass: Prophet of freedom*. Simon & Schuster.

Boshoff, J. J. (2018, January). *The search for the slave ship Meermin. Developing a methodology from finding intertidal shipwrecks*. University of South Africa. https://uir.unisa.ac.za/bitstream/handle/10500/24734/dissertation_boshoff_j.pdf;sequence=1

Bradt, S. (2010). *'One-drop rule' persists racial hierarchy*. Harvard Gazette. https://news.harvard.edu/gazette/story/2010/12/one-drop-rule-persists/

Bradt, S. (2010). *'One-drop rule' persists racial hierarchy*. Harvard. https://news.harvard.edu/gazette/story/2010/12/one-drop-rule-persists/

Bridgewater State University. (2007). In Massachusetts hall of Black achievement: *Malcolm X (Item 13)*. BSU. https://vc.bridgew.edu/hoba/13

Bringing Them Home. (n.d.). *Historical context: The stolen generations*. BTH. https://bth.humanrights.gov.au/significance/historical-context-the-stolen-generations?msclkid=e1774539cf4711ec8c533f37dc49e321

Brown, C., Esq. (2020, November 30). *What amendment does police brutality violate?* Brown Firm. https://www.brownfirmpllc.com/what-amendment-does-police-brutality-violate/

Browning, J. (n.d.). *Anti-miscegenation laws in the United States*. Duke University. https://scholarship.law.duke.edu/cgi/viewcontent.cgi?article=1544&context=dlj&msclkid=17bb897bcfb411eca933b9a1cad5723c.

Buckland, W. W. (1908). *The Roman law of slavery: The condition of the slave in private law from Augustus to Justinian*. Cambridge University Press.

Burns, J. F. (1977, September 14). Young black leader dies in detention in South Africa, raising fears of unrest. *New York Times*, p. 3. https://www.nytimes.com/1977/09/14/archives/young-black-leader-dies-in-detention-in-south-africa-raising-fears.html

C. B. S. Inc. (2016, September 15). Lawyer: $1.9 settlement reached in Sandra Bland case. *CBS*. https://www.cbsnews.com/video/lawyer-1-9m-settlement-reached-in-sandra-bland-case/#x

C. B. S. Inc. (2020, June 9). Police fired 41 shots when they killed Amadou Diallo. His mom hope's today's protests will bring change. *CBS News*. https://www.cbsnews.com/news/amadou-diallo-kadiatou-protests-george-floyd-police/

Cambridge University Press. (2022). *Tribe.* Cambridge University Press. https://dictionary.cambridge.org/dictionary/english/tribe?msclkid=0c83111dd03d11ec9f800a425784bb04

Carnegie Corporation of New York. (2022). *Our approach.* Carnegie. https://www.carnegie.org/programs/

Carter, E.L., Kemper, K.R., Brown, A. & Phillips, J.C. (2009). *"Executing the powers with which it is in trusted": Justifications, definitions and limitations of government speech. 14 Communications, Law and Policy, 14*(4), 453-478. doi:10.1080/10811680903238019

Central Intelligence Agency. (n.d.). *Field listing: Government type.* CIA. https://www.cia.gov/the-world-factbook/field/government-type/

Cha-Jua, S. K. (2014, Spring). We believe it was murder: Mobilizing black resistance to police brutality in Champaign, Illinois. *The Black Scholar, 44*(1), 58–85. doi:10.1080/00064246.2014.11641212

Chang, C. (2019, January 21). How early Australians treated Aboriginal people. *News.com.* https://www.news.com.au/national/politics/how-early-australians-treated-aboriginal-people/news-story/e984d3a453382c59a1d5d81f99a9ad8c

Chestnut, T. (2008). *Lynching: Ida B. Wells-Barnett and the Outrage over the Frazier Baker Murder.* Archives. https://www.archives.gov/files/publications/prologue/2008/fall/lynching.pdf

Cission, U. S. Inc. (2022). HBO sports to celebrate 'What's my name: Muhammad Ali.' *PR News Wire.* https://www.prnewswire.com/news-releases/hbo-sports-to-celebrate-whats-my-name--muhammad-ali-documentary-with-nyc-pop-up-experience-300842993.htm

City of New York. (2022). *New York patrol guide.* NYC Gov. https://www1.nyc.gov/site/ccrb/investigations/nypd-patrol-guide.page#:~:text=The%20NYPD%27s%20Patrol%20Guide%20contains%20the%20rules%20that,must%20follow%20in%20carrying%20out%20their%20official%20duties

Columbia University Center for Teaching and Learning. (n.d.). *The autobiography of Malcolm X: Speeches and interviews.* CUCTL. https://ccnmtl.columbia.edu/projects/mmt/mxp/speeches/mxt29.html

Commonwealth Consolidated Acts. (n.d.). *Racial discrimination act 1975.* CCA. http://www.austlii.edu.au/cgi-bin/viewdb/au/legis/cth/consol_act/rda1975202/

Commonwealth Secretariat. (2019). *Commonwealth declarations.* Commonwealth Secretariat. https://production-new-commonwealth-files.s3.eu-west-2.amazonaws.com/s3fs-public/202201/Commonwealth%20Declarations%20Booklet.pdf?VersionId=V5eWs7gRYjOcPeco80v0nJ0UrOcS3iNb

Commonwealth Secretariat. (2022). *Commonwealth charter.* Commonwealth Secretariat. https://thecommonwealth.org/charter?msclkid=64c91d17d08311ec9ec693da6e83bf9a

Community Oriented Policing Services. (2014). *Community policing defined.* USDOJ. https://cops.usdoj.gov/RIC/Publications/cops-p157-pub.pdf#:~:text=Community%20policingis%20a%20philosophy%20that%20promotes%20organizational%20strategies,of%20crime.%20Community%20policing%20comprises%20three%20key%20components%3A

Constitution, U. S. com. (2022). *List of the 27 amendments.* Consitiutionus.com. https://constitutionus.com/constitution/amendments/constitutional-amendments/?msclkid=3272ff80cfa911ecab22099cf1237eab

Dahrendorf, R. (2003, October). A definition of democracy. *Journal of Democracy, 14*(4), 101–114. doi:10.1353/jod.2003.0067

Davis, D. L. (2021). From the field: Why I founded black cops against police brutality. *Journal of Ethnicity in Criminal Justice, 19*(3-4), 201–222. doi:10.1080/15377938.2021.1979159

Digital Panopticon. (2020). *Convicts and the colonization of Australia, 1788-1868.* Digital Panopticon. https://www.digitalpanopticon.org/Convicts_and_the_Colonisation_of_Australia,_1788-1868

Dubow, S. (2000). *The Africa national congress.* Jonathan Ball Publishers.

Dubow, S. (2000). *The African National Congress.* Johannesburg, South Africa: Jonathan Ball Publishers.

Ellis, D. (2019, Summer). Apartheid. *Israel Studies, 24*(2), 63–71. doi:10.2979/israelstudies.24.2.06

Encyclopedia Britannica. (2022). *Democracy.* Britannica. https://www.britannica.com/topic/democracy

Encyclopedia Britannica. (2022). *Steve Biko.* Encyclopedia Britannica. https://www.britannica.com/biography/Steve-Biko

Equal Justice Initiative. (2022). *About EJI.* EJI. https://eji.org/about/

Equal Justice Initiative. (2023). *Equal justice initiative.* EJI. https://eji.org/

Equal Justice Initiative. (2023a). *Plan your visit.* EJI. https://museumandmemorial.eji.org/visit/

Ewing, E. L. (2020, August 25). *Blue bloods: America's brotherhood of police officers.* Retrieved on April 30, 2022 from https://www.vanityfair.com/culture/2020/08/americas-brotherhood-of-police-officers

Fabian, A. (Director). (2008). *Skin.* [Film]. MPI Media Group.

Fagan, J., & Harcourt, B. (2014, November 26). *Questions and answers for Columbia Law students about grand juries.* Columbia. https://www.law.columbia.edu/news/archive/fact-sheet-michael-brown-case/

Fanon, F. (2008). *Black skin, White masks.* Grove Press.

Fasenfest, D. (2010, October). Government, governing, and governance. *Critical Sociology, 36*(6), 771-774. file:///C:/Users/janel/Downloads/36_6.pdf. DOI: . doi:10.1177/0896920510378192

Federal Bureau of Investigation. (2006). *Emmett Till.* FBI. https://www.fbi.gov/history/famous-cases/emmett-till

Feinberg, A. (n.d.). Police brutality/Excessive force assignment. *Share My Lesson.* https://sharemylesson.com/teaching-resource/police-brutality excessive-force-assignment-267266

Find and Connect. (2021). *The Aborigines protection act 1886 (1887-1890).* Find and Connect. https://www.findandconnect.gov.au/guide/vic/E000432?msclkid=ec9ee398cf4511ec9b478069421f9580

Finton, L. (2023, April 7). *Activists to host Tyre Nichols photo exhibits, lantern ceremony before city hall.* Retrieved on April 10, 2023 from https://www.yahoo.com/entertainment/activists-host-tyre-nichols-photo-152701684.html

Finton, L. (2023, April 7). *Activists to host Tyre Nichols photo exhibits, lantern ceremony before city hall.* Yahoo. https://www.yahoo.com/entertainment/activists-host-tyre-nichols-photo-152701684.html

Fulbright, L. (2000, March 6). "*Wanted: Female cops.*" file:///C:/Users/janel/OneDrive/Desktop/Publications/Examining%20Black%20Deaths%20in%20Custody%20-%202022/Women_may_be_solution_to_polic.pdf.

Gardbaum, S. (2013, February). *The new commonwealth model of constitutionalism.* Cambridge University Press.

Gardbaum, S. (2013, February). *The new commonwealth model of constitutionalism.* Cambridge, UK: Cambridge University Press. doi:. doi:10.1017/CBO9780511920806

Genius Media Group. (2022). *Lemme breathe – Locksmith*. Genius. https://genius.com/Locksmith-lemme-breathe-lyrics

Gerber, M. (2016, September 20). $1.9-million settlement in Sandra Bland death is the latest big payout in police misconduct lawsuits. *LA Times*. https://www.latimes.com/nation/la-na-police-death-settlement s-20160920-snap-htmlstory.html

Gibson, N. C. (2011). *Fanonian practice in South Africa: From Steve Biko to Abahali base Mjondola*. University of KwaZulu-Natal Press.

Gipps, G. (1840). *1840: 4 Victoria, No. 8. An act to prohibit the Aboriginal natives of New South Wales from having fire arms or ammunition in their possession, without the permission of a magistrate*. Kathy Stavrou. https://www.kathystavrou.net/caught-in-the-act/act5-1840.htm l?msclkid=86b2337bcf4711ecb557cec86ca930f3

Glaser, M. A., & Denhardt, J. (2009, August 5). Community policing and community building: A case study of officer perception. *American Review of Public Administration*, *40*(3), 309–325. doi:10.1177/0275074009340050

Golden, M. (2014, Winter). *Carnegie corporation in South Africa: A difficult past leads to a commitment to change*. Carnegie Media. https://media.carnegie.org/filer_public/f3/54/f354cbf9-f86c-4681-8573-c697418ee786/ccny_cresults_2004_southafrica.pdf

Golden, M. (2014, Winter). *Carnegie corporation in South Africa: A difficult past leads to a commitment to change*. Carnegie. https://media.carnegie.org/filer_public/f3/54/f354cbf9-f86c-4681-8573- c697418ee786/ccny_cresults_2004_southafrica.pdf

Golden, M. (2014, Winter). *Carnegie corporation in South Africa: A difficult past leads to a commitment to change*. Carnegie. https://media.carnegie.org/filer_public/f3/54/f354cbf9-f86c-4681-8573-c697418ee786/ccny_cresults_2004_southafrica.pdf

Gooding, P. (2017). The government is the cause of the disease, and we are stuck with the symptoms: Deinstitutionalization, mental health advocacy and police shootings in 1900s Victoria. *Continuum (Perth)*, *31*(3), 436–446. doi:10.1080/10304312.2016.1275146

Grobbelaar, P. (1987). *Reader's digest Afrikaans-Engelse Woordeboek English-Afrikaans*. Reader's Digest Association of South Africa.

Grosse Point Historical Society. (n.d.). *Dr. Martin Luther King's 1968 speech at Grosse Pointe High School*. GP Historical Society. http://gphistorical.org/mlk/index.htm

Hansen, C. (2019, July 10). *Slave patrols: An early form of American policing*. NLEOMF. https://nleomf.org/slavhttpse-patrols-an-early-form-of-ameri can-policing

Harmon, R. A. (2017). Legal remedies for police misconduct. In Academy for Justice, a Report in Scholarship and Criminal Justice reform. *Virginia Public Law & Legal Theory Research Paper No. 40.* https://law.asu.edu/sites/default/files/pdf/academy_for_justice/2_Reforming-Criminal-Justice_Vol_2_Legal-Remedies-for-Police-Misconduct.pdf

Harrison, K. (2020, June 10). I can't breathe: The suffocating truth of Australia's race relations. *Newsroom.* https://newsroom.unsw.edu.au/news/social-affairs/i-cant-breathe-suffocating-truth-australia%E2%80%99s-race-relations

Hatungimana, W. (2020). How people approve their governments: Corruption perceptions of police legitimacy in Africa. *Journal of Modern Studies, 60*(1), 1-22.. doi:10.1017/S0022278X21000392

Haygood, W. (2013). *The butler: A witness of history.* Atria Books.

Healing Foundation. (2022). *Who are the stolen generations?* Healing Foundation. https://healingfoundation.org.au/who-are-the-stolen-generations/#:~:text=The%20Stolen%20Generations%20refers%20to%20a%20period%20in,Aboriginal%20children%20to%20be%20removed%20from%20their%20parents

Hillsdale College. (n.d.). *Political readings: From the Declaration of Independence.* Hillsdale College. https://www.hillsdale.edu/america/

Hilton, B. T. (2011). Frantz Fanon and Colonialism: A Psychology of Oppression. *Journal of Scientific Psychology*, 45–59.

Hilton, B. T. (2011, December). Frantz Fanon & colonialism: A psychology of oppression. *Journal of Scientific Psychology*, 45–59. http://psyencelab.com/uploads/5/4/6/5/54658091/frantz_fanon_and_colonialism.pdf

History and Social Justice Website. (2022). *Howell, MI.* Howell - History and Social Justice (tougaloo.edu).

History, W. edu. (2019, March 16). How Malcolm X died. *World History.* https://www.worldhistoryedu.com/how-malcolm-x-died/

Holcombe, M., Moshtaghian, A., & Akbarzai, S. (2021, July 19). Eric Garner's family commemorates his death as judge allows litigation against police and city officials. *CNN.* https://www.cnn.com/2021/07/19/us/eric-garner-family-commemoration-judge-litigation/index.html

Holcombe, M., Moshtaghian, A., & Akbarzai, S. (2021, July 19). *Eric Garner's family commemorates his death as judge allows litigation against police and city officials.* https://www.cnn.com/2021/07/19/us/eric-garner-family-commemoration-judge-litigation/index.html

Holland, H. (1989). *The struggle. A history of the African National Congress.* Grafton Paperback.

Holland, H. (1989). *The struggle: A history of the African National Congress.* Toronto, CA: Grafton Paperback.

Hook, D. (2004). *Frantz Fanon, Steve Biko, 'psychopolitics' and critical psychology. LSE Research Online*. Juta Academic Publishing.

Hughes, L. & Meltzer, M. *A pictorial history of the negro in America.* New York, NY: Crown Publishers.

Hughes, L., & Meltzer, M. (1956). *A pictorial history of the negro in America.* Crown Publishers.

IMDb. (2002). *Inside man.* IMDb. https://www.imdb.com/title/tt0454848/?msclkid=9b40a20bce8111ecbe7d45cc09b5ed2f

IMDb. (2022). *John F. Kennedy: Biography.* IMBd. https://www.imdb.com/name/nm0448123/bio

IMDb. (2022). *Just mercy.* IMDb. https://www.imdb.com/title/tt4916630/

IMDb. (2022). *Loving (2016).* IMDb. https://www.imdb.com/title/tt4669986/?msclkid=4a10d795cfb411ec971d1432e11b4317

Indianapolis Public Schools. (n.d.). *"Say their names" toolkit.* Indianapolis Public Schools. https://myips.org/get-involved/racial-equity/say-their-names-toolkit/

Indianapolis Public Schools. (n.d.). *"Say their names" toolkit.* IPS. https://myips.org/get-involved/racial-equity/say-their-names-toolkit/

International Work Group for Indigenous Affairs. (n.d.). *Indigenous peoples of Australia.* IWGIA. https://iwgia.org/en/australia#:~:text=The%20Indigenous%20World%202022%3A%20Australia%20Written%20on%2001,Australians%20in%202021%20was%20estimated%20to%20be%20881%2C600

Irons, P. (2002). *Jim Crow's children: The broken promise of the Brown decision.* Strand Books.

John Jay College of Criminal Justice. (2012). *Harry Belafonte, Dr. Hawa Abdi, Vivian Nixon and the late justice William O. Douglas to receive 2012 John Jay medal for justice.* John Jay College. http://johnjay.jjay.cuny.edu/newsroom/5715.php

Johnson, A. G. (2006). *Privilege, power, and difference.* McGraw Hill Companies.

Jones, J. (2021). Frazier Baker: Black postmaster and infant daughter lynched in Lake City, South Carolina '1898.' *Black Then.* https://blackthen.com/frazier-baker-black-postmaster-and-infant-daughter-lynched-in-lake-city-south-carolina-1898/

Jones, J. M. (2017). Killing fields: Explaining police violence against persons of color. *The Journal of Social Issues, 73*(4), 872–883. doi:10.1111/josi.12252

Journeyman Pictures. (2000). *The incredible apartheid story with a difference.* [Video]. Youtube. https://www.youtube.com/watch?v=cYZyvxpsCjQ&list=PLFE71DB5172BB3D46

Kaba, M. (n.d.). *Yes, we mean literally abolish the police.* https://drive.google.com/file/d/1KR-D1GBoOQzT_IljgqOoEaPOareRQ0xD/view

Karimi, F. (2013, December 5). Nelson Mandela, anti-apartheid icon and father of modern South Africa, dies. *CNN.* https://www.cnn.com/2013/12/05/world/africa/nelsonmandela/index.html?msclkid=15894e81ced611ecbfb54ac0c0c85ad5

Kihato, C. W. (2014). Lost dreams? Tales of the South African city twenty years after apartheid. *African Identities*, *12*(3-4), 357–370. doi:10.1080/14725843.2015.1009616

Klamer, M. (1995). Whitman, slavery, and the emergence of leaves of grass. University, PA: The Pennsylvania State University Press.

Kuumba, C. (2021, February 14). *The United Nations follow-up on police brutality and abuse.* Bing. https://www.bing.com/search?q=united+nations+and+police+brutality&cvid=03773022b10848cf991013caa37b8d2b&aqs=edge.69i57j69i64.40944j0j1&pglt=2211&FORM=ANNTA1&PC=HCTS

Lafraniere, S. (2005, August 24). Tracing a mutiny by slaves off South Africa in 1766. *New York Times.* https://www.nytimes.com/2005/08/24/world/africa/tracing-a-mutiny-by-slaves-off-south-africa-in-1766.html

Laurence, P. (2010). *Race classification: Then and now.* Politics Web. https://www.politicsweb.co.za/news-and-analysis/race-classification-then-and-now

Lee, S. (1992). *Malcolm X.* [Video file]. Amazon. https://www.amazon.com/Malcolm-X-Denzel-Washington/dp/B0097JUG86/ref=sr_1_2?crid=2FGRH3CVPI161&keywords=malcolm+x&qid=1680501278&s=instant-video&sprefix=malcolm+x%2Cinstant-video%2C141&sr=1-2

Legends of America. (2022). *Native American tribes list.* Legends of America. https://www.legendsofamerica.com/na-tribelist/?msclkid=e81c0039d03c11ecaf9b4525ddec4ae0

Levine, K. (2016). How we prosecute the police. *The Georgetown Law Journal*, *104*(4), 745–776.

Library of Congress. (n.d.). *The Constitution of the United States.* Library of Congress. https://constitution.congress.gov/constitution/?msclkid=6ec01f36cff511ecbfcd5e5be68fe779

Library of Congress. (n.d.). *The fifteenth amendment.* Library of Congress. https://constitution.congress.gov/constitution/amendment-15/

Library of Congress. (n.d.). *The fourteenth amendment.* Library of Congress. https://constitution.congress.gov/constitution/amendment-14/

Library of Virginia. (1924). *The "one-drop" rule and racial identification by Whites, Blacks and Native Americans.* Library of Virginia. http://www.virginiaplaces.org/population/onedrop.html

Lockwood, L. (1970). *Conversation with Eldridge Cleaver (Algiers).* Dell Publishing Co., Inc.

Lyle, P., & Esmail, A. M. (2016). Sworn to protect: Police brutality – A dilemma for America's police. *Race, Gender. Class, New Orleans, 23*(3/4), 155–185.

Lynch, H. (Ed.). (1976). *The great contemporary issues series – Black Africa. (Vol. 5)* New York, NY: The New York Times Arno Press.

Lynch, H. (Ed.). (1976). *The great contemporary issues series – Set 1, Vol. 5: Black Africa.* New York, NY: The New York Times Arno Press.

Lynch, H. (Ed.). (1976). *The great contemporary issues series: Black Africa (vol. 5).* New York, NY: The New York Times Arno Press.

Lynch, J. (2023, January 17). Memphis police relieve officers pending investigations into the arrest of man who later died, chief says. *CNN.* https://www.cnn.com/2023/01/16/us/memphis-tennessee-arrested-man-dies-hospital/index.html/

Macabasco, L. W. (2022, March 8). Lynching postcards: A harrowing documentary about confronting history. *The Guardian.* https://www.theguardian.com/film/2022/mar/08/lynching-postcards-a-harrowing-documentary-about-confronting-history

Macabasco, L. W. (2022, March 8). Lynching postcards: A harrowing documentary about confronting history. *The Guardian.* https://www.theguardian.com/film/2022/mar/08/lynching-postcards-a-harrowing-documentary-about-confronting-history/

Magnolia Pictures. (2017, January 5). *I am not your negro: Official trailer.* Bing. https://www.bing.com/videos/search?q=I+Am+Not+Your+Negro&docid=608001557737573582&mid=EE7CB61FA93C401B7FB1EE7CB61FA93C401B7FB1&view=detail&FORM=VIREHT

Malcolm, X. (2012). *The House negro and the field negro.* Bing. https://www.bing.com/videos/search?q=I+Am+Not+Your+Negro&&view=detail&mid=4CC268E118D2B546E9A24CC268E118D2B546E9A2&rvsmid=EE7CB61FA93C401B7FB1EE7CB61FA93C401B7FB1&FORM=VDMCNR

Marshall, B. (2019, September 17). *U.S. Constitution signed September 17, 1787.* MLWGS. https://mlwgs.com/u-s-constitution-signed-september-17-1787/

Martinez, M. M. (2017). Blackcreole: Too white to be black, too black to be white: Recollections of a mixed-race New Orleans colored creole. Wilmington, NC: DoorKnobFilms.Com.

Maule, B. A. (2017). *Police misconduct in Brooklyn: Documenting, understanding and preventing*. Springer Publications. doi:10.1007/978-3-319-66814-7

Maxwell-Stewart, H., & Oxley, D. (2020). Convicts and the colonization of Australia, 1788-1868. *Digital Panopticon.* https://www.digitalpanopticon.org/Convicts_and_the_Colonisation_of_Australia,_1788-1868

Maylam, P. (1995, March). Explaining to apartheid city: 20 years of South Africa urban histography. *Journal of Southern African Studies*, *21*(1), 19–38. doi:10.1080/03057079508708431

McGovern Library and Dakota Wesleyan University. (2022). *Martin Luther King, Jr.: The civil rights movement.* DWU. https://library.dwu.edu/martin_luther_king/civil_right

McGrath, A. (2016, February 11). *Celebrating white men and their black lovers.* SMH. https://www.smh.com.au/opinion/love-and-living-in-early-australia-the-epitome-of-valentines-day-fervour-still-enflaming-a-big-divide-20160211-gmr23y.html#:~:text=Australia%27s%20anti-miscegenation%20laws%20came%20under%20the%20guise%20of,whose%20lacy%20gown%20ignited%20the%20%22white%20wedding%22%20trend%29.?msclkid=241ff2d0cfb611ec9cdc968b2b869935

McMichael, C. (2016). Police wars and state repression in South Africa. *Journal of Asian and African Studies*, *51*(1), 3–16. doi:10.1177/0021909614541086

Meeks, C. (2011, October 5). Racism is fueled by fear. *Huffington Post.* https://www.huffpost.com/entry/post_2501_b_992066

Merriam-Webster, Inc. (2022). Fear. *Meriam Webster.* https://www.merriam-webster.com/dictionary/fear

Merriam-Webster, Incorporated. (2022). *Racism.* Meriam-Webster. https://www.merriam-webster.com/dictionary/racism

Michigan State University. (n.d.). *The death of Steve Biko.* Michigan State University. https://overcomingapartheid.msu.edu/sidebar.php?id=65-2584&msclkid=1b8fd8d7cecb11eca0ec014ea8fc762e

Miller, M. (2013, December 18). Sharpeville massacres marked turning point in South Africa's history. *CBS News.* https://www.cbsnews.com/news/sharpeville-massacre-marked-turning-point-in-south-africas-history/

Moorehouse, B. (2018, February 21). Still no KKK in Howell: Updated "hate map" shows all the groups in Michigan. *The Livingston Post.* https://thelivingstonpost.com/still-no-kkk-in-howell-updated-hate-map-shows-all-the-groups-in-michigan./

Morales, E.P. (2022, January). *Unraveling abolition: Legal culture and slave emancipation in Columbia.* New York, NY: Cambridge University Press.

Murray, K. R., & Haberfield, M. R. (2021). *Use of force training in law enforcement: A reality based approach.* Springer. doi:10.1007/978-3-030-59880-8

Museum of Australian Democracy. (n.d.). *Commonwealth of Australia Constitution Act 1900 (UK).* FoundingDocs. https://www.foundingdocs.gov.au/scan-sid-91.html

Museum of Australian Democracy. (n.d.). *Commonwealth of Australia Constitution Act 1900 (UK).* Museum of Australian Democracy. https://www.foundingdocs.gov.au/scan-sid-91.html

NAACP. (2022). *History of lynching in America.* NAACP. https://naacp.org/find-resources/history-explained/history-lynching-america/

National Geographic Society. (2022). *Ku Klux Klan.* National Geographic Society. https://www.nationalgeographic.org/article/ku-klux-klan/

National Museum of African-American History and Culture - Smithsonian. (n.d.). *Jim Letherer, Selma to Montgomery march.* NMAAHC. https://nmaahc.si.edu/object/nmaahc_2015.129.58

National Park Service. (2016a). *Voting Rights Act of 1965.* National Park Service. https://www.nps.gov/articles/votingrightsact.htm

National Park Service. (2018a). *Jim Crow laws.* National Park Service. https://www.nps.gov/malu/learn/education/jim_crow_laws.htm

National Park Service. (2018a). *Jim Crow laws.* Retrieved on February 3, 2022 from https://www.nps.gov/malu/learn/education/jim_crow_laws.htm

Nelson Mandela Foundation. (2022). *The archive at the center of memory: Timeline.* Nelson Mandela Foundation. https://www.nelsonmandela.org/content/page/timeline?msclkid=320c32c9ced611ecb984658f100a6b7f

New York City Police Department. (2019, April 3). *Patrol guide.* NYCPD. https://www1.nyc.gov/assets/nypd/downloads/pdf/public_information/public-pguide1.pdf

News, W. G. N. (2019, May 7). *Sandra Bland's own cellphone video surfaces.* Bing. https://www.bing.com/videos/search?q=sandra+bland&docid=608009482127036521&mid=BE7E3AB9998EBE414DD6BE7E3AB9998EBE414DD6&view=detail&FORM=VIRE

Newtown, J. (1788). *Thoughts upon the African slave trade.* London: Printed for J. Buckland, in Pater-Noster Row, & J. Johnson, in St. Paul's Church-yard.

Newtown, J. (1788). *Thoughts upon the African slave trade.* J. Buckland, in Pater-Noster Row, and J. Johnson in St. Paul's Church-yard.

Nexus Partnerships Limited. (2020). *The commonwealth.* Commonwealth of Nations. https://www.commonwealthofnations.org/commonwealth/

Nieftagodie, N. (2014). The Soweto uprising. Auckland Park, South Africa: Jacana Media (Pty.) Ltd.

Noah, T. (2019). *Born a crime: Stories from a South African childhood.* Spiegel and Grau.

Normore, A. H., & Scott, W. R. (2021). Police brutality and the militarization of Black and Brown communities: Transforming the culture of policing through education and training. *New Directions for Adult and Continuing Education, 2021*(170), 79–88. doi:10.1002/ace.20427

Obama, B. (2020). *A promised land.* Crown.

Open Education Sociology Dictionary. (2022). Government. *Sociology Dictionary.* https://sociologydictionary.org/government/?msclkid=69710078d03911ec896ef2ae3a565911

Peck, R. (Director/Producer). 2017. *I am not your negro.* [Film]. Magnolia Pictures and Amazon Studios.

Petersen, T.T. (2022, August 12). *Military conquest of the prairie: Native American resistance, evasion & survival, 1865-1890.* Liverpool University Press.

Petersen, T.T. (2022, August 12). *Military conquest of the prairie: Native American resistance, evasion & survival, 1865-1890.* Liverpool, UK: Liverpool University Press.

Petersen, T.T. (2022, August 12). Military conquest of the prairie: Native American resistance, evasion and survival, 1865-1890. *Liverpool, UK: Liverpool University Press.*

Phillips, J. H. (2001, May 1). Room 6/9 – The tragedy of Steve Biko. *Journal of Forensic Sciences, 33*, 3–8.

Philpott, D. (2010). *A guide to federal terms and acronyms* (2nd ed.). The Scarecrow Press, Inc.

Pose, M. (2009). *Indigenous protest, Australian bicentenary, 1988 in museums Victoria collections.* Victoria Museums. https://collections.museumsvictoria.com.au/articles/2835

Potter, G. (n.d.). *The history of policing in the United States.* file:///C:/Users/janel/Desktop/Publications/Examining%20Black%20Deaths%20in%20Custody%20-%202022/The%20History%20of%20Policing%20in%20the%20United%20States.GaryPotter.8.22.2021.pdf.

Project, N. I. A. (2020, October 13). *Defund police.* [Video]. Youtube. https://www.youtube.com/watch?v=bT0YpOmk8NA

PsyPost. (2016, October 16). Fear causes Whites high in implicit racism to be more supportive of voter ID laws. *PsyPost.* https://www.psypost.org/2016/10/fear-causes-whites-high-implicit-racism-supportive-voter-id-laws-45408

Public Broadcasting Service. (2019). *Slave ship mutiny.* PBS. https://www.pbs.org/black-culture/shows/list/slave-ship-mutiny/

Radio, M. (2017, September 12). *Why is Howell Considered the KKK capitol of the klan?* Michigan Radio. https://www.michiganradio.org/arts-culture/2017-09-12/why-is-howell-considered-the-kkk-capital-of-klan/

Redden Law, P. L. L. C. (2022). *The case of Sandra Bland as an example of police brutality in Texas.* Redden Law. https://www.reddenlawtexas.com/the-case-of-sandra-bland-as-an-example-of-police-brutality-in-texas/

Schaeffer, F. A. (2005). *How should we then live?* Crossway Books.

Sebok, A. J. (2004, January 12). *The Amadou Diallo case was New York City's $3 million settlement too low, too high, or a just amount?* Find Law. https://supreme.findlaw.com/legal-commentary/the-amadou-diallo-case.html

Shaer, M. (2013, September 30). 134 minutes with Frank Serpico – NY Magazine: A Hudson troll with the NYPD's most famous whistle-blower and aging Casanova. *NY Magazine.* https://nymag.com/news/intelligencer/encounter/frank-serpico-2013-10

Sharpton, A. (2022). *Righteous trouble makers: Untold stories of the social justice movement in America.* Hanover Square Press.

Simmons, J. C. (2014, May 30-June 1). *Seeing evil, hearing evil, speaking good: Social media as a tool for transformative justice.* [Conference presentation]. Left Forum, New York, NY.

Simmons, J. C. (2011). *Kept by Jesus.* Lu Lu Self-Publishing.

Smith, W. (2021, February 17). *Amend: The fight for America.* [Net Series]. Netflix.

Snipp, C. M., & Liebler, C. A. (2012). *The end of the "one-drop" rule?: Hypodescent in the early 21st century.* Princeton. https://paa2012.princeton.edu/papers/121933?msclkid=32762c9fd00211ec9876b854623994a5

South African History Online. (n.d.). *English settlement in South Africa.* SA History. https://www.sahistory.org.za/article/english-settlement-south-africa?msclkid=913ee8bfcdba11eca89fcce63fef6f72

South African History Online. (n.d.). English settlement in South Africa. *South African History Online.* https://www.sahistory.org.za/article/english-settlement-south-africa?msclkid=913ee8bfcdba11eca89fcce63fef6f72

South African History Online. (n.d.). *Pass laws in South Africa 1800-1994.* SA History. https://www.sahistory.org.za/article/pass-laws-south-africa-1800- 1994#:~:text=In%201866%20a%20Pass%20law%20was%20passed.%20Any,the%20Eureka%2C%20was%20found%20in%20Hopetown%20in%201867.?msclkid=7248423ecf6011eca7f20b2ad750dcf5.

Spielvogel, J. J. (2014). *Discovering our past: A history of the world.* McGraw Hill Education.

Spruill, L. H. (2016). Slave patrols, "Pack of Negro dogs," and policing Black communities. *Phylon*, *53*(1), 42–66.

Srividhya, S., Hutchings, K., & Wright, J. M. (2009). *Debating the slave trade: Rhetoric of British national identity, 1759-1815*. Taylor & Francis Group.

Stanford University. (n.d.). *Say their names: Green Library supporting the Black lives matter movement.* Stanford University. https://exhibits.stanford.edu/saytheirnames

Statutes and Stories. (2022). Enforcement of the fourteenth amendment. *Statues and Stories.* https://www.statutesandstories.com/blog_html/the-ku-klux-klan-act-of-1871/

Swift, J. (2022). *The curious history of slavery in Africa.* Cornell. https://research.cornell.edu/news-features/curious-history-slavery-west-africa

The Amadou Diallo Foundation. (2022). *Amadou Diallo.* ADF. https://www.amadoudiallo.com/about-amadou/

The Arizona Board of Regents. (2022). *Tribe.* AZ Regents.https://azregents.edu/

The Arizona Board of Regents. (2022). *Tribe.* Azregents. https://azregents.edu/

The Guardian. (2014, December 4). 'I can't breathe': Eric Garner put in chokehold by NYPD officer – video. *The Guardian.* https://www.bing.com/videos/search?q=eric+garner&view=detail&mid=C6A4C096C0122EFC50D8C6A4C096C0122EFC50D8&FORM=VIRE

The New Yorker. (2020, June 14). Kadir Nelson's "Say their names." *The New Yorker.* https://www.newyorker.com/culture/cover-story/cover-story-2020-06-22

The Sentencing Project. (2022). *Race & justice news: Blacks disproportionately arrested for marijuana in Alabama: October 30, 2018.* The Sentencing Project. https://www.sentencingproject.org/news/race-justice-news-blacks-disproportionately-arrested-marijuana-alabama/

The Telegraph. (2014, August 20). *Eyewitness describe Michael Brown killing as new footage released.* Bing. https://www.bing.com/videos/search?q=Michael+Brown+Video+Footage&&view=detail&mid=46AFF2A1F65D860B5E0046AFF2A1F65D860B5E00&&FORM=VRDGAR&ru=%2Fvideos%2Fsearch%3Fq%3DMichael%2BBrown%2BVideo%2BFootage%26FORM%3DVARSQP

The U.S. National Archives and Records Administration. (n.d.). *Angela Davis (January 26, 1944).* US National Archives. https://www.archives.gov/research/african-americans/individuals/angela-davis

Thompson, B. C. (1958, September 25). Screen: A forceful social drama; 'The Defiant Ones' has debut at Victoria. *New York Times*. https://www.nytimes.com/1958/09/25/archives/screen-a-forceful-social-drama-the-defiant-ones-has-debut-at.html

Timetoast. (2022). Apartheid game. *Timetoast*. https://www.timetoast.com/timelines/apartheid-regime

Trigger, D.S. (1985, June). *Doomadgee: A study of power relations and social action in North Australian Aboriginal settlement*. [Doctoral dissertation, University of Queensland].

Tupper, N. M. (2021). Working with victims of police brutality: Conducting and documenting multistoried interviews. *The International Journal of Narrative Therapy and Community Work, 2*, 48–57.

Turner, C. (2021). *Lynching postcards: A harrowing documentary about confronting history*. [Video file]. Paramount Plus. https://www.paramountplus.com/movies/video/hselCM7fYyRK6mazd5ooDmdhlYiMrNYH/

U.S. Commission on Civil Rights in New York City. (2000, August). *Police practices and civil rights in New York City*. GPO. https://permanent.access.gpo.gov/lps13167/main.htm

U.S. Department of Health and Human Services. (2021). *Tuskegee experiment*. CDC. https://www.cdc.gov/tuskegee/timeline.htm?msclkid=9d69f9a7cd4711ecba7d3de204e661d5

United Nations. (2021, July 17). *"The blood we sacrificed was worth it": Sharpeville Massacre*. UN. https://southafrica.un.org/en/135812-blood-we-sacrificed-was-worth-it-sharpeville- massacre?msclkid=9b9122c8ceea11ec9d5355ec4615bbe1.

United Nations. (2021, July 17). *"The blood we sacrificed was worth it": Sharpeville Massacre*. UN. https://southafrica.un.org/en/135812-blood-we-sacrificed-was-worth-it-sharpeville- massacre?msclkid=9b9122c8ceea11ec9d5355ec4615bbe1.

United Nations. (2022, March 25). *Resistance to slavery and unity against racism: Rhythms of resistance*. UN. https://www.youtube.com/watch?v=VUhHhW1__sg

United Nations. (2022, March 25). *Resistance to slavery and unity against racism: Rhythms of resistance*. UN. https://www.youtube.com/watch?v=VUhHhW1__sg

United States Citizenship and Immigration Services. (n.d.). *Intermediate level: Establishing independence*. USCIS. https://www.uscis.gov/sites/default/files/document/lesson-plans/Intermediate_establishing_independence_handouts.pdf?mscl kid=5152e848d10611ec849a49e419e34f13

United States Department of Justice. (n.d.). *About us*. USDJ. https://www.justice.gov/about

United States Department of Justice. (n.d.). *Shooting death of Michael Brown – Ferguson. Missouri: 2014*. USDJ. https://www.justice.gov/crs/timeline-event/shooting-death-michael-brown-ferguson-mo/

United States Holocaust Memorial Museum. (n.d.). *Mein kampf.* USHMM. https://encyclopedia.ushmm.org/content/en/article/mein-kampf

University of Minnesota Human Rights Library. (n.d.). *All Amendments to the United States Constitution.* HR Library. http://hrlibrary.umn.edu/education/all_amendments_usconst.htm?msclkid=2ff06db1cff911eca379a664ac2ef6af

University of Minnesota Human Rights Library. (n.d.). *All Amendments to the United States Constitution.* University of Minnesota. http://hrlibrary.umn.edu/education/all_amendments_usconst.htm?msclkid=2ff06db1cff911eca379a664ac2ef6af

Van der Westhuizen, C. (2008). *White power and the rise and fall of the National Party.* Struik Publishers.

Van Vuuren, H. (2015). Apartheid, guns and money: A tale of profit. Auckland Park, South Africa: Jacana Media (Pty) Ltd.

Virginia, A. A. R. P. (2022). *Sunday sit-ins with AARP Virginia and Richmond ASALH.* [Video]. Youtube. https://www.youtube.com/watch?v=JQATlH1lRWE

Vrieland, D. (2022). *Dr. King comes to Grosse Pointe.* Academia Letters. *Article, 4541.* doi:10.20935/AL4541

Waheeda. (2015, January 22). Civil rights charges highly unlikely for Michael Brown case. *The Source.* https://thesource.com/2015/01/22/fbi-has-completed-investigation-into-the-shooting-of-michael-brown-civil-rights-charges-not-expected/

Weatherby, W. J. (1989). *James Baldwin: Artist on fire.* Dell Publishing.

Wells, D., Umansky, E., & Syed, M. (2020, July 26). *The NYPD files: Search thousands of civilian complaints against New York City police officers.* Prop Publica. https://projects.propublica.org/nypd-ccrb/

Willoughby-Herald, T. (2015). *Waste of a White skin.* University of California Press. doi:10.1525/california/9780520280861.001.0001

Woodward, C. V. (1966). *The strange career of Jim Crow.* Oxford University Press.

Worland, J. (2014, November 28). U.S. panel sharply criticizes police brutality in US. *Time.* https://time.com/3609811/police-brutality-united-states-un-ferguson-torture

World, T. R. T. (2021, February 22). *New evidence: NYPD and FBI allegedly conspired in the murder of Malcolm X.* Bing. https://www.bing.com/videos/search?q=malcom+x+and+surveillance&docid=608038232636278311&mid=E7F121B84F99E605B75BE7F121B84F99E605B75B&view=detail&FORM=VIRE/

Xu, V., Fiedler, M.L. & Flaming, K.H. (2005, May 1). Discovering the impact of community policing: The broke windows thesis. Collective efficacy, & citizens' judgment. *Journal of Research in Crime and Delinquency, 42*(2), 147-186. . doi:10.1177/0022427804266544

About the Contributors

Janelle Christine Simmons earned her B.A. in psychology from Michigan State University, She went on to earn her M.A. in Forensic Psychology from John Jay College of Criminal Justice, an M.Div. from Torch Trinity Graduate School of Theology and and Ed.S. in Curriculum and Instruction from Liberty University and an Ed.D. in Educational Leadership from Liberty University. Dr. Simmons is actively looking for a post-doctorate fellowship or a full-time lecturer position to apply what she has learned thus far.

Index

G

H

I

J

L

M

N

O

P

R

S

T

U

X

www.ingramcontent.com/pod-product-compliance
Lightning Source LLC
LaVergne TN
LVHW061545290926
849162LV00004B/906